The Skilled Facilitator

Roger M. Schwarz

Institute of Government
The University of North Carolina
at Chapel Hill

The Skilled Facilitator

Practical Wisdom for Developing Effective Groups

Jossey-Bass Publishers · San Francisco

Substantial discounts on bulk quantities of Jossey-Bass
books are available to corporations, professional
associations, and other organizations. For details and
discount information, contact the special sales
department at Jossey-Bass Inc., Publishers.
(415) 433-1740; Fax (415) 433-0499.

For sales outside the United States, please contact your local Simon
& Schuster International Office.

Jossey-Bass Web address: http://www.josseybass.com

Library of Congress Cataloging-in-Publication Data

Schwarz, Roger M., date.
    The skilled facilitator : practical wisdom for developing
effective groups / Roger M. Schwarz. — 1st ed.
        p.   cm. — (The Jossey-Bass management series) (The Jossey-
Bass public administration series) (The Jossey-Bass nonprofit
sector series)
    Includes bibliographical references and index.
    ISBN 1-55542-638-7
    1. Communication in management.   2. Communication in personnel
management.   3. Work groups.   4. Conflict management.   I. Title.
II. Series.   III. Series: The Jossey-Bass public administration
series.   IV. Series: The Jossey-Bass nonprofit sector series.
HD30.3.S373   1994
658.4'036—dc20   93-48662
                                                                          CIP

FIRST EDITION
HB Printing   10 9 8 7   *Code 9442*

A joint publication in

The Jossey-Bass
Management Series

The Jossey-Bass
Public Administration Series

and

The Jossey-Bass
Nonprofit Sector Series

To Kathleen, Noah, and Hannah,
who are my developmental facilitators
in so many ways
and who bring so much joy to my life

Contents

Preface

This book is about how facilitators and others help work groups become more effective. I wrote it after I searched unsuccessfully for a group facilitation book. My colleague Richard McMahon and I were designing and preparing to teach a one hundred-hour group facilitation workshop for managers. During the years in which I have taught people how to facilitate groups, I have pieced together readings by a number of authors on various topics, but the goals of the workshop required a book in which all the subjects were integrated. I searched for a book that would clearly describe the process of facilitation, the issues that arise during it, and how facilitators deal with them—a book that would convey much of what I have learned through my years of facilitating and studying groups. I wanted a book that was conceptually based but practical in focus, addressed to both the thinking practitioner and the practical scholar.

The search was frustrating. I found many books about the theory of group dynamics and even some books about the theory of intervening in groups. Many books gave practical advice about how to make groups and meetings effective. My search identified only a few books that bridged the gap between theory and practice—that is, books that were rooted in theory and that clearly described how to apply the theory in a broad range of situations. I had used these books for years, and they have strongly influenced me: works by Chris Argyris and Donald Schön (for example, Argyris, 1970; Argyris & Schön, 1974, 1978) and Edgar Schein (1969, 1987, 1988). Yet no single book adequately reflected what has become my approach to facilitation and to teaching others to facilitate.

The Skilled Facilitator is designed to integrate the theory and practice of group facilitation. It does not present a comprehensive theory of group facilitation. Instead, it describes a set of core values and congruent principles—elements of a theory—and shows how to use various techniques to apply the principles in practice. In doing so, the book seeks to answer two questions for the reader who wants to facilitate: What do I say and do in this situation? and What are the underlying principles that explain why I say and do this? By answering the two questions, the reader can understand techniques, how to modify them, and how to design new techniques while remaining consistent with the core values and principles of effective facilitation. No book can address all the situations in which facilitators find themselves or all the techniques they use to help groups. That is why the core values and principles are important. Having learned them, facilitators can apply them to new situations and extend their ability beyond situations they have already encountered. This approach reflects a fundamental principle that underlies the book: effective facilitators base their thoughts and actions on a model of effective groups and on models of diagnosis and intervention, all of which are internally consistent.

The core values and principles serve another, related purpose. Because facilitators help groups reflect on and articulate the reasons for their actions, facilitators must be able to do the same for their own work. If they cannot, it is doubtful that they can help their clients. As consultants, facilitators also must address issues that arise from the general nature of client-consultant relationships.

This is not a book about research, but I use relevant research to develop the facilitation principles and techniques. Unfortunately, the existing research does not address many of the questions for which facilitators need answers in order to be effective. To fill the gaps, this book, like others that discuss interventions, goes beyond research findings and draws on practitioners' experiences, including my own.

Audience

The Skilled Facilitator is written primarily for people who want to become or already are facilitators and secondarily for people who want to use facilitation skills without formally filling the facilitator role. This audience includes people who consult with groups or organizations and people who lead and manage groups or organizations. The book addresses both internal and external consultants, including facilitators who work with boards, management teams and other work groups, and special groups, such as quality teams, labor-management committees, interorganizational committees, and community action committees. It is also written for organization development consultants, who need facilitation skills to help groups manage the process of change, whether the substantive change involves creating a total quality management process, self-managing work teams, a learning organization, or a new budgeting system or installing a new computer system. In addition, mediators who want to work with organizations will find the book helpful in making the transition to facilitation.

The book is useful for people who act as consultants by giving expert technical advice to organizations—budget, finance, and legal experts, human resource managers, and trainers as well as their external consultant counterparts. The advice of expert consultants can easily be rejected or fail to work, not because the advice is technically poor but because it does not address the underlying process by which the group works. For example, a technically excellent budgeting system will probably not produce valid data if members believe the data will be used against them. To be effective, all consultants require some facilitation skills, even if they do not formally serve as facilitators (Schein, 1990).

Managers and leaders whose work calls for facilitation skills will also appreciate the book. First, chairs of committees and boards can improve their groups by applying the facilitation principles described here. Many groups use some form of Robert's Rules, which—as the full name states—were designed to maintain order. Group facilitation principles are designed to improve problem solving and decision making.

Second, managers and leaders who meet with representatives of other organizations to coordinate activities can also benefit from applying the principles and techniques described in the book. Managers who play the coordinating role often have no authority over the other participants. Consequently, success depends on the support of all the parties involved.

Third, managers and leaders who seek information from their customers, clients, and other interested parties will find the principles of facilitation relevant—for instance, managers in government organizations that hold meetings to find out how proposed regulations will affect various stakeholders.

Finally, managers and leaders who want to improve their professional effectiveness in all situations will find the book helpful. In the future, the effective manager and leader will be a consensus builder, problem solver, process leader, team builder, source of empowerment, change agent, and facilitator of conflict resolution (International City Management Association, 1991). To master these roles, managers and leaders will need to learn how to identify and challenge the assumptions that guide members' actions and that prevent the group or organization from becoming more effective. *The Skilled Facilitator* provides core values, principles, and techniques for accomplishing this. The book is also well suited to the interests of practical scholars, including faculty members who teach courses on conflict management, groups, consultation, or organization development, whether in the field of management, public administration, planning, psychology, social work, education, or public health or in other applied fields.

Overview of Contents

Part One (Chapters One and Two) provides the context for the book. Chapter One describes two types of group facilitation and the role of the facilitator for each type. Topics of discussion include the objectives of facilitation and the core values and assumptions that guide it, and what happens when a facilitator leaves the facilitator role.

Chapter Two begins by considering why a model of group effectiveness is valuable for facilitators. Next, the chapter considers what it means for a group to be effective and identifies the elements within a group and outside it that contribute to group effectiveness. The second part of the chapter describes how the model of group effectiveness helps facilitators.

Part Two (Chapters Three and Four) focuses on establishing the foundation for effective facilitation. Chapter Three describes a step-by-step process that a facilitator and a client use to agree on whether and how they will work together.

Chapter Four explores how a facilitator observes a group, decides whether group members are acting effectively or ineffectively, and decides whether to intervene. The chapter introduces a six-step cycle that facilitators can use to diagnose and intervene in groups, and it explains the diagnostic steps in the cycle. It includes a set of ground rules for effective groups that facilitators can use to diagnose behavior in a group and that group members can use to increase their own effectiveness.

Part Three (Chapters Five through Eleven) focuses on how a facilitator intervenes in a group—that is, what a facilitator says and does. Chapter Five explores the different factors that a facilitator considers when intervening in a group. Examples include when to intervene, the specific behaviors to focus on, and which members to address.

Chapter Six describes in detail how facilitators intervene. It first describes the types of interventions facilitators use and the situations in which they are appropriate. Next, it returns to the six-step diagnosis-intervention cycle, this time to discuss how to say what the facilitator needs to say when intervening in groups. Because words are so important in facilitation, the chapter also examines specific types of words that facilitators should use and words that they should avoid.

Chapter Seven focuses on interventions that facilitators make at the beginning and end of meetings.

Chapter Eight focuses on interventions that facilitators make to help groups solve problems. The interventions help groups use a problem-solving model similar to the models that many groups learn when they are trained in problem-solving techniques.

Chapter Nine returns to the set of ground rules introduced earlier and, using many specific statements, shows how facilitators intervene to help group members follow their ground rules.

Chapter Ten deals with emotions, especially negative emotions, that pose a special challenge for a facilitator and the group. The chapter begins by considering how emotions are generated and expressed. Then, by applying the values and principles discussed earlier in the book, it shows how facilitators intervene to help group members express their emotions effectively, including emotions directed at facilitators.

Chapter Eleven examines how two facilitators work together with a group. The chapter begins by describing the advantages and disadvantages of cofacilitating and the conditions under which cofacilitators can work together successfully. Next, it discusses different ways that cofacilitators can divide and coordinate their work. Finally, it describes how cofacilitators can learn from each other by jointly reflecting on their work. Readers who do not have the opportunity to cofacilitate may wish to skip this chapter.

Part Four (Chapters Twelve and Thirteen) describes how to use facilitation skills in your own organization. Chapter Twelve begins by describing how the internal facilitator's role develops and the advantages and disadvantages of the role. Next, it discusses general strategies that internal facilitators can use to improve their roles. Last, it revisits earlier chapters to discuss issues that internal facilitators specifically face in contracting, diagnosing, and intervening with groups and to describe ways to deal with each issue.

Chapter Thirteen explores how members in organizations can incorporate the core values and principles of facilitation into their everyday roles to become facilitative leaders. The chapter begins by identifying recent organizational innovations (for example, employee empowerment, quality improvement, self-managing teams, and learning organizations) and then considers the kind of leader that is needed in innovative organizations—a facilitative leader. It then outlines the role of a facilitative leader and examines how the facilitative leader applies the core values and principles of facilitation and how facilitative leaders help groups increase their effectiveness. The chapter concludes with some thoughts about becoming a facilitative leader.

There are seven resources at the end of the book. Resource A details the development of an effective contract between a facilitator and client. Resources B and C contain sample facilitator-client agreements for two types of facilitation. Resource D discusses how facilitators use self-knowledge instruments and experiential exercises consistent with the approach described in the book. Resource E is a guide that cofacilitators can use for deciding whether and how to work together. Resource F discusses contracting issues for internal facilitators and their supervisors and includes a contracting questionnaire for internal facilitators and their supervisors. Resource G lists additional readings.

Features of the Book

A book cannot substitute for the skill-building practice that facilitation training provides. Still, I have tried to write the book in a way that provides readers with the kind of details they would learn in training. I have included many examples to illustrate how to (and how not to) apply the principles in practice. Most examples come from my experiences as a group facilitator. In presenting the examples, I sometimes describe not only what occurred but also my thoughts and feelings at the time, because reactions affect how a facilitator works with clients. I have also included examples of my own ineffective facilitation. I have learned from my mistakes and assume that readers will too.

I have included verbatim examples of dialogue that illustrate how a facilitator intervenes, but I have disguised the names or types of the client organizations and the names of individual members. Also, throughout the book, I have called attention to the principles of facilitation by putting them in boldface type so readers can easily identify them.

In *The Skilled Facilitator,* I describe one approach to group facilitation, while recognizing that others exist. Rather than provide an overview of different approaches, I have tried to offer one relatively comprehensive and integrated approach, so that readers can apply it and use it as a point of reference when examining other approaches. I refer to the approach described in this book as a *low-level inference approach*. Essentially, this means that facilitators diagnose and intervene in groups by making the fewest and the smallest inferential leaps possible. For example, consider two facilitators with different approaches who are facilitating the same group together. The low-level inference facilitator may point out that several members have stated their opinions but have not inquired whether others agree or disagree. Observing the same behavior, a facilitator using a different approach may infer that the same several members do not seem interested in others' opinions or that they are controlling the group.

Within the low-level inference approach, I describe two types of facilitation, recognizing that groups use facilitators for different purposes. Basic facilitation helps a group temporarily improve its process long enough to solve a specific, substantive problem. Developmental facilitation helps a group learn how to continually improve its process so that it can generally solve problems more effectively.

The techniques described throughout the book are based on a core set of values: valid information, free and informed choice, and internal commitment (Argyris, 1970). When facilitators use the techniques but do not hold the core values, at best they will be less effective; at worst they can be manipulative. As facilitators come to hold the core values, the techniques of facilitation come more naturally.

I believe I have become a more effective facilitator as I have developed an approach that I can call my own. To be sure, my approach incorporates much of what I have learned from others. But I have also had to select from, add to, and modify what I have learned. I trust that readers will ultimately do the same.

Chapel Hill, North Carolina   Roger M. Schwarz
February 1994

Acknowledgments

Many people helped me while I was writing this book, and I want to thank them. By asking for my help, my clients provided an opportunity for me to learn and to test the ideas in the book. They appear in examples throughout, but I have disguised their identities for purposes of confidentiality.

Several of my colleagues—Margaret Carlson, Douglas Cowherd, Richard McMahon, and A. John Vogt—read various versions of the entire manuscript, as did Laura Dell, Philip Dixon, Jack Loftis (reviewers for Jossey-Bass), and Lawrence Frey (a reviewer for Sage Publications). Margaret Carlson and Richard McMahon also reviewed the final version of the manuscript, sometimes receiving chapters on short notice and giving me feedback within hours. Their comments helped me structure parts of the book, and their editorial zeal helped me write more precisely.

A number of clients who have participated in the Institute of Government's intensive workshop Group Facilitation and Consultation, which my colleagues Richard McMahon and Margaret Carlson and I offer, reviewed parts of the manuscript and provided encouragement: Anne Davidson, Thomas Elmore, Susan Ennis, Debra Henzey, Patrick LaCarter, Michael McDaniel, William Riemer, Nita Sims, Lynn Stelle, James Stokoe, Patricia Thomas, and Rebecca Veazey. As my internal cofacilitator on a long-term project, Michael McDaniel also helped me think about issues in cofacilitation and the role of the internal facilitator. By asking important questions, many other workshop participants helped me clarify my ideas. My colleagues David Abramis, Frayda Bluestein, Kurt Jenne, Laurie Mesibov, and Andrew Sachs, also provided suggestions for parts of the manuscript. My sister Dale Schwarz and brother-in-law Guillermo Cuellar, both facilitators and therapists, critically evaluated the manuscript while enthusiastically supporting me.

Cortlandt Cammann, my doctoral advisor at The University of Michigan, provided me with my first opportunities to learn and practice facilitation. Together we developed a set of ground rules for effective groups, an expanded version of which is a central part of the book.

John Sanders, former director of the Institute of Government, supported Richard McMahon and me in offering the group facilitation and consultation workshop, for which the book was initially designed. Michael Smith, the current director of the Institute of Government, who strongly encourages the work of group facilitation, agreed (in what was admittedly less than a free and informed choice) to my working almost exclusively on the book in order to complete it. Gordon Whitaker, a colleague in the Political Science Department, agreed to swap offices during this time, so each of us could work uninterrupted.

I am fortunate to be a member of a work group that practices the core values and principles described in the book. I have learned much about collaboration and work groups from Margaret Carlson, Kurt Jenne, and Richard McMahon, my colleagues in the management group at the Institute of Government, as we continually work to improve our group's ability to provide quality services, enhance our functioning, and meet our individual needs. In this spirit, those people also agreed to cover my teaching and consulting responsibilities during the summer, while I completed the book.

At Jossey-Bass, my editor, Sarah Polster, and her associates, Barbara Hill, Luana Morimoto, and Alice Morrow Rowan, have given me sound editorial advice and responded to my concerns; they have been a pleasure to work with.

Other people at the Institute of Government have supported me as I completed the book, in ways other than reviewing manuscripts. Patricia Langelier, Marsha Lobacz, Alexander Hess, and their assistants conducted literature searches and located reference material. Dorothy Smith provided secretarial support. Charles Bennett and Marc Sutherland made copies of manuscript chapters under tight deadlines. Whenever my computer crashed, John Gullo diagnosed the problem and fixed it, saving me from missing several deadlines.

The book reflects the influence of two people in particular. It should be clear to readers that Chris Argyris has provided a framework for my thinking about facilitation and human behavior in general. In the early 1980s, I was one of Argyris's students; his approach to improving organizational life continues to have a profound influence on my work. The influence of a second person cannot be seen by readers. Richard McMahon and I have spent hundreds of hours together facilitating groups, teaching others how to facilitate, and reflecting on our experiences. The book reflects his ideas. His greatest influence was getting me to focus on what I believe about facilitation rather than accept the approaches of others. In short, he was my conceptual and spiritual facilitator for the book. For that I am extremely grateful.

Finally, my wife, Kathleen Rounds, and son, Noah, have supported me in the project from the beginning. Kathleen believed in my work, gave me feedback on chapters, and even took on some of my home responsibilities temporarily when I needed to meet a deadline. More important, she and Noah helped me recognize when the book was consuming too much of my life and helped me regain my balance. So did my daughter, Hannah, who was born shortly before the book was completed.

Acknowledgments **xix**

As I watch Noah at age four communicate with others, I marvel at his directness. He tells people what he thinks and feels and why; openly disagrees with people; and even asks them what they think. I trust that Hannah will do the same. Yet when I think about them growing up, I become concerned, because I know that people in organizations often do not work together with such openness. Somewhere along the way, as children mature, they recognize this and learn to adapt to organizations, becoming less open and honest. The quality of our organizations and the quality of our work lives suffer for it. I hope that this book in some way can help people create the open, honest working relationships that are essential for people to work together effectively.

R.M.S.

The Author

Roger M. Schwarz is associate professor of public management and government and assistant director at the Institute of Government, The University of North Carolina at Chapel Hill. He received his B.S. degree (1978) in psychology from Tufts University, his A.M. degree (1980) in organizational psychology from The University of Michigan, his M.Ed. degree (1981) from the Harvard University Graduate School of Education, and his Ph.D. (1986) in organizational psychology from The University of Michigan.

At the Institute of Government, Schwarz teaches, writes, conducts research, and acts as a consultant to public officials in North Carolina. His areas of interest include managing organizational change and conflict, developing effective work groups, and improving service quality. He has published articles on these topics. He has served as a group facilitator to numerous groups in public, nonprofit, and private organizations, and he teaches workshops on group facilitation and facilitative leadership.

Part One How Facilitation Helps Groups Achieve Their Goals

Chapter One Group Facilitation and the Role of the Facilitator

People depend on groups to accomplish what individuals alone cannot. Yet, groups are often disappointing. Consider these examples:

- A department head and his section heads meet weekly to discuss the performance of the department. The department head does most of the talking. The section heads occasionally share their observations, being careful not to challenge the department head's opinions directly. After each meeting, the section heads discuss privately how the department's performance would improve if the department head understood how he contributed to the problems. Down the hall, the department head confides in his assistant that he questions how well the section heads can manage their units if they act like yes-men with him. No one ever discusses in the full group the concerns aired after each meeting.
- A top management team meets to solve a complicated problem that affects the entire organization. All are experienced, successful managers, and they quickly identify a solution and implement it. Just as they think they have solved the problem, it returns in a different form, and the problem gets worse. Despite many attempts, the team cannot get rid of the problem.
- A board meets every other week to make policy decisions. Each time an issue comes up, members take sides, pushing their positions. They rarely share their reasons for taking their positions and no one asks. Members leave the meetings frustrated, sometimes even when they have won the vote. Despite all the decisions they make, members feel the board has no unified direction.

■ A newly formed group comprising representatives from local business organizations, the police department, community groups, and the schools meet to
try to figure out how to reduce crime in their community. All members agree
on the group's goals and are willing to devote time, energy, and money to
solve the problem. Yet the group members' optimism quickly evaporates as
they blame each other for causing the problem.

Groups do not have to function in ways that lead to ineffective performance and frustrate group members. Groups can improve the ways they work.

This book is about helping work groups to improve their effectiveness by
using facilitation skills. It is about helping all types of work groups: top management teams, boards, committees, work teams, quality groups, task forces, and
employee-management groups.

Consultants and managers need facilitation skills to be effective. Organizational consultants—both internal and external—use facilitation skills when
they contract with clients and diagnose and intervene in organizations. Managers
use facilitation skills to help employees learn to identify and solve problems for
themselves. Most of these activities occur in groups.

As organizations have made significant changes, the need for facilitation
skills to improve their effectiveness has increased. Examples include efforts to
improve the quality of products and services, empower employees, develop shared
visions, develop self-managing work teams, create learning organizations, and
develop organizational cultures that make these changes possible. Organizations
use groups of employees to plan and implement most of the changes, and the
groups typically require some form of facilitation. In addition, facilitation skills
have become more important as organizations try to openly and constructively
manage conflicts that arise from these and other changes they try to create.

At the heart of improving group effectiveness lies the ability of group
members to reflect on what they are doing, in order to create the conditions
necessary to achieve their goals. Groups find it difficult to openly examine their
behavior on their own; they often need the help of a facilitator.

What Is Group Facilitation?

**Group facilitation is a process in which a person who is acceptable to all
members of the group, substantively neutral, and has no decision-making authority intervenes to help a group improve the way it identifies and solves problems
and makes decisions, in order to increase the group's effectiveness.**

To intervene means "to enter into an ongoing system" for the purpose of
helping those in the system (Argyris, 1970, p. 15). The definition implies that the
system—or group—functions autonomously—that is, the group is complete without a facilitator. Yet the group depends on a facilitator for help. Consequently,
**to maintain the group's autonomy and to develop its long-term effectiveness, the
facilitator's interventions should decrease the group's dependence on the facili-**

tator. Ideally, the facilitator accomplishes this by intervening in a way that teaches group members the skills of facilitation.

Although the ideas in this book are relevant for many types of groups, the book focuses on work groups, which have certain characteristics. First, a group has a collective responsibility for performing one or more tasks, the outcome of which can be assessed (Hackman, 1989). The outcome may be a product, service, or decision. Second, a work group is an open social system. It has boundaries that distinguish members from nonmembers, its members are interdependent, and they have specific roles (Alderfer, 1977). Sometimes, a group is formed from two or more other interdependent groups that are in conflict but want to improve their relationship. Examples include union-management groups, environmentalist–real estate developer groups, and town-university groups. Third, a work group operates in an organizational context, which requires it to manage its transactions with other individuals and groups (Hackman, 1989). Examples of groups that have the three characteristics include emergency medical service teams, personnel departments, task forces, school faculties, basketball teams, selection committees, city councils, boards of directors, and quality teams.

To ensure that the facilitator is trusted by all group members and that the group's autonomy is maintained, the facilitator should be acceptable to all members of the group, be substantively neutral—that is, the facilitator should display no preference for any of the solutions the group considers—and not have decision-making authority. In practice, the facilitator can meet these three criteria only if the facilitator is not a group member. While a group member may be acceptable to other members and may not have decision-making authority, the person has a substantive interest in the group's issues. **By definition, a group member cannot *formally* fill the role of facilitator. Still, a group member can use the principles and techniques described in this book to help the group.** Effective leaders regularly facilitate their groups as part of their leadership role.

The facilitator's client is the entire group, not certain members. Consequently, the facilitator's interventions should not help certain members at the expense of others. Nor can the facilitator accept the views of one member as automatically representing those of other members.

The facilitator's main task is to help the group increase its effectiveness by improving its process. *Process* refers to how a group works together. Process includes how members talk to each other, how they identify and solve problems, how they make decisions, and how they handle conflict. In contrast, *content* refers to what a group is working on. For example, the content of a group discussion may be whether to move the organization's offices, how to provide higher-quality service to customers, or what each group member's responsibilities should be. Whenever a group meets, it is possible to observe both its content and process. For example, in a discussion about how to provide higher-quality service, suggestions about installing a customer hotline or giving more authority to those with customer contact reflect content. However, members responding to only certain members' ideas or failing to identify their assumptions are facets of the group's process.

Underlying the facilitator's main task is the fundamental assumption that **ineffective group process reduces a group's ability to solve problems and make decisions.** While research findings on the issue are mixed (Kaplan, 1979), the premise of the book is that by increasing the effectiveness of the group's process, the facilitator helps the group improve its performance. The facilitator does not intervene in the content of the group's discussions; to do so would require the facilitator to abandon neutrality and would reduce the group's responsibility for solving its problems.

Basic and Developmental Facilitation

Facilitation can be divided into two types, which are based on the objectives of the group (Table 1.1). In *basic facilitation,* the group seeks only to solve a substantive problem, such as developing an incentive pay program or establishing long-term goals. The group uses a facilitator to *temporarily* improve its process in order to solve the substantive problem. When the group has solved its problem, the facilitation objective has been achieved, although the group may not have necessarily improved the effectiveness of its process. Consequently, if another difficult substantive problem arises, the group will likely again require a facilitator.

In *developmental facilitation,* the group seeks to *permanently* improve its process while solving a substantive problem. The group uses a facilitator to learn how to improve its process and applies its newly developed skills to solve its substantive problem. When the group has accomplished its objectives, it will—as in basic facilitation—have solved its substantive problem. But just as important, the group will have improved its ability to manage its process. Consequently, if another difficult substantive problem arises, the group will be less dependent on a facilitator.

The two approaches mean different roles for the facilitator. **In basic facilitation, although the group can influence the process at any time, in general it expects the facilitator to guide the group using what he or she considers effective group process. In developmental facilitation, members expect to monitor and guide the group's process and expect the facilitator to teach them how to accomplish this goal.**

Think of process as the vehicle a group uses to reach its desired destination (goal). The basic facilitator is a mechanic who fixes the group's car well enough to get the group to its destination. If the group wants to take another difficult trip, it may need a mechanic again. In contrast, the developmental facilitator is a teacher, instructing members in how to monitor, repair, and redesign their vehicle so they can use it to reach whatever destination they seek.

Basic and developmental facilitators intervene for different reasons. In general, **a basic facilitator intervenes when the group's process or other factors affecting the group interfere with its accomplishing specific, substantive goals.**

Table 1.1. Basic and Developmental Facilitation.

Characteristic	Basic Facilitation	Developmental Facilitation
Group objective	Solve a substantive problem	Solve a substantive problem while learning to improve its process
Facilitator role	■ Help group temporarily improve its process ■ Take primary responsibility for managing the group's process	■ Help group permanently improve its process ■ Share responsibility for managing the group's process
Outcome for group	Dependence on facilitator for solving future problems	Reduced dependence on facilitator for solving future problems

The interventions are designed to help the group accomplish its substantive goals without necessarily learning how to improve its process.

A developmental facilitator intervenes under the same conditions as a basic facilitator. But in addition, a developmental facilitator intervenes when the group's process or other factors affecting the group hinder the group's long-term effectiveness or when reflecting on the process will help members develop their process skills. The interventions are designed to help the group learn how to diagnose and improve its process. A fundamental difference between basic and developmental facilitation is the difference between doing something for a group and teaching a group how to do the same thing for itself.

As noted earlier, both basic and developmental facilitators intervene when factors other than group process hinder the group. Chapter Two discusses the other factors. Throughout the book, the terms *basic facilitators* and *basic groups* refer to facilitators and groups using basic facilitation. Similarly, the terms *developmental facilitators* and *developmental groups* refer to facilitators and groups using developmental facilitation.

Given that ineffective group process hinders a group's ability to solve substantive problems, basic facilitation is essentially limited. It helps a group solve one substantive problem without exploring why it has trouble solving problems in general. In contrast, developmental facilitation focuses on why the group has trouble solving substantive problems.

Still, developmental facilitation is not always the best approach for every group. Whether a facilitator uses a basic or developmental approach with a particular client depends on several factors. Obviously, the group's primary goal is a major factor. A second important factor is time. Groups unable to devote the time necessary for developmental facilitation should not pursue it. Even when adequate time is available, if the group is a temporary one (such as a task force), the investment required for developmental facilitation may not be worth it. A third factor is group stability. Even if the initial group learns to facilitate itself, if the group membership changes frequently or drastically, it may not be able to sustain the skill. A final factor is control over process. Unless the group has control over its process, including how it makes decisions, developmental facilitation may be of limited use.

This discussion has assumed that basic and developmental facilitation are pure types. In practice, facilitation occurs on a continuum from purely basic to purely developmental.

Core Values That Guide Facilitation

Every third-party role is based on a set of assumptions about human behavior. Assumptions include values (things worth striving for) and beliefs (things considered to be true) that typically are accepted as valid without testing. Because assumptions clarify biases, identifying them is important.

This book's approach to facilitation is based on three values: valid information, free and informed choice, and internal commitment to those choices. The three core values are listed in Table 1.2 and come from the work of Chris Argyris and Don Schön (Argyris, 1970; Argyris & Schön, 1974). *Valid information* means that people share all information relevant to an issue, using specific examples so that other people can determine independently whether the information is true. Valid information also means that people understand the information that is being shared with them.

Free and informed choice means that people can define their own objectives and the methods for achieving them and that their choices are based on valid information. When people make free choices, they are not coerced or manipulated. Consequently, **facilitators do not change peoples' behavior. Facilitators provide information that enables people to decide whether to change their behavior. If they decide to change their behavior, the facilitator helps them learn how to change.**

Internal commitment to the choice means that people feel personally responsible for the decisions they make. Each person is committed to the decision because it is intrinsically compelling or satisfying, not because the person will be rewarded or penalized for making that decision.

The core values create a reinforcing cycle. People require valid information to make an informed choice. When people make free and informed choices, they become internally committed to the choices. When people are internally committed to their decisions, they take responsibility for seeing that the decisions are implemented effectively. Finally, people who value valid information continually seek new information to determine whether their decisions remain sound or should be changed.

The core values serve two parallel purposes—they guide effective group behavior, and they guide effective facilitator behavior. To examine how the values serve as a guide for effective group behavior, consider what happens when groups' actions are inconsistent with the core values.

Table 1.2. Core Values Guiding Facilitation.

Core Value	Description
Valid information	■ People share all relevant information. ■ People share information in a way that others understand it. ■ People share information in a way that others can independently validate it. ■ People continually seek new information to determine whether previous decisions should be changed.
Free and informed choice	■ People define their own objectives and methods for achieving them. ■ People are not coerced or manipulated. ■ People base their choices on valid information.
Internal commitment to the choice	■ People feel personally responsible for their decisions. ■ People find their choices intrinsically compelling or satisfying.

Source: Adapted from the work of Chris Argyris and Don Schön (Argyris, 1970; Argyris & Schön, 1974).

For example, members often try to influence decisions by sharing information that supports their positions and withholding information that undermines them. They often withhold information that they believe will make them look bad. They place a higher value on winning the discussion or protecting their own interests than on sharing valid information. Because valid information has been withheld, groups often make poor decisions. The example of the department head and his section heads at the beginning of the chapter is one illustration of withholding valid information. The Challenger Shuttle disaster—caused by the failure of an O-ring, which some organizational members believed might malfunction—is a vivid and tragic example of what can happen when valid information is withheld.

Group members are often asked to commit to achieving a goal without having any control over how they will accomplish the goal or what the goal should be. They often become compliant. They may do only what is minimally necessary to complete the job, expending extra effort only when they believe others are watching. Because of the lack of internal commitment, the group fails to accomplish the goal.

Facilitators help groups improve their process by helping them to act in ways that are consistent with the core values. **In developmental facilitation, the group members develop the ability, over time, to identify when they have acted inconsistently with the core values and to correct their behavior—without a facilitator's help. In basic facilitation, the group uses a facilitator to help it act consistently with the core values, temporarily, while working with the facilitator.**

Facilitators should also use the core values to guide their own behavior. They should provide valid information by sharing their observations with the group about how members have acted consistently and inconsistently with the core values and other principles of group effectiveness. By helping group members to see the consequences of their behavior and by asking them whether they want to change, facilitators enable the group to make free and informed choices. Consequently, members become committed to the choices they make during facilitation.

Central to this approach to facilitation is the assumption that effective facilitator and effective group behaviors are guided by the same core values. This means that when facilitators act effectively, they are models of effective behavior for group members. The notion that using the core values leads to effective process is not an untested assumption. It has been borne out by more than twenty years of research (Argyris, 1982, 1985, 1987, 1990; Argyris, Putnam, & Smith, 1985, Argyris & Schön, 1974, 1978).

Throughout the book, key principles as well as other values and beliefs that stem from the core values are identified in boldface type.

The Role of the Facilitator

Essentially, the facilitator's role is to help the group improve its process in a manner consistent with valid information, free and informed choice, and internal commitment to the choices. The facilitator accomplishes this by helping the group establish ground rules for effective group process, identifying behavior that is both inconsistent and consistent with the ground rules, and helping members learn more effective behavior.

The role of a facilitator becomes clearer by considering what a facilitator is *not*. First, a facilitator is not a group member. The facilitator has no role in the content of the group's decisions. For example, if the group is deciding when to start a project, the facilitator does not vote or even express an opinion. Second, a facilitator is also not a clerical or errand person for the group. Third, a facilitator is not an intermediary between the group and the larger organization. The facilitator's client is the group. The group and other parts of the organization are responsible for their own communications with each other. Finally, the facilitator is not an arbitrator or judge. The group is responsible for making its own decisions and resolving its own conflicts.

Facilitators need a variety of skills and abilities to fill their role, including accurately listening to, observing, and remembering behavior and conversation; communicating clearly; identifying similarities and differences among statements; understanding multiple perspectives; analyzing and synthesizing issues; identifying assumptions; diagnosing and intervening on effective and ineffective behavior; being a model of effective behavior; providing feedback without creating defensive reactions; accepting feedback without reacting defensively; monitoring and changing one's own behavior while working with a group; developing the trust of clients; empathizing with clients; providing support and encouragement; and having patience. This list is not exhaustive. But no list can capture the complexity of the facilitator's role.

The Facilitator's Responsibility for the Group's Outcomes

What responsibility does the facilitator have for the group's failure or success? Some inexperienced facilitators may feel totally responsible for a group's actions;

if the group fails, the facilitators believe they are to blame. On the other hand, other facilitators may feel that they have no responsibility for a group's success or failure.

The extent to which facilitators are responsible for a group's effectiveness depends on their own behavior. **So long as they act effectively, facilitators are not responsible for the group's ineffective behavior or its consequences.** However, a facilitator is responsible for the group's ineffective behavior and its consequences to the extent that it stems from the facilitator's ineffective behavior. Consider, for example, a top management group that commits to making decisions by unanimous agreement but then votes six to four to install a new organization-wide computer network, although several managers insist that the network will not meet their departments' needs. Once installed and debugged, the computer network remains unused, largely because it fails to perform critical tasks needed by several departments. The facilitator would be partly responsible for the effect of the group's poor decision if the facilitator had not shared with the group that several members' interests were not met in the decision, that the group was violating its own ground rule by voting, and that negative consequences could develop as a result of these behaviors.

Basic facilitators fulfill their responsibilities to their groups by acting consistently with the core values, identifying for the groups when members have acted inconsistently or consistently with principles of effective group behavior, and letting the groups make free and informed choices based on the facilitators' interventions. In addition, developmental facilitators help group members learn how to identify when they have acted inconsistently with principles of effective group behavior, and they help group members correct their behavior.

Because the facilitator does not get involved in the content of decisions, the facilitator is not directly responsible for *what* the group decides. However, because facilitators are involved in the decision *process,* they are responsible for helping the group consider *how* its process may lead to more or less effective decisions. For example, imagine that a group is trying to decide what data to use to predict the size of the market for its services. The facilitator does not offer an opinion about what would be the best data to use. However, the facilitator does help the group consider what criteria it is using to make the decision. When members disagree about what would be the best data to use, the facilitator helps them design ways to test their disagreement.

When the group does make mistakes, the facilitator is responsible for helping the members analyze the process they used to make the decision that led to the mistake. By determining where the group went wrong (for example, it may have made an erroneous assumption), members can agree on what they will do differently next time.

If the content of a group's decisions improves as the process improves, does it not follow that all mistakes in content flow from poor process—and therefore are partly the facilitator's responsibility? The answer is no, for several reasons.

First, effective group process, and problem solving in particular, is based on assumptions that all relevant information is available and accurate and that the consequences of actions can be predicted accurately. Obviously, such assumptions are often incorrect. When the assumptions are violated, groups can make content mistakes even when their process is effective.

Second, as Chapter Two describes, effective group process is necessary but not sufficient for creating an effective group. An effective group also requires an effective structure and a supportive organizational context. An effective structure includes such elements as members who have appropriate knowledge and skills; well-designed, motivating jobs; and adequate time for members to complete the task. A supportive organizational context includes aspects of the larger organization that influence the group, including a supportive culture, rewards consistent with the group's objectives, and various resources.

Finally, a facilitator must respect a group's free and informed choice to use an ineffective group process that may lead to poor content decisions. For many facilitators, this is the hardest test of whether they will enable their groups to make free and informed choices. Yet it may also be the most important test. If, by trying to help a group avoid poor process, the facilitator prevents the group from making its own choice, the facilitator acts inconsistently with the core values. Ultimately, this reduces the credibility of the facilitator. Also, this may suggest incorrectly to clients that the core values can be ignored when they seem inconvenient.

Comparing Facilitation and Mediation

Basic and developmental facilitation and the role of the facilitator can be clarified by comparing them to mediation. People often use the words *facilitation* and *mediation* interchangeably. While there are similarities between the two, there are also important differences. According to Moore (1986, p. 14), "Mediation is the intervention into a dispute or negotiation by an acceptable, impartial, and neutral third party who has no authoritative decision-making power to assist disputing parties in voluntarily reaching their own mutually acceptable settlement of issues in dispute."

Before comparing facilitation and mediation, a warning is in order. There are no single, agreed-upon definitions of facilitation and mediation. Some people who call themselves facilitators may act more like what this book describes as mediators. Some mediators will find that this book reflects their own approach. In describing facilitation and mediation, this book focuses on the most basic differences, recognizing that some readers may disagree.

Facilitation and mediation are similar in that both involve interventions by a neutral third party who is acceptable to the clients and who has no decision-making authority. Both seek to help groups reach decisions that are acceptable to all members. Facilitators and mediators share many of the same skills and techniques, but they apply them in different situations and sometimes to accomplish different objectives. In general, mediation is more similar to basic facilitation than to developmental facilitation.

Objectives. Facilitation and mediation have different objectives. The objective of mediation is to help the parties negotiate a settlement to a particular conflict (Wall, 1981). Parties who seek a mediator have a conflict they have been unable to settle.

The objective of facilitation, on the other hand, is to help a group improve its process for solving problems and making decisions so that it can achieve its goals and increase its overall effectiveness. Although dealing with conflict can be a significant part of facilitation, it is not always the primary focus. In addition, developmental facilitation seeks to help the group permanently improve its process for solving problems. By transferring the skills of the facilitator to the group, the group becomes less dependent on the facilitator. In short, developmental facilitators seek to work themselves out of a job.

Entering into the Process. Because mediators help parties resolve their conflicts, the parties typically seek a mediator after they reach impasse—that is, when they believe they can progress no further. When facilitators help groups resolve conflicts, they too are sometimes called in after the groups have reached an impasse. But often they become involved earlier. For example, a group may seek basic facilitation because members understand that they do not have skills sufficient to manage the process of what is expected to be a difficult discussion. Facilitators often enter the process after a group has gone through a critical incident, such as a significant change in group membership or group mission. Less often, groups seek a facilitator solely for development, without external pressure to change.

Controlling the Process. Facilitators and mediators help groups by influencing the process that they use to work with one another. Yet, mediators exert greater control over the process than facilitators do. The mediator controls the process by determining who should talk when and by having the disputants follow certain ground rules and a set procedure and discuss the conflict in a specific order. **Facilitators and their clients jointly control the process of facilitation.** A basic facilitator guides much of the group's process, so the group can focus on the content, but the group can actively share control whenever it chooses. In developmental facilitation, the group and facilitator actively share control of the process.

Leaving the Role of Facilitator

Sometimes, it is appropriate for the facilitator to temporarily leave the role of facilitator and play another role. This section considers the different roles, when it is beneficial to play them, and what risks the facilitator faces in doing so.

The Facilitator as Mediator

Another difference between facilitators and mediators is that a facilitator works in the presence of the entire group, whereas the mediator may work with the parties together as well as separately. The problem with a facilitator's playing the role of a mediator is illustrated by the differences in the roots of the two words. *Mediate* comes from a word meaning "to come between"—in this context, to come between group members. *Facilitate* comes from a word meaning "to make easy"—in this context, to make it easy for the group to be effective. (It is worth noting that facilitated groups work hard in order to make it easier for them to be effective.) **One of the facilitator's goals is to improve group members' ability to work together effectively; serving as an intermediary usually limits the achievement of this goal because members are not required to deal directly with each other.**

However, in some situations it is reasonable for the facilitator to temporarily play the role of mediator—to come between the different parties that constitute the group. One such situation arises when the facilitator is beginning to work with the group and different subgroups have concerns about whether the facilitator will be impartial and sensitive to their needs. Because the subgroups may not raise their concerns in the full group, it is reasonable for the facilitator to meet separately with the subgroups to hear their concerns. Similarly, when a subgroup is reluctant to even meet in the larger group, it is reasonable for the facilitator to talk with the subgroup and explore its concerns.

A facilitator may also reasonably act as a mediator when one or more members of the group want to raise an issue in the larger group but do not know how to do it. Here, the facilitator can help the members figure out how to raise the issue in the larger group. In any event, the facilitator should avoid raising the issue for the members. Doing so would increase the group's dependence on the facilitator. It could also set the facilitator up if, after raising the issue for certain members, the members deny raising the issue with the facilitator.

Facilitators face a dilemma when a subset of the client group engages them in a conversation about the group. For example, before a session is to begin, two members approach the facilitator to say that another group member is creating problems for the group and that they want the member "brought back into line." Further, they may request that the facilitator raise the issue. If the facilitator discusses with these members how the other member is acting out, in order to see whether they are willing to raise the issue, the facilitator collects information about the group that the facilitator cannot act on and cannot share with others, unless those raising the issue agree to share it. On the other hand, if the facilitator immediately stops the conversation, members are less likely to raise the issue in the group. One way to avoid the dilemma is for facilitators to tell the entire group at the outset that they cannot guarantee to keep confidential any conversation about the group that members have with them outside the group. In addition, the facilitator can help the members discuss how to raise an issue without discussing the issue itself.

A facilitator may temporarily act as mediator when conflict between subgroups causes communication to almost completely break down. For example, I facilitated a union-management cooperative effort in which the seven union members of the union-management committee simultaneously closed their notebooks and walked out in the middle of a meeting. The discussions had become tense, and union members were frustrated by what they perceived to be management's efforts to undermine the process. As the facilitator, I saw two choices. I could stay in the room, let the union leave, and see the process unravel, along with the progress the committee had made. Or, I could temporarily assume the role of mediator and talk with the union members, trying to find a way to help union and management members to work together again. I chose the latter course and spent the next six hours mediating in meetings and phone calls. The next morning, the union and management subgroups were back in the room, discussing why the process had broken down and exploring ways to prevent it from recurring.

When conflict is so great that subgroups are not willing to talk with each other and the facilitator decides to mediate by conveying information between subgroups, the facilitator must decide what information to share. Here, the facilitator should have a clear agreement with each subgroup about the kinds of information that may be shared with the other subgroup.

The facilitator as mediator can sometimes prevent a difficult conflict from escalating to the point where the group essentially breaks down and ceases to function. However, by agreeing to mediate, the facilitator may reduce the likelihood that the group will develop the skills to resolve conflicts. Also, working with subgroups may lead group members to question the facilitator's neutrality. Therefore, the facilitator should serve as a mediator only when the benefits to the group seem to outweigh the costs. When doing so, the facilitator should state clearly that she or he is serving in the mediator role.

Colluding with Clients

Collusion is a secret agreement or cooperation, especially for a deceitful purpose. When a facilitator colludes with a group, the facilitator often is asked to act in a particular way but to deny doing so. **Collusion is inconsistent with the facilitator's role, because it requires the facilitator to withhold valid information and consequently prevents free and informed choice for certain group members, and it places the interests of some group members above the interests of the group as a whole.** Often, clients implicitly invite a facilitator to collude when they ask the facilitator to mediate.

The facilitator might collude in several ways: with one or more group members against one or more other group members, with one or more group members against a nongroup member, and with a nongroup member against one or more group members. The following examples illustrate the types of collusion:

- A group member approaches the facilitator before a meeting. The member says he wants to raise an issue in the meeting but does not want the group to know it is his issue. He is concerned that the issue will not get the attention it deserves if the group thinks he is raising it. He asks the facilitator to raise the issue "at an appropriate time" but to not tell the group where it originated. The facilitator agrees.
- A task force is about to meet with the department head to which it reports

(the department head is not a member of the task force) to recommend changes in the department. It has been agreed that the task force facilitator will facilitate the meeting. Before the meeting, the task force members realize that they have made some assumptions about the department head that they have not confirmed with her. The recommendations will work only if the assumptions are true. But they are reluctant to ask the department head about the assumptions, because they involve a sensitive issue. They ask the facilitator not to raise the assumptions in the meeting or to pursue them if the department head mentions them. The facilitator agrees.

- A group leader's supervisor (who is not a member of the group) tells the facilitator that the group is spending too much time on an issue. The supervisor is especially concerned that the group is spending time discussing issues that are not within its charge. The supervisor asks the facilitator to attend fewer group meetings and, when facilitating, to steer the group away from the issues. The facilitator says, "OK, I'll see what I can do."

One way to avoid colluding with the group is to discuss, as part of the contract, what the facilitator can and cannot do. Facilitators can give examples of requests that they cannot fulfill because they would lead to collusion.

When facilitators receive a request that would require them to collude with the group, facilitators should explain how fulfilling the request would require that they act outside the role of facilitator. The facilitator should then invite the individual to ask questions and to disagree. In this way, the facilitator can work with the person making the request to find a way for that person to raise the issue directly with the relevant individuals. For example, the facilitator might begin by saying, "I think it is important that the group hear your concern, and I think it is appropriate for you to discuss it with them. Would you be willing to talk with me about how you can have that conversation with the group?"

The Facilitator as Evaluator

The facilitator faces a role conflict when someone in the organization asks the facilitator to evaluate the performance of one or more members in the group. For example, a department head, who is not a member of the facilitated group, may be concerned about the performance of one of the group members. She may ask the facilitator to evaluate the member to help her decide whether to take any corrective action. Alternatively, she may be considering promoting one of several members of the group and may ask the facilitator to evaluate the members to help her make the promotion decision.

The facilitator has a role conflict because evaluating group members jeopardizes the members' trust in the facilitator. One reason members trust the facilitator is that the facilitator has no authority and adheres to the principle that **the facilitator does not use information obtained within facilitation to influence decisions about group members (or any organization members) that are made outside facilitation.** Evaluating group members increases the facilitator's power in the organization. Therefore, it decreases the likelihood that members will discuss openly information that could prove harmful to them.

The Facilitator as Content Expert or Information Resource

When a facilitator has information that may be relevant to a group's task, the facilitator is a potential content expert or information resource for the group. For example, the facilitator may know how to establish a recycling program or a valid performance appraisal system. Or, the facilitator may simply know who the group can contact to obtain such expertise. Periodically, members may ask the facilitator to share information or opinions the facilitator has on a subject.

The group is able to quickly obtain information to solve its problem when the facilitator serves as a content expert or information resource. But the quick fix creates other risks. One risk is that the group will begin to see the facilitator as a substantively non-neutral third party, which reduces the facilitator's credibility and, ultimately, effectiveness. A second risk is that the group will become more dependent on the facilitator. Group members may become sensitive to whether the facilitator approves of their decisions, which affect the decisions they make.

The facilitator as content expert or information resource is an acceptable role only when the facilitator and group have explicitly contracted for it. Even when this is the case, the facilitator can take several steps to reduce the risk that any expert interventions will negatively affect the facilitation role. First, the facilitator should act as information resource or expert only when asked by the group and only when the group reaches consensus to do so. Second, before doing so, facilitators always should announce to the group that they are temporarily leaving the role of facilitator to serve as an information resource or expert. This makes it clear to the group that the facilitator is sharing the information other than as a substantively neutral third party. When the information has been provided, facilitators should announce that they are resuming the role of facilitator. Third, facilitators should limit their expert role to factual information and should not indulge in opinion. Finally, in the early stages of working with a group, the facilitator should avoid filling the role of content expert or information resource. The group's heavy dependency on the facilitator at this point creates greater risks.

People who facilitate groups in their own organization—known as *internal facilitators*—are often asked by members of the group to play an expert role. Chapter Twelve discusses how internal facilitators can provide expert information and facilitate effectively.

The Myth of Total Neutrality. It is a myth that facilitators can always be neutral about the substance or content of a group's discussions while being partial about what constitutes effective group process. Recall that *substantively neutral* means that a facilitator conveys no preferences for any solutions the group considers.

Facilitators are partial about what constitutes effective group process because that is their substantive area of expertise. They know what kinds of behaviors are more or less likely to lead to effective problem solving and other important group outcomes—and they convey this knowledge in several ways. When they ask group members to follow certain ground rules (such as sharing all relevant information) or when they identify how members have acted inconsistently with the core values, they identify their beliefs about what constitutes effective group process. When facilitators use the core values to guide their own behavior, their behavior is a reflection of their theory of effective interpersonal process. In fact, embedded in each of the facilitator's interventions is some prescription for effective behavior. In other words, because facilitators are always modeling behavior, and because embedded in their behavior are beliefs about effective group process, facilitators are constantly conveying their beliefs through their actions.

Consequently, **the facilitator is not neutral about the content of a group's discussion when it involves how to manage group or interpersonal process more effectively.** In such cases, the facilitator's theory about what makes group process effective can be used to address the group's substantive discussion about how to manage process more effectively. As the group's process becomes the subject of discussion, the facilitator's comments about process focus on the group's content. Consequently, the facilitator becomes involved in the content of the discussion. Because many management issues involve some aspect of interpersonal or group process, the facilitator's theory of group effectiveness has implications for how groups handle many issues.

However, the facilitators' role is not to impose the principles that guide their interventions with the group on the group's substantive solutions. To do so would be inconsistent with the facilitator's role. The chapters on intervention describe some ways that the facilitator can deal with this issue.

Summary

Group facilitation is the process by which a person who is acceptable to all members of the group, substantively neutral, and has no decision-making authority intervenes to help a group improve the way it identifies and solves problems and makes decisions, in order to increase the group's effectiveness. Basic facilitation seeks to help groups solve a substantive problem. Developmental facilitation seeks to help members solve a substantive problem while learning to improve their group process. Both types of facilitation are based on the core values of valid information, free and informed choice, and internal commitment. The facilitator's role is designed to help groups act consistently with the core values. While temporarily leaving the role of facilitator is appropriate at times, it may also jeopardize the facilitator's and the group's ability to act consistently with these values.

Chapter Two What Makes Work Groups Effective?

Readers probably have had a variety of experiences working in groups. For most people, those experiences are mixed. In some groups, the members worked well together, accomplished the task, and met some of each member's needs. In other groups, the task was done poorly (if at all), the members did not get along, and members felt frustrated. What factors might members say contributed to the group's success? For example, did they have clear goals? Did the members agree on how they should work together? What factors might members say contributed to the group's ineffectiveness? Were there undiscussed conflicts? Were members not motivated by the tasks? Were they missing certain expertise?

The answers to these questions begin to describe a model of group effectiveness. A model is like a pair of glasses for looking at a group. The glasses enable a facilitator to see and understand patterns that are affecting the group's effectiveness, for good or for ill. Every facilitator formulates a model about what makes a group effective, even if the model includes only two or three elements. Even if facilitators are not conscious of their models, they still use them as diagnostic and intervention guides, to decide where to look when things go wrong and what to change. Like glasses, the model is valuable only as a tool, to help facilitators better observe and understand groups. Unfortunately, facilitators' models often are of limited use because they do not identify all the major elements that contribute to effectiveness.

The elements that contribute to group effectiveness are not random. Groups need to have and do certain things to be effective. **To help groups become more effective, facilitators must understand the elements that contribute to group effectiveness and how those elements interact. The knowledge enables facilitators**

Figure 2.1. Group-Effectiveness Model.

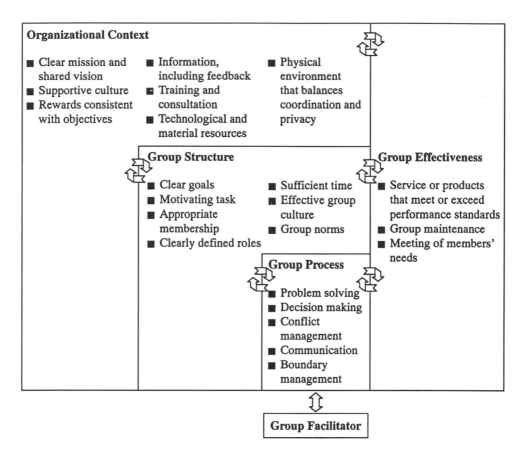

to determine how members' behaviors and others factors contribute to and detract from group effectiveness and to recognize the limits of group facilitation.

As we discussed in Chapter One, groups become more effective when their process is consistent with their core values. But group process is only one of the factors that makes groups effective. This chapter describes a model of group effectiveness that facilitators can use to guide their diagnosis and intervention. The model helps facilitators determine whether a group is being effective, identify which factors and elements that contribute to effectiveness are missing or present, and decide how to intervene to help a group become more effective and determine whether facilitation alone can improve the group's effectiveness.

A Model of Group Effectiveness

The model described here (see Figure 2.1) builds largely on the work of J. Richard Hackman (1987) and Eric Sundstrom, Kenneth P. De Meuse, and David Futrell (1990).

What Makes a Work Group Effective?

Before answering the question of what elements contribute to a work group's effectiveness we must first consider what it means for a group to be effective. An effective work group meets the three criteria listed in Exhibit 2.1. Rather than measure the quality and quantity of the service or product against some objective standard, the first criterion uses the expectations and satisfaction of the group's customers to determine whether the group's service or product is acceptable. There are two reasons for this. First, many groups do not have objective standards of performance that can be measured clearly or easily. Second, what happens to a group often depends more on those outside the group, who either evaluate its performance directly or receive its products or services, than on any objective performance index alone. The criterion reinforces the idea that groups must respond to the demands of their customers in order to be effective (Katz & Kahn, 1978; Zeithaml, Parasuraman, & Berry, 1990). Groups must meet the demands of two types of customers: internal customers—those inside the organization who either receive the group's work or evaluate its performance—and external customers—those outside the organization who receive the group's work.

The second criterion takes into account that most groups work together over an extended period on a series of tasks. Unlike a task force, which is formed to perform a specific task and is then disbanded, most groups must continue working together on subsequent tasks. Consequently, the processes they use must enable them to continue working together effectively. For example, group processes that burn out members or that erode trust among members would reduce members' capability to work together on subsequent group tasks.

The third criterion recognizes that group members' needs must also be satisfied. For example, members may have a need for challenging and interesting work. If the group's work is boring and fails to motivate members, the quality of the work is likely to suffer eventually. Similarly, the service or product the group provides must meet members' own standards of quality. In the long run, groups that do not meet their members' needs will be less effective.

To be effective, the group must meet all three criteria, which are interrelated. For example, if a group's process reduces the members' ability to work together or if members' needs are not being met, the quality of the group's service

Exhibit 2.1. Three Criteria for Effective Groups.

1. The services that the group delivers or the products it makes meet or exceed the performance standards of the people who receive it, use it, or review it.

2. The processes and structures used to carry out the work maintain or enhance the capability of members to work together on subsequent group tasks.

3. The group experience, on balance, satisfies rather than frustrates the personal needs of group members.

Source: Adapted from Hackman (1987).

or product is likely to drop in the long run. Groups are not, however, either effective or ineffective; their effectiveness is measured on a continuum that ranges from completely effective to not at all effective.

Three factors contribute to group effectiveness: group process, group structure, and the organizational context (Hackman, 1987; Hackman, 1989). Each factor has a number of elements (Figure 2.1). On the one hand, group process and group structure can be thought of as characteristics of a group. The organizational context, on the other hand, comprises elements of the larger organization that are relevant to the group's structure and process. The interrelationships among group process, group structure, and organizational context are complex. For now, it is sufficient to say that each element can influence the others, as illustrated by the arrows in the diagram. As Figure 2.1 shows, **facilitators intervene directly through a group's process, enabling the group to examine and perhaps change its process, structure, and organizational context.**

Group Process

Process refers to *how* things are done rather than *what* is done (Schein, 1987). To be effective, groups must manage a number of processes, which are shaded in Figure 2.2. **The two primary group processes are problem solving and decision making.**

Problem Solving. Except for groups that have a mission to carry out orders without asking questions or making judgments, problem solving is at the core of a group's activities. A problem is simply a gap between what is desired and what exists. For example, a problem exists when social work cases are closed within sixty days when the standard requires that they be closed within forty-five days. Problem solving is the systematic approach a group uses to identify a problem, establish criteria for evaluating potential solutions, collect relevant information, identify the causes of the problem, evaluate and select a solution, implement it, and evaluate it.

A group with an effective problem-solving process meets two conditions. First, members use a systematic process for solving problems. This seems obvious, but many groups are not systematic. Members often begin to solve the problem by suggesting solutions before agreeing on the problem or its causes. Consequently, potential causes are not considered, and the group's solution does not solve the problem. The second condition for effective problem solving is that all members focus on the same step of the process at the same time. Groups get off track when some members are trying to identify causes of the problem and other members are already suggesting solutions.

Decision Making. Decision making involves reaching a conclusion or making a choice. In a problem-solving process, people think of the decision as the point at which the group selects the best solution from among several choices. But groups make many decisions in the process of solving a problem, such as how

Figure 2.2. Group-Effectiveness Model.

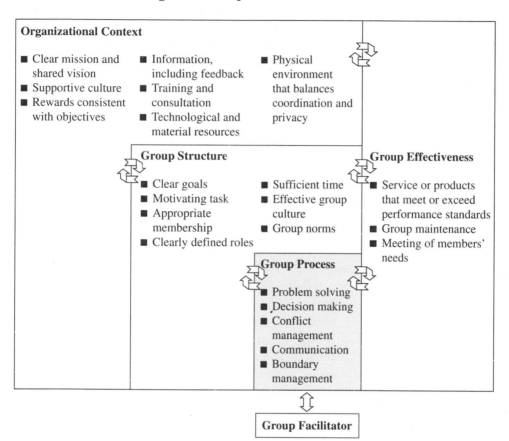

to define the problem and what information should be considered in evaluating solutions. Decision making includes *who* should be involved *when,* in *what* decisions, and *how* those involved will decide.

Who should be involved? When solving problems, four types of people can be involved: those responsible for planning, those responsible for implementing the decision, those affected directly by the decision, and those affected indirectly or who can influence whether or how the solution is implemented.

When should members be involved? Members can become involved in decisions in the problem-solving process at one of three major steps: before the problem has been clearly identified, after the problem has been identified but before a solution has been selected, or after the solution has been selected but before it has been implemented.

How should members decide? Groups have different ways of deciding. In some cases, the leader of the group decides alone, with or without consulting other members. In other cases, the leader becomes a member of the group with the same influence (theoretically) as other members. In still other cases, the leader turns the problem over to the other group members, agreeing to implement any decision they reach (sometimes within certain constraints) (Vroom & Yetton, 1973). Whenever more than one person is to make the decision, they must decide whether they will make their decisions by consensus, majority vote, or by some other means. **The core value of internal commitment implies that groups are more effective when they make decisions by consensus (unanimous agreement).**

What decisions should members be involved in? The question points out that the answers to who should be involved, when, and how will be different and depend on the nature of the problem that needs to be solved. Leaders (or members of self-managing groups) can decide the answers to who should be involved, when, and how by answering the following questions: Who has information necessary to solve the problem? Who has the knowledge and skills necessary for solving the problem? Do members need to be committed to the solution in order to implement it successfully? If so, who needs to be committed to the solution?

Conflict Management. How a group manages conflict will affect its ability to solve problems, be creative, and to integrate the different interests of group members with the demands placed on the group. Researchers have identified five general ways that individuals manage conflict: competing, accommodating, avoiding, compromising, and collaborating (Hall, 1969; Thomas & Kilmann, 1974). Each approach can be described in terms of two dimensions: the extent to which people attempt to satisfy their personal goals and the extent to which people attempt to maintain or improve the relationship with someone with whom they are in conflict (Hall, 1969). Competitive individuals seek to win, and they tend to see things in win-lose terms; only one party can win. Therefore, they focus on achieving their personal goals, with little concern for the relationship. Individuals who accommodate seek primarily to maintain the relationship. Because they believe they cannot do so and also achieve their personal goals, they give in to the other person. Individuals who use avoidance see conflict as futile and withdraw, neither satisfying their own goals nor improving the relationship. Individuals who compromise believe that everyone must give a little to resolve a conflict. They attempt to meet as many of their own goals as possible without seriously harming the relationship. Unlike the other four approaches, individuals who collaborate believe that it is possible both to meet one's personal goals and to improve the relationship. To do this, they seek ways to integrate their interests with those with whom they are in conflict.

Effective groups consider conflict a natural part of group life that, when managed well, improves members' ability to accomplish their tasks, work together, and contribute to their personal growth. They use conflict to increase their understanding of each other, share previously hidden thoughts and feelings, and openly test differences of opinion. Members present their views while accepting that others' views may be more valid. Members disagree with each other without fear of retribution. Unlike groups that avoid conflict to help a member save face, members of effective groups openly confront each other, believing that each person is strong enough to receive negative feedback directly (Argyris & Schön, 1978). Ultimately, effective groups resolve conflicts not only in a way that the conflict remains resolved but also so that members understand how the conflict arose and how they were able to resolve it (Eiseman, 1978).

Communication. The communication process is embedded in all other group processes. Essentially, communication involves exchanging information in a way that conveys meaning. Effective groups communicate in a way that uses fully the members' knowledge and skills and that maintains their motivation to perform the task. The patterns of how group members communicate can be identified by answering a number of questions. Although members communicate nonverbally (for example, body movements and writing), the focus here is primarily on verbal communication.

Who communicates? Group members do not all talk the same amount. Sometimes, who talks more and less indicates a person's perceived importance in the group. For example, in meetings the group leader often talks more than other members. In other groups, senior members may talk more than junior members. In still other groups, those who have the most information about the subject talk most. And in still other groups, those who need the most information talk most (by asking questions). The order in which members talk can also be revealing. Here again, all senior members may speak before any junior members do. Certain members may speak only after their immediate supervisor has spoken. In some cases, one member may always try to speak after a particular member in order to support or refute a point.

Who communicates with whom? Whether people speak depends in part on whether they are spoken to. In some groups, members address their comments to one or a few members present. For example, members sometimes speak directly to the group chair (sometimes as if other members are not present). To whom members direct their comments affects the group's ability to solve problems. For example, if each member speaks only to the leader, it is difficult for members to react to each others' comments. In its extreme, meetings become a series of unrelated monologues in which member after member states her or his views. Using formal rules, such as *Robert's Rules of Order,* in an effort to control large groups can increase the probability of unrelated monologues. Part of who communicates with whom is who interrupts and who gets interrupted. Typically, members who have higher status in the group interrupt those with lower status. Also relevant is who disagrees with whom. In effective groups, members openly express their disagreements with any other member, regardless of differences in position or status.

How do members communicate with each other? There are several ways to identify how members communicate with each other. First, when members are attempting to solve a problem, observe whether their comments build on, compete with, or are unrelated to each other. When members' comments build on each other, the group attempts to identify that part of the individual's comments that it supports in order to incorporate it in the solution. When members' comments compete with each other, members attempt to show the superiority of their views without inquiring about each other's views. Finally, members' comments are unrelated when they do not refer to earlier comments by other members. The monologues discussed earlier fall into this category. In effective groups, members identify how their ideas are similar and inquire about how others see things differently.

Second, group communication occurs at different levels of abstraction. Some members communicate at abstract levels without discussing specific examples. For example, a supervisor might say, "We need to be more careful about scheduling work for our editors." In contrast, other group members communicate using concrete examples. For example, another supervisor might say, "Last week Bob and Jill gave the copy editors a thousand pages that needed to be edited in two days." Similarly, groups that use the passive voice rather than the active voice make it difficult to determine who has done what with whom. Using the passive voice, a member might say, "Some cases of violation of confidentiality have been reported." In contrast, a member using an active voice might say, "Bob reported two cases in which filing clerks in the downtown unit have violated confidentiality." Group members who communicate using concrete examples and active voice are better able to determine the validity of members' statements and solve problems based on the information.

Related to the level of abstraction is the extent to which the group members identify and test the assumptions and inferences they make. Members often misunderstand each other when they hold different assumptions about the topic of discussion yet fail to recognize the dynamic. Similarly, members misunderstand each other when they make inaccurate inferences. For example, upon observing that a member is regularly late to meetings, another member may remark, "You don't care about the work of this group." Whether the member cares about the group is an inference based on the behavior—coming late to the meetings. To determine whether the inference is accurate, the member making the inference needs to ask the late member about it. Members miscommunicate when they make false inferences or assumptions, do not discuss them with the relevant members, and act as if they are true.

What do members communicate and not communicate about? Most groups have undiscussable issues (Argyris & Schön, 1974)—important issues relevant to the group's task that members believe they cannot discuss openly in the group without negative consequences. Examples include a member's poor performance, special relationships within the group, how funds are allocated or spent, future plans for the organization or group, and reluctance to disagree with others. When an undiscussable issue is related to a problem the group is trying to solve, the group forces itself to solve the problem either in a way that does not take into account all the relevant information or in a way that does not address the cause of the problem. Undiscussable issues are important to identify, which is difficult because group norms usually prevent members from raising them. Effective groups learn how to discuss undiscussable issues.

What about nonverbal communication? Members also communicate nonverbally by using their bodies. Examples include raising eyebrows, frowning, staring at the ceiling, and leaving the room. Members can use nonverbal behavior to emphasize, repeat, substitute for, regulate, or contradict their verbal behavior (Knapp, 1972). Many books have been written to help people identify what certain types of body language mean. Like verbal communication, nonverbal communication serves its purpose only when the person receiving the message interprets it as the sender meant it. Group communication becomes ineffective when members infer inaccurately the meaning of a message. For example, in some cultures putting one's feet on the table is considered a sign of disrespect. In a meeting I facilitated, one member accused another of not having respect for her because he had propped his feet on the table. It turned out that he had an illness that required him to keep his legs elevated.

A staggering number of aspects of the communication process can be observed; only a few have been identified here. Additional aspects are discussed in Chapter Four.

Boundary Management. **Effective work groups manage their relationships with the larger organization by simultaneously differentiating themselves from and integrating themselves into the larger organization.** On the one hand, groups need to be separate in order to function as a group. Though it seems obvious, without boundaries a group cannot remain a group. For example, a group that fails to differentiate its work from the work of the larger organization can end up taking on tasks unrelated to the group's purpose and outside the group's expertise. By differentiating itself from the larger organization, a group clarifies who its members are, what tasks it is responsible for accomplishing, and what kind of authority and autonomy it has. A group accomplishes this by differentiating its members from nonmembers (for example, through titles and dress) and controlling who can be a member, differentiating its work from that of other parts of the organization, and sometimes by differentiating where it is located physically (Sundstrom, De Meuse, & Futrell, 1990).

On the other hand, groups need to integrate into the larger organization, in part because their survival depends on it. The larger organization provides the group with materials, supplies, technology, people, and information needed to accomplish the group's task. The larger organization also decides whether to accept the group's work and, as a result, whether to continue providing it with more resources.

Groups also need to integrate their work into other parts of the larger organization in order to agree on timing and practice and to avoid redundancy. For example, a team of county tax collectors must coordinate its collection schedules with the county budget office so the latter will have current revenue data to use in completing the budget.

Some groups also need to manage their boundaries directly with the customers of the organization. Groups differentiate themselves from customers and establish boundaries by dressing differently (for example, wearing badges), restricting the physical areas that customers may enter, and restricting the information and services they provide. Simultaneously, effective groups must coordinate their schedules with those of their customers and provide a service or product that meets clients' needs.

The degree of differentiation and integration a group requires depends on its tasks (Sundstrom, De Meuse, & Futrell, 1990). However, the more a group needs to integrate its work into other groups inside or outside the organization, the more susceptible it is to conflict with those groups, which in turn may reduce its effectiveness (Brown, 1983).

The Relationship Among Group Processes. Although this chapter discusses each of the processes separately, in reality a group uses many processes simultaneously when its members work together. For example, when a group solves a problem, it also makes decisions about who will be involved and manages conflicts that arise when members disagree about what to do. And, of course, all of the group's conversation is communication. Similarly, when a group manages its boundaries, it also solves problems, manages conflicts, and communicates with other parts of the organization or people outside the organization. Segmenting the group's behavior into different processes simply helps a facilitator understand more clearly how the group is acting effectively or ineffectively, which is useful for intervening in the group process.

How Group Processes Increase Group Effectiveness. Groups apply their problem-solving, decision-making, and other processes to solve problems associated with the particular services for which they are responsible or products they are responsible for making. For example, a group of auto engineers may use a problem-solving process to determine how to improve the fuel efficiency of cars, while a group of sanitation workers may use a problem-solving process to determine how to reduce the amount of trash that residents generate.

But groups also use their processes to identify and solve problems that arise from their processes, structure, and organizational context. The group's process is the means by which the group increases its effectiveness. In other words, the group relies on its processes to help it identify and solve problems caused by ineffective group structure, organizational context, and even ineffective group process. **In one way, group processes, especially a group's problem-solving process, represent the group's ability to diagnose and intervene on any elements that limit its effectiveness.** This is why developmental facilitation increases the group's ability to monitor and manage its own processes.

Group Structure

An effective group requires an effective structure. Group structure (shaded in Figure 2.3) refers to the relatively stable characteristics of a group, including its

Figure 2.3. Group-Effectiveness Model.

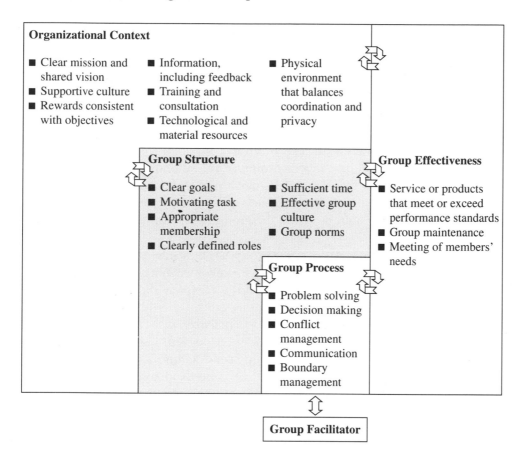

tasks, the membership, the roles each member fills, the time members have available, its members' shared values and beliefs, and its norms. Unlike the structure of a building or the human body, group structure has no physical counterpart. In fact, group structure is simply a stable, recurring group process that results from group members continually interacting with each other in certain ways (Allport, 1967). When members change the patterns of interactions, they change the structure. Because structure develops from group process, the distinction between the two is somewhat arbitrary.

Clear Goals. Whether a group sets its own goals or receives them from the larger organization, a group cannot reach its goals systematically if the goals are ambiguous or missing. The goals should be clear enough that the group can measure its progress toward them. The group's goals should also be consistent with the mission and vision of the organization.

A Motivating Task. The group's task is the work the group performs to accomplish its goal. However, the task and the goal are different. For example, if a group's goal is to ensure that the public has safe housing, the group may perform the tasks of inspecting dwellings and educating the public. In order for a task to motivate group members, it should meet the following conditions (Hackman, 1987, p. 324):

- A group task should require members to use a variety of their skills.
- A group task should be a whole and meaningful piece of work with a visible outcome.
- The outcomes of a group task should have significant consequences, either for customers or others in the organization.
- A group task should give members significant autonomy over how they accomplish the task so that they feel ownership of their work.
- Working on a group task should generate regular and trustworthy feedback to group members about how well the group is performing.

Appropriate Membership. An effective group has a membership that is carefully selected according to several criteria. First, the members must bring an appropriate mix of knowledge and skills to successfully complete the task. For example, a task force formed to resolve conflicts among groups should include a representative of each group to represent that group's perspective.

Second, the group should be just large enough to handle the task. Every additional member requires that the group spend additional time coordinating activities. A group with more members than it needs to complete the task will spend time on coordination that could be spent working directly on the task. In addition, as the group grows, members can lose interest in the work and reduce their effort.

Finally, the composition of the group should be stable enough that the group can maintain its continuity of effort yet fluid enough to ensure that members do not all think the same way and discourage new or different ideas (Janis, 1972). Groups that are continually losing and replacing members spend much time orienting the new members and learning how to work together (Schwarz, 1991).

Clearly Defined Roles. Because groups are made up of individuals who fill interdependent roles, members must understand clearly what role each member plays and what behaviors people expect of each role. For example, in a team of operating-room nurses, members must know who will directly assist the surgeon, who will get supplies, and who will handle paperwork. When roles are understood clearly and agreed upon, members can coordinate their actions more easily to complete the task. Without clear, agreed-upon roles, members can experience conflict and stress (Katz & Kahn, 1978).

In some groups, each member fills only one role; in other groups, the members are capable of filling all the roles in the group and often shift roles. An example of the latter occurs when members take turns leading the group.

In theory, a position description identifies the set of behaviors expected for that role so the behaviors are consistent, regardless of who fills the role. In practice, the role a person plays results from a combination of the formally defined role, the individual's personality, the person's understanding of the role, the expectations that others have for that role, and the interpersonal relationships that the person has with others in the group (Katz & Kahn, 1978). This means that different people may fill the same role somewhat differently. Consequently, group members need to clarify their roles.

Sufficient Time. Obviously, a group needs enough time to complete its task. Specifically, a group needs two kinds of time: performance and process time. During performance time, the group prepares to and produces its product or its service. During process time, the group reflects on how it can improve its performance. Process time enables the group to systematically learn from its experience in order to improve its overall effectiveness. For example, a fire-fighting team's performance time occurs when responding to a call. Process time includes such activities as reviewing the approach the fire fighters used to suppress the fire and identifying their team's strengths and weaknesses. In other groups, it is more difficult to distinguish performance and process times because the groups switch frequently between the two activities.

Typically, groups spend too little time on process, underestimating how process time can enhance the time spent on performance. Occasionally, groups spend a disproportionate amount of their time on process, leaving insufficient time to accomplish the task.

Effective Group Culture. Group culture is the set of values and beliefs that members of a group share and that guide their behavior. Beliefs are assumptions about what is true (for example, people are naturally motivated to do a good job). Values are assumptions about what is worthwhile or desirable (for example, honesty). In a group with a strong culture, members take actions and make decisions that are consistent with the shared values and beliefs. When a group's culture is consistent with effective management principles, the group can be positively influenced by the culture. For example, groups that value quality service are more likely to seek and respond to customers' suggestions for improving service. However, when a group's culture is inconsistent with effective management principles, groups can be negatively influenced. For example, if a group of line workers believes that managers should think and line workers should do, the group is less likely to look for ways to increase productivity.

If a group's culture includes the core values of valid information, free and informed choice, and internal commitment, the culture will positively influence a group's process. Unfortunately, groups—and organizations more generally— rarely have the core values as part of their culture (Argyris, 1990).

A group's culture is not identified simply by listening to what members say they value or believe. Members often espouse values and beliefs that are inconsistent with their actions and are often unaware of their inconsistencies (Argyris & Schön, 1978). The values and beliefs that constitute the group's culture can be inferred by observing the artifacts of the culture (Schein, 1985), including how members act (Argyris, 1990). Artifacts are products of the culture, including the policies, procedures, and structures that members create. Inferring values and beliefs is a primary method that developmental facilitators use to help groups examine their process.

Group Norms. Norms are expectations about how people should or should not behave that all or many group members share. Some examples of norms are that members should let each other know when someone plans to be absent, that members should not talk negatively about the group to nongroup members, and that members should not openly question the leader's decisions. Take, for example, a group norm that members will do whatever needs to be done to ensure that they produce their product or deliver their service on time. In this case, group members who are facing a deadline for a report may work around the clock to finish it.

Norms are important because they help integrate members into the group (Katz & Kahn, 1978) by helping them predict how others will act in a given situation and by providing a guide for members' behavior. Not all group norms help a group become effective, however. For example, the norms of some groups may be "we shouldn't work too hard" or "don't take customer complaints too seriously." In addition, a group norm may be different from an individual member's personal view (Katz & Kahn, 1978). A member may prefer not to dress formally, believing it puts off the clients with whom he deals. However, he may wear a suit and tie each day because that is the expectation. In this way, norms also influence conformity.

As a group forms, it can develop a set of norms in several ways. First, members can develop a set of norms by default. This occurs when different members bring similar expectations to the group because of common social backgrounds or the influence of their membership in the same organization. If members are used to addressing each other by their last names, the group is likely to adopt this practice.

Second, norms can emerge when members who have different expectations work together. Assume, for example, that some members expect that conflicts should be confronted openly, while others expect that conflicts should be avoided. When the group encounters its first few potential conflicts, some members will attempt to confront the conflict openly, while others will attempt to smooth it over. If the group ends up avoiding the conflict, the norm that is likely to develop is that members are expected to avoid conflict.

Although norms exert a powerful influence on group members' behavior, they are difficult to observe simply because they are expectations that members have in their minds. Many norms develop implicitly; that is, without the group ever talking directly about the norm. For example, the norm of many groups is that during meetings, the leader should be solely responsible for keeping the group on track, yet rarely do groups talk explicitly about who is responsible for this.

Unfortunately, when norms develop implicitly, members may learn about a norm only by violating it. This often occurs with new members, who are then told, "That's not the way we do things here." But even group members who have worked together for a long time can have different understandings about a particular norm. In the extreme, each member can personally prefer the same type of behavior while assuming falsely that most other members prefer another. As a result, a norm develops that most members do not support. Developing norms explicitly ensures that members are aware of the norms and enables the group to determine how much members support them personally.

It should be clear that groups can have norms about many things, including how problems should be solved, how decisions should be made, how conflict should be handled, and all the other processes in which groups engage. Norms help keep the processes in place.

Organizational Context

The organizational context includes aspects of the larger organization that influence the group but that the group does not control. The organizational context (shaded in Figure 2.4) should include a clear mission, a shared vision, a supportive culture, rewards consistent with group objectives, information about performance, training and consultation, technology and material resources, and a physical environment that balances coordination and privacy. Understanding the organizational context helps facilitators identify how the larger organization is likely to help or hinder a group's efforts to improve its effectiveness. It also helps identify the extent to which facilitation alone can help a group.

A Clear Mission and a Shared Vision. A mission is the purpose of an organization; it answers the question "Why do we exist?" (Senge, 1990). An organization attempts to achieve its mission by accomplishing various goals, which in turn are achieved by performing various tasks. A vision is a mental picture of the future that an organization seeks to create (Senge, 1990). Whereas a mission clarifies why the organization exists, a vision identifies what the organization should look like and how it should act as it seeks to accomplish its mission (Bryson, 1988). Together, a mission and a vision provide meaning that can inspire and guide members' work.

However, members often have difficulty understanding the mission or vision of their organization, either because it has never been explained to them or because different and powerful groups in the organization disagree about what the mission or vision should be. Agreeing on a mission or vision is important work for boards and top management groups, whch are responsible for shaping the mission and vision of the organization. But the value of a mission and vision

Figure 2.4. Group-Effectiveness Model.

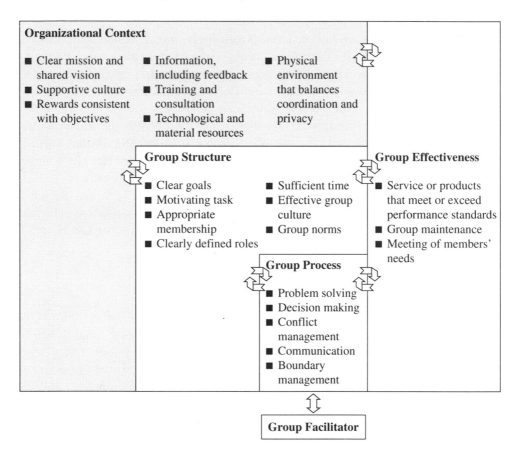

lies in the shared commitment that members make to achieving them, not in simply having them written on a piece of paper or displayed on the walls of the organization. Consequently, the process of developing a mission and vision of the organization must involve the larger organization.

A Supportive Organizational Culture. While *group culture* refers to the set of values and beliefs that are generally shared by members of a group, *organizational culture* refers to the set of values and beliefs that employees of an organization generally share and that guide their behavior. Because each group can have its own culture and because groups are different with respect to their functions, the type of professionals they may employ, and the demographic characteristics of their members, a group's culture may be different from the overall culture in the organization.

For a group to be effective, the organizational culture must be supportive. This means the organizational culture is consistent with effective management principles, including the core values of valid information, free and informed choice, and internal commitment. Unfortunately, as noted earlier, organizations rarely have the core values as part of their culture (Argyris, 1990) and changing an organizational culture is perhaps the most difficult kind of organizational change to create. Therefore, a strong, ineffective organizational culture can make it difficult for a group to sustain increases in its effectiveness.

Rewards Consistent with Group Objectives. An organization influences groups by rewarding certain behaviors. To create an effective group, the organization needs to reward behaviors that are consistent with the group's objectives. For example, if a construction crew's objective is to build quality homes, rewarding the group solely according to the number of homes it builds unintentionally encourages members to increase their rewards at the expense of work quality. It would be more consistent with the group's objective to reward members also for the quality of their construction.

Rewarding the group in a way that is consistent with its objectives also means rewarding the right members. If the task is genuinely a group task that requires the effort of all members, the reward should be made to the group as a whole or to members equally. Unfortunately, organizations often reward a few individuals within a group, even when the entire group completed the task. This can create conflict among group members that reduces effectiveness (Kerr, 1975).

Information, Including Feedback About Performance. A group needs information from the organization to perform effectively. For example, groups charged with making decisions that will affect the entire organization need to know how its various solutions could affect various departments. An organization enables the group to be effective by providing valid and relevant information to the group. Information about the group's performance is critical to its effectiveness. Feedback about performance enables the group to analyze its performance and to improve.

Training and Consultation. Sometimes, a group has all the knowledge and skills it needs to perform its task. Other times, the group needs help understanding either technical matters or learning skills necessary to perform the task. The skills may be task related, such as learning how to prepare a budget, or process related, such as learning how to effectively coordinate group members' efforts. In any event, a group needs to be able to obtain help from the organization. This can be difficult if the group does not have the authority to call on other parts of the organization for assistance (Hackman, 1987).

Technology and Material Resources. Technology is the means by which a group converts or transforms its raw materials into a product or service. For example, health care teams use medical technology and health education to help sick people become healthy and to keep healthy people from becoming sick. Top management teams use organizational mission and vision, and information about the marketplace and the strengths and weaknesses of the organization, to make strategic choices. Faculty members use various teaching and learning methods to help uneducated students become learned students. Material resources include the tools, supplies, and raw materials needed to provide the finished product or service.

The technology that the organization provides a group can affect greatly how the group accomplishes and experiences its tasks. For example, technology such as computers can help groups accomplish their work more quickly. Technology can also affect the group's autonomy. A group of workers who assemble small appliances has relatively little autonomy if the appliance moves down an assembly line and the workers do not control its pace. Alternatively, if the group works around a workbench, members have more control over the pace of their work.

A Physical Environment That Balances Coordination and Privacy. Within the organization, the *physical environment* refers to where and how members are physically located. The group's physical location affects members' ability to work with each other and to serve those who receive their product or service. The members of a group do not necessarily need to be physically located in the same office or building or site. Yet the more members are physically separated from each other or from their customers, the more effort they must spend to coordinate their activities or serve their customers. For example, a police department that has stations throughout a city will be able to respond more quickly to any call in the city than one that operates from a central headquarters. However, the different stations must coordinate their responses to ensure adequate coverage.

During planning or process sessions, groups need a physical environment that minimizes interruptions. This may mean meeting in a conference room off site or simply away from clients or customers. Groups should change their working environment to match their needs for coordination and privacy.

Interorganizational Groups

To simplify the discussion about what makes groups effective, this discussion has assumed that all group members work for the same organization. However, such is not always the case. First, facilitators help groups whose members form an umbrella organization, such as an association of organizations. Here, members share a common cause, but each member represents the interests of one organization to the umbrella organization. Second, facilitators also assist groups that are not an organization or part of a larger organization but whose members represent different organizations. One example is a group that deals with environmental issues and includes representatives from business, labor, and environmental groups and government.

Interorganizational groups have structural and process elements that are similar to other groups'. However, interorganizational groups are subject to the organizational cultural influences of each organization that the group represents. Consider a group composed of a representative from a division of state government, an environmental organization, a home builder's association, and a real estate association. The environmental organization will influence the group's functioning through its representative, the state government agency will influence the group's functioning through its representative, and so on. In addition, the group is subject to the influences of related organizations not represented. In short, interorganizational groups operate in complex organizational contexts, which makes group facilitation more challenging.

How the Model Helps Facilitators

As noted earlier, the model of group effectiveness helps facilitators determine whether a group is being effective, identify which factors and elements that contribute to effectiveness are missing or present, decide how to intervene to help a group become more effective, and determine whether facilitation alone can improve the group's effectiveness.

First, facilitators can use the three criteria for group effectiveness to help determine initially whether and how a group is working ineffectively. Ineffective groups will fail to meet at least one criteria.

Next, facilitators can consider how each element identified in the model may contribute to the group's ineffectiveness. The model implies that there are predictable issues that groups must resolve to be effective. **Each element of the model of group effectiveness (for example, supportive culture, clearly defined roles, group norms) represents a foreseeable problem that a group must solve and keep solved in order to be effective.** Each factor (structure, process, and organizational context) and each constituent element play a unique role in making a group effective. The strength of one factor or element cannot compensate for the weakness of another. For example, by itself a good structure cannot guarantee competent group behavior; it can only create conditions that make it easier for group members to take advantage of their knowledge and skills and process. Similarly, effective group process can take advantage of a sound structure and supportive organizational context but cannot alone create the resources necessary to sustain a group. Finally, a supportive organizational context can provide ongoing resources and reinforce effective group process but by itself cannot ensure effectiveness.

It is not possible to specify which elements the facilitator should look at when a group fails to meet a particular effectiveness criterion. Groups are too complex to permit such predictions. Because any element in a group can affect any other element, any element or combination of elements could be contributing to the group's ineffectiveness. The model simply gives the facilitator the places to consider.

Third, the model helps a group decide what changes to make to become more effective. Because groups are open systems, **all elements of the group's** process, structure, and organizational context can influence each other, and changes in one element can lead to changes in other elements. In addition, the model implies that **the elements of a group and its organizational context must be congruent. It is not enough for each element to function well; the relationships among the elements must also be harmonious.** Therefore, facilitators must also consider the interrelationships of the elements when diagnosing the causes of group ineffectiveness and when helping groups to change. As groups change, facilitators can help them consider potential ripple effects.

The Potential and Limitation of Group Facilitation

Group facilitators intervene largely on process to help groups improve their process, structure, and organizational context. Therefore, facilitation can directly improve the group's effectiveness to the extent that the group has the direct authority to change the character of the elements that make up these factors.

However, groups are different in the extent to which they have authority to change the character of the elements of group effectiveness. In recent years, organizations have begun to establish self-managing work groups, which have the potential to perform at levels much higher than typical groups. Although the groups are often referred to generically as *self-managing,* to be more accurate Richard Hackman (1986) has given different names to the groups that are based on the elements of group effectiveness over which group members have authority. Figure 2.5 (adapted from Hackman, 1986) shows the elements over which each type of group has authority.

In *manager-led groups,* group members do not have authority over any elements of group effectiveness. Their sole responsibility is to perform the tasks assigned to the group. All authority rests with either the manager of the group or with managers above the group's level. Members of *self-managing groups* have authority for monitoring and managing their own group processes and two elements of their structure (group norms and group structure). As Hackman (1986) points out, self-managing groups are common among groups of managers and among professional workers. Another example is interorganizational groups, in which the members work together to coordinate the services among the organizations they represent. *Self-designing groups* have all the authority of self-managing groups as well as the authority to design their group's structure and parts of their organizational context. Self-designing groups include task forces that are given free rein to accomplish a predetermined goal (for example, a team formed to develop a new program and allowed to organize itself, call on the larger organization for necessary resources, and carry out its tasks). Finally, members of *self-governing groups* have authority for all the functions of self-designing groups as well as for setting the overall mission, vision, and culture within which the group operates. Examples of self-governing groups include city councils, boards of directors, and cooperatives. Hackman has noted (1986) that in prac-

Figure 2.5. Group Members' Authority over the Elements of Group Effectiveness in Four Types of Groups.

	Manager-led Group	Self-managing Group	Self-designing Group	Self-governing Group
Organizational Context			■ Rewards consistent with objectives ■ Information and feedback ■ Training and consultation ■ Technological and material resources ■ Physical environment that balances coordination and privacy	■ Clear mission and shared vision ■ Supportive culture ■ Rewards consistent with objectives ■ Information and feedback ■ Training and consultation ■ Technological and material resources ■ Physical environment that balances coordination and privacy
Group Structure		■ Effective group culture ■ Group norms	■ Clear goals ■ Motivating task ■ Appropriate membership ■ Clearly defined roles ■ Sufficient time ■ Effective group culture ■ Group norms	■ Clear goals ■ Motivating task ■ Appropriate membership ■ Clearly defined roles ■ Sufficient time ■ Effective group culture ■ Group norms
Group Process		■ Decision making ■ Problem solving ■ Conflict management ■ Communication ■ Boundary management	■ Decision making ■ Problem solving ■ Conflict management ■ Communication ■ Boundary management	■ Decision making ■ Problem solving ■ Conflict management ■ Communication ■ Boundary management

Source: Adapted from Hackman (1986).

tice, groups often do not fall neatly into one category but instead may fall in between two types of groups.

Still, by understanding which type of group a facilitator is working with, the facilitator can determine how much control the group has over the various elements that help and hinder its effectiveness. As groups move from being manager-led to being self-governing, the group as a whole has more responsibility for managing its process, structure, and organizational context. At the same time, **as the group as a whole assumes more responsibility for managing its effectiveness, it can benefit more from group facilitation, particularly developmental facilitation.**

Group facilitation, however, is not a panacea. In fact, one researcher (Kaplan, 1979) reports that research on group facilitation—perhaps because of poor research design—has not found that group facilitation enhances the group's performance of tasks. Facilitators and their groups need to understand the inherent limitations of facilitation so they can make informed choices about creating change.

First, as the model illustrates, three factors contribute to a group's effectiveness. In practice, a group's problems often arise from a combination of poor process, structure, and organizational factors. **When the group's problems are caused in part by elements of factors that the group does not control, group facilitation can help identify the problems but cannot solve them.** In this situation, other ways of changing the problematic factors are needed, including joint facilitation of the group that controls the problematic elements and the affected group. For this reason, the potential power of group facilitation increases as groups move from being manager-led to being self-governing, thereby increasing the range of issues over which they can make free and informed choices and be internally committed.

Second, group facilitation also has limits as a method for creating large-scale change in organizations, because successful changes within a group do not automatically spread to the larger organization. When an organization attempts to create large-scale change throughout the organization, it sometimes starts by creating a pilot group, hoping that the changes in the pilot group can be replicated throughout the organization, in part by having the pilot group serve as a model that will influence the larger organization. However, an organization typically has greater influence on its groups than any group has on its organization. Therefore, to help the pilot group change, its organization often permits it to operate outside the normal organizational processes or structures to buffer it from the negative influences of the larger organization. This enables group members to develop new ways of working without being overcome by managers who do not yet practice the new methods.

But buffering a pilot group from the larger organization typically isolates it from other groups. This prevents the pilot group from influencing other groups to change. Therefore, **to seed its changes throughout the organization, a pilot group must ultimately be able to interact with other organizational groups**

and still maintain its changes. This is difficult to do unless the group has substantial influence in the organization, as top management teams do. Groups with less influence can use processes and structures that are in conflict with the larger organization for a period of time. But, as discussed earlier, eventually the group's changes are likely to be displaced if the group cannot get sufficient organizational support for them, because groups ultimately depend on the larger organization for their survival. Consequently, to create change throughout an organization, facilitated pilot groups can be expanded to include members from other groups, or additional facilitated groups can be started.

Summary

This chapter concludes the overview by discussing how a group-effectiveness model helps facilitators determine whether a group is being effective, identify which factors and elements that contribute to effectiveness are missing or present, decide how to intervene to help a group become more effective, and determine whether facilitation alone can improve the group's effectiveness. The chapter identified criteria for assessing a group's effectiveness and discussed how a group's process, structure, and organizational context contribute to its effectiveness. The chapter concluded by showing that the group-effectiveness model implies that facilitation can directly improve a group's effectiveness to the extent that the group has the direct authority to change the character of the elements that make up these factors.

Part Two Establishing the

Foundation for Facilitation

Chapter Three Contracting: Deciding Whether and How to Work Together

A facilitator does not simply get together with a group that needs help and begin facilitating. Effective facilitators need first to find out whether they can help a group. Groups that seek facilitators usually want to know what the facilitators will do. Because the facilitator-group relationship is an important one, the parties need to explore whether and under what conditions they want to enter into the relationship. The process in which a facilitator and group develop an agreement about whether and how they will work together and what they will accomplish is known as *contracting*.

Although the term contracting refers to the process by which the client and facilitator agree to the conditions of facilitation, I use the term with some reluctance. Contracting connotes a legal process often arrived at through negotiation. In facilitation, the primary purpose of contracting and the actual contract has nothing to do with creating a legally enforceable agreement. **The primary focus is on developing an agreement that reflects clear expectations about how the facilitator and group will work together.** This chapter identifies the stages in contracting for facilitation, describes the issues that typically arise in the contracting process and principles for dealing with them, and identifies the elements of an effective facilitation contract.

Why Contract?

Contracting occurs generally between the time the facilitator initially speaks with someone from the client organization and when the facilitator reaches agreement with the group about the goals of the facilitation and the conditions under which

45

the facilitator and group will work together. Although contracting at this stage of the relationship is essential, additional contracting may—and often does—occur at any time during the facilitation process.

Contracting has several related purposes. First, and most obvious, contracting ensures that the facilitator and group understand and are committed to the conditions that will govern their working relationship. This involves clarifying expectations that each party has for the other. The expectations include the objectives and boundaries of the facilitation, the ground rules the group will use, issues of confidentiality, the roles of the facilitator and group members, how decisions will be made, and when the facilitation will end. **Ineffective contracting almost invariably results in problems later in the facilitation process.**

Second, contracting provides the group members and facilitator with an opportunity to observe how each other works and to make somewhat informed choices about whether each party wants to work with the other. In some ways, contracting represents a microcosm of the larger facilitation process. Agreeing on objectives and roles, and generally clarifying expectations are elementary interventions; the contracting stage gives the group an opportunity to watch the facilitator's approach. Similarly, the group members' reactions to the contracting process are likely to foreshadow problems in facilitation. The facilitator uses the information gained in the early contacts to determine whether facilitation is likely to be appropriate and beneficial for the group's situation and to determine whether the facilitator is interested in working with the particular group. When a facilitator decides to work with a client, the information obtained during the contracting stage is used to anticipate problems the facilitator may encounter when working with the group.

Third, the contracting process provides a psychological foundation for the relationship between the facilitator and the group. As part of contracting, I ask group members to describe the problems their group faces, the solutions they have tried and those that have failed, and sometimes how the individuals have contributed to and helped to reduce the problem. All the questions make group members vulnerable. Trust develops when clients make themselves vulnerable to the facilitator and find that the facilitator not only does not take advantage of their disclosures but also that the facilitator responds with empathy and support, even while recognizing the ineffectiveness of the group's behaviors. When handled effectively, the contracting process generates a group's trust in the facilitator, which means the facilitator can be effective later.

Stages of Contracting

Contracting occurs in the fairly predictable stages shown in Figure 3.1, beginning with a discussion between the facilitator and some member of the client organization and ending with discussions between the facilitator and the entire client group. **Because the contract sets conditions under which the group and facilitator will work together, ultimately all members involved directly in the facilitation**

Figure 3.1. Stages of Contracting.

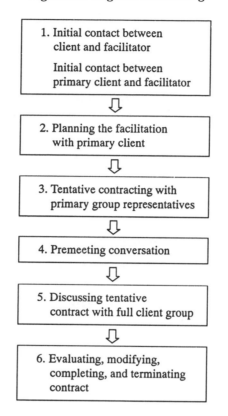

need to agree to the terms of the contract. Their agreement ensures that members develop a contract based on valid information and with free and informed choice. To accomplish this, the facilitator must first determine who the primary client is, that is, the members of the group that will work directly with the facilitator.

In developmental facilitation and in long-term basic facilitation (that is, basic facilitation lasting more than a few sessions), all members of the client group can and should be involved in the contracting process after the initial contact. In short-term basic facilitation, it is often not feasible to include the whole primary client group in the entire contracting process. It is not necessary that all members participate in the entire contracting process. However, the full group must ultimately agree to the terms of the contract. Until this occurs, all agreements between the facilitator and the primary client group are tentative.

Stage One: The Initial Contact

The initial contact has a number of purposes. First, it enables the facilitator to determine whether the contact person is part of the group asking for help and, as a result, whether and how to continue the initial discussion. Second, it enables the facilitator to understand the nature of the client's problems, the extent to which the client contact can articulate the results the group wants, and the extent to which the client has already identified ways to solve the problem. Third, the facilitator uses the discussion to assess the likelihood that the facilitation will be effective if the facilitator agrees to work with the client. The facilitator explores the client's motivation and the factors that may help or hinder the client in solving the problem. Fourth, the facilitator assesses whether he or she has the skills and interest and is available to help the client. Finally, the initial contact provides the potential client with information about the facilitator's approach so the client can make a free and informed choice about whether to use or pursue using the facilitator's services.

Determining Who the Client Is

In determining who the client is, the facilitator seeks to identify and talk with the group that has accepted responsibility for the problem—the group with which the facilitator will ultimately work. This is the *primary client* (Schein, 1987) and the only group that can contract with the facilitator because **only the primary client group has the information necessary and the ability to contract with the facilitator.**

However, as Edgar Schein has described it (1987), the facilitator comes in contact with other categories of clients who may or may not also be members of the primary client group (Figure 3.2). The *contact client* makes the initial contact with the facilitator. Sometimes, the contact client is a staff member or a secretary who is not a member of the primary client group but who has been asked to contact a facilitator on behalf of the primary client. *Intermediate clients* serve as links between contact clients and primary clients and are involved in early parts of contracting. For example, the facilitator may get a call from a secretary (contact client) who asks whether the facilitator is available to help his manager work with a group experiencing conflict. In conversation with the manager, it becomes clear that she is not seeking help for herself but for a group of employees. Personnel managers frequently serve as intermediate clients, when they help find consultants for other managers. Other intermediate clients include staff members who help plan the initial facilitation session.

Finally, *ultimate clients* are "stakeholders whose interests should be protected even if they are not in direct contact with the consultant or manager" (Schein, 1987, p. 125). The ultimate clients include the organization as a whole, the customers who use the services of the organization or buy its products, and the larger community or society. As Figure 3.2 shows, an individual may fall into more than one category. For example, when a top-level executive contacts the facilitator directly to ask for help in working with the top management group, the executive will be a contact client, intermediate client, and primary client simultaneously.

Figure 3.2. Four Types of Clients.

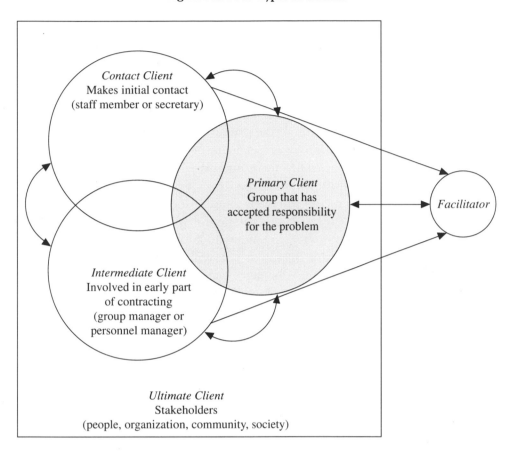

Contact Client
Makes initial contact
(staff member or secretary)

Primary Client
Group that has
accepted responsibility
for the problem

Facilitator

Intermediate Client
Involved in early part
of contracting
(group manager or
personnel manager)

Ultimate Client
Stakeholders
(people, organization, community, society)

Working with the Contact Client

Because only the primary client group has the information necessary and the ability to contract with the facilitator, it is important to quickly determine whether the contact client is a member of the primary client group. The facilitator does this by asking specifically who or what group would be using the facilitator's services and whether the caller is a member of that group. Once the facilitator has determined whether the contact client is also a member of the primary client group, the facilitator asks a series of appropriate questions and shares relevant information. Exhibit 3.1 lists questions that facilitators ask a contact client to obtain the information necessary.

If the facilitator determines that the contact client is not the primary client, the purposes of the conversation with the nonprimary client are to identify the primary client, explain why it is not possible to contract with the contact client, and provide the contact client with sufficient general information to share with the primary client, who can decide whether to contact the facilitator.

Exhibit 3.1. Questions for the Contact Client.

1.   Who (what group) is seeking the facilitation services?
2.   Are you a member of this group?
3.   Has the group committed to particular times for this facilitation work? How much has the group already planned for this work?
4.   What objectives does the group want to accomplish?
5.   What problems is the group experiencing? Can you give me some specific examples?

Determining the identity of the primary client is not always easy. In one case, a county manager called me to seek help for his public works director, who some employees felt had acted in a racist manner when he fired a black employee. The manager stated that the public works director was interested in getting help and asked if I would come in, interview people, and give the manager a report. I described my role and explained that giving him a report would be inconsistent with my role as facilitator. I then said that if the director was interested in working with me, I would be happy to talk with the director. I stated that if I did work with the director, the manager was, of course, free to talk with the director about the facilitation, but I would not discuss the content of the facilitation with the manager. Because the manager had described the public works director and his staff as having the problem, I defined my primary client as the group that included the public works director and his employees.

In another case, a human resources executive from an international bank called to see if I could help a line executive and one of the line executive's subordinates. The employees who reported to the subordinate and the line executive considered the subordinate autocratic. The line executive also believed he needed to improve his own relationship with his subordinate. In this case, the line executive was a primary client because he had expressed responsibility for part of the problem—his relationship with his subordinate. The subordinate's employees were also primary clients because they were willing to discuss their ineffective relationship with their supervisor. However, the subordinate was only potentially a primary client, because he had not yet expressed an interest in working on the problem identified by his supervisor. The principle here is that **individuals are not primary clients until they have made a free and informed choice to ask for the facilitator's help.**

The definition of the primary client often shifts, typically to be more inclusive, as the facilitator finds out more about the problems facing the organization. In contracting with a group of school administrators and faculty members who were in conflict over the form of school governance, it became clear to me that the group did not adequately represent the range of opinions among the faculty and administration. At my suggestion, the group decided to expand its number, thereby increasing the size of the primary client group. However, one faculty member, who was president of the faculty, declined an invitation to join the group. The incident illustrates that there is sometimes a difference between who might be expected to be part of the primary client group and who chooses to be part of it.

In some cases, the contact client may represent a primary group that does not yet exist. The executive director of a health care foundation called to ask whether I would be interested in facilitating a large commission to deal with health policy. The commission would comprise public and private leaders, and its report would be used to draft legislation. The foundation would appoint the commission, but no members had been appointed nor had the commission chair been selected. Further, no member of the foundation, including the executive director, would be a member of the commission, so there was no primary client. I talked with the executive director about how I could work with the commission but stated that the commission members, when appointed, would need to decide whether they wanted to work with me. The situation is not unusual. Organizational planners, working on such projects as total quality management or union-management cooperative efforts, which may use third-party facilitators, often try to identify facilitators who can be available to groups immediately after they are formed.

After determining that the contact client is not a primary client, the facilitator might say something like, "I'd be glad to talk with you in general about what I do as a facilitator. However, to figure out whether I can be of help to your organization, I'll need to talk with the person who heads the group I would be meeting with. This gives the person and me a chance to make sure that we clearly understand the situation. Does that sound reasonable?" Following the core values of valid information, free and informed choice, and internal commitment to the choice requires that the facilitator contract only with the primary client group. However, facilitators can elicit from and share with the contact client certain information that helps facilitators decide whether they could meet the primary client's request or help the primary contact decide whether to pursue discussions with the facilitator.

I prefer that primary clients call me if they are still interested. My preference is based on the principle that **the primary client is responsible for seeking help and ultimately cannot delegate that responsibility.** Underlying the principle is the assumption that clients who take responsibility for seeking help will be more committed to the facilitation process.

When the Contact Client Is a Primary Client

When the contact client is a primary client, facilitators use the initial conversation to diagnose the client's problem, identify factors affecting the success of the facilitation, determine whether they have the skills and interest to facilitate, discuss their approach to facilitation, and agree on next steps.

For facilitators to make a free and informed choice about whether and how to help the potential client, they need to make an independent judgment about the client's situation. Therefore, **facilitators should assume neither that the client**

has accurately diagnosed nor inaccurately diagnosed the situation. So that clients do not misinterpret the reason for facilitators' questions, facilitators should share their assumption with clients. After clients briefly describe their situation, facilitators can say, "To figure out whether I can help you, I need to determine whether I see the situation the same way you do. I'd like to ask you some questions that will help me understand your situation, and then we can talk about whether I see things similarly to or differently from you. Is that OK with you?" Such a statement also helps the client understand how the facilitator would like to proceed, and it checks for the client's agreement.

Diagnosing the Problems and Factors Affecting Facilitation

Exhibit 3.2 lists questions that a facilitator asks in the initial conversation with the primary client. The questions help identify the client's problem behaviors, the consequences for the group's effectiveness, and the potential causes. The questions also help explore the client's motivation and resources for change as well as experiences the client has had with consultants and how the current request for help came about. Facilitators may need to modify some questions according to the specific purpose of the facilitation.

The facilitator's goal in the conversation is not to develop a complete diagnosis of the client's problem—that is impossible to achieve in one conversation—but rather to begin the diagnosis and determine whether facilitation is an appropriate method for helping the client. A skilled facilitator is flexible enough to start diagnosing where the client begins the story rather than forcing the client to respond in an order predetermined by the facilitator. In fact, **a general principle underlying diagnosis and intervention is to begin with the client's interests and concerns.**

Identifying Problems, Consequences for Effectiveness, and Potential Causes. Together, the questions about problems, consequences for effectiveness, and potential causes focus on the elements of the group-effectiveness model discussed in Chapter Two. The questions about problems do not correspond to a particular element in the model. Instead, the questions give clients a chance to begin describing the problem as they see it.

How Clients Define Their Problems, Causes, and Solutions. Clients are different in the extent to which they have identified the methods for solving the problem. The *confident* client has already defined the problem, its causes, and a method for solving it and wants to know whether the facilitator can deliver the service requested. For example, the client may say that her top management team has conflicts because there is little agreement about priorities for goals. The client wants to get the team together to develop a consensus and wants me to help the group reach the consensus. The client often ends her description with a request such as, "Can you help me accomplish this?" The confident client believes that

Exhibit 3.2. General Questions for Diagnosing the Problems of the Primary Client.

Identifying Problems

1. Describe to me the problems the group is having. What are some specific examples?
2. What do members in the group do (or not do) that you see as a problem? What are some specific examples?
3. How widespread are the problems? Do they occur all the time or only under certain conditions or with certain individuals?
4. When did the problems begin? What else was occurring at that time or shortly before the problems began?
5. In what ways do members contribute to the problems? In what ways do you contribute to the problems?

Consequences for Group Effectiveness

6. What are the consequences of these problems? How do the problems affect the group's ability to produce quality products or deliver quality services? work together? meet individual members' needs? What are some specific examples?

Potential Causes—Process, Structure, Organizational Context

7. What do you think are the causes of the problems? What have you seen or heard that leads you to think these are the causes?
8. How does the group solve problems and make decisions? communicate and manage conflict? coordinate its work with others in the organization? Do any of these seem related to the problems you described? If so, how?
9. Does the group have clear goals? Are members motivated by their tasks? Does the group have the right kind of members to do its work? Do members understand and agree on their roles? Do they have enough time to do their work? What kinds of behaviors do members expect of each other? What are the core values and beliefs that members share about work? Do any of these seem related to the problems you described? If so, how?
10. In what ways does the organization help or hinder the group? Is there a clear mission and a shared vision? Is the culture supportive? How are group members rewarded? Does the group get enough information to do its work? enough training and other resources? appropriate physical space to work in? Do any of these seem related to the problems you described? If so, how?
11. What is the history of the group? How has the membership and leadership changed?
12. How do you think other people in the group would identify the problems and their causes? Would others disagree?

Motivation and Resources for Change

13. What have you tried to do to improve the situation? What were the results?
14. Why does each member want to work with a facilitator? How motivated is each member?
15. What are the group's strengths? How does the group act in ways that are effective?

Experience with Consultants and Current Request for Help

16. Have you used other consultants or facilitators in the past, either for this situation or others? What role did the consultant or facilitator play? What were the results? What did the consultants do that members liked or disliked?
17. What has led you to contact someone now? What has happened or is about to happen in the group or organization?
18. How did the idea to call me in particular come about? Who initiated it? How was it received by other group members?
19. How do you see me helping the group accomplish its objectives?

she has accurately diagnosed the situation and that the help she is requesting is the appropriate intervention.

The *searching* client has identified the problem but has not determined its causes or what methods to use to solve the problem. This client wants to know how the facilitator can help the organization solve the already-identified problem. For example, the client may say that customers have begun complaining about poor service in the past year. The client does not know the cause of the increase in complaints and wants to improve service in a way that involves those directly working with customers. The client often ends his description by asking, "How can you help us with this problem?"

The *puzzled* client has not yet clearly identified the problem. For example, a client may say simply that morale is low in a particular department and people are leaving. The client ends the description of the problem by asking, "Can you help us figure out what is going on and what to do about it?"

Clients also vary in their willingness to reconsider their own diagnosis of the problem and its causes. A confident client can be more reluctant to reexamine the diagnosis because the solutions he has developed based on his diagnosis mean he has a vested interest in the diagnosis.

To varying degrees, clients present the facilitator with an identified problem and some solution. However, as mentioned previously, to be most helpful to the client, the facilitator cannot assume that the client has accurately diagnosed the problem, its causes, or an effective solution. In the contracting phase, the facilitator and the primary client are jointly responsible for identifying the problem that the group is facing.

Accepting the client's diagnosis at face value or, worse yet, when the facilitator has data that suggest a different diagnosis, may lead the facilitator to provide services that will be ineffective. For example, a manager asked that I work with him and his board to develop funding priorities for the county. According to the manager, the board had functioned by funding projects on a piecemeal basis, without a consensus on a larger set of goals to be accomplished. In our conversation, the manager also said that his relationship with the board was strained. The board had circumvented his hiring authority and did not involve him in other important decisions. It became clear to me that the strained relationship between the manager and board would make it difficult for the group to set funding priorities. The manager agreed with me but was reluctant to discuss the relationship, fearing that the situation would become worse. If I had accepted the manager's definition of the problem, I would have worked with the board without understanding the full problem and could have led the group to approach a task with little chance of success.

Returning to the three types of clients, in each case the facilitators need to let the client know that they want to find out more about the problem and make some initial independent judgment.

Motivation and Resources for Change. Groups need a threshold level of motivation to change their behavior. In other words, groups need to experience a certain level of pain (Levinson, 1972) or aspiration before they are willing to devote their energy to changing their behavior. The motivation may be internal, coming from group members' own interests, or external, from sources outside the group. One major premise of this book is that members are more committed to actions taken when they are internally motivated. Not all motivation for change, however, stems from dissatisfaction with past or current performance. Some groups that are satisfied with their current performance are motivated to improve their effectiveness because they anticipate that future conditions will require a higher level of performance.

As Robert Blake and Jane Mouton (1983) have noted, because a group seeks help does not necessarily mean that the group is interested in changing its behavior. For example, a group may seek a facilitator, hoping that person will take responsibility for actions that the group finds threatening. For developmental facilitation, identifying the level and source of the motivation for change can help determine whether the group will be able to sustain the energy to change its behavior and to maintain new behaviors.

Sometimes, a critical incident has occurred that provides the proximal motivation for change. Consider, for example, a group in which racial tension has led members to fail to adequately coordinate their activities. The group may seek help after a meeting in which the lack of coordination has had a serious negative consequence and resulted in members accusing each other of being racist. In addition to conflict, other critical incidents that provide motivation for change may include a change in the group's composition, the beginning of a new project, or a change in the group's organizational context.

Groups need resources to change, including time and organizational support, which means information, training, and money. As with other significant group changes, a group's performance level is likely to decrease temporarily as it learns new behaviors that result from developmental facilitation (Beer, 1980). This requires that the group have enough organizational slack (Cyert & March, 1963)—some unused capacity—to buffer it from negative consequences that might otherwise flow from decreased performance.

A more subtle resource is a group's strengths. When a group approaches a facilitator for help, it is easy to focus only on its weaknesses, ignoring its strengths. Understanding the group's strengths, however, helps the facilitator assess the foundation upon which the group can design its new behavior.

Experience with Other Consultants and Current Request for Help. The group's experience with facilitators or other consultants creates expectations about future efforts. A group that has had a negative experience working with a facilitator is likely to be reluctant to work with one again if members use their experience to generalize about all facilitators. By learning how previous facilitators worked with the group and in what ways the group found those facilitators helpful and not helpful, the new facilitator can infer what the group expects from a facilitator and what issues are likely to arise between the facilitator and the group. In addition, the facilitator should ask directly how the group believes the facilitator can help it.

Understanding how the client came to contact the facilitator is also important diagnostic information. Knowing who referred the client to the facilitator can provide information about the client's expectations. Finding out whose idea it was to contact the facilitator, how the idea was received, and who was involved in deciding to make the contact can also provide some information about support for the facilitator and facilitation in general.

Describing One's Approach to Facilitation. At some point during the conversation with the primary client, facilitators should share their approach to facilitation so that the client can make a more informed choice about whether to use them. Describing one's approach to facilitation includes identifying the core values and beliefs that guide the facilitator's behavior, the uses of basic and developmental facilitation, the role as the facilitator defines it, and explaining how these would translate into working with the client. For example, the facilitator might explain that it is the facilitator's responsibility to provide valid information about how the group is spending its time, but how it spends its time remains the group's choice. Consequently, when the facilitator believes the group has gotten off track, the facilitator would share that information with the group, but the group would decide whether the conversation is off track and whether the group wants to pursue the digression. It is also useful for the facilitator to describe the types of behaviors that are inconsistent with the facilitator's role, especially behaviors that clients might expect of the facilitator, such as serving as a go-between among group members or becoming involved in the substance of discussions. Finally, if the facilitator models the use of the core values in talking with the client, the client experiences the facilitator's approach and can use the information to decide whether to pursue working with the facilitator.

Assessing One's Interest in and Ability to Help the Client. Assuming that facilitation is appropriate for the client's request, during the initial conversation with the primary client facilitators need to assess their interest in and ability to help the client and convey the assessment to the client. Facilitation is psychologically demanding work that requires intense concentration. It is difficult to facilitate effectively when one's interest is low. This does not mean that the facilitator needs to be interested in the subject matter the group will discuss; Resource A describes how strong interest in the group's substantive issues can actually reduce the facilitator's effectiveness. Rather, it means that facilitators must have enough interest in providing the help to give the group their undivided attention.

Some facilitators are not interested in working with groups that seek to accomplish objectives at odds with their own strongly held values. For example, a facilitator who believes that women have the right to control their reproductive lives may not be interested in facilitating a group that is seeking ways to make abortion illegal. Whether a facilitator's interest in working with a client should be influenced by such personal values is an individual choice. In any event, facilitators need to be aware of their personal values and how they may affect their interest in working with particular client groups.

Before the end of the conversation with the primary client, facilitators should tell the client whether they are able and/or interested in helping the client. If facilitators are not interested or are unable to help, they should explain why. For example, facilitators may point out that it is not an effective use of their time to work with a group whose membership will soon change significantly.

Summarizing and Agreeing on Next Steps. When facilitators have enough information to make an initial diagnosis, they should share it with the primary client group and check whether the client agrees. Assuming the problem lends itself to facilitation and the facilitator is interested and able to help the client, facilitators should describe how they think they can most effectively help the group and determine whether the client agrees. This entails describing the role of the facilitator, including whether the facilitation would be basic or developmental.

The facilitator should identify any decisions or tentative decisions the client group has made that are likely to reduce its ability to achieve its stated objectives and determine whether the client group is willing to reconsider the decisions. For example, the facilitator may note the time the group has allocated is insufficient for the objectives it seeks to accomplish. Or, the facilitator may point out that excluding certain individuals is likely to reduce the group's ability to actively discuss the issues on which it seeks consensus. If any of these group decisions is likely to reduce the group's effectiveness to the point where the facilitator is unwilling to facilitate unless the decisions are changed, the facilitator needs to state this when raising the issue.

Finally, the facilitator and client should agree on the next steps. If the client is interested in pursuing the facilitator's help, the next step is for the contact client to discuss the conversation with the facilitator with representatives of the different parts of the primary client group. If members remain interested, the contact client can arrange a conference call or meeting of the facilitator and the primary client group representatives. The objectives of the meeting would be to help the facilitator further understand the client's problems, to further share information about the facilitator's approach, and to jointly plan the facilitation.

Stage Two: Planning the Facilitation

In the planning stage for basic facilitation, the facilitator typically meets with a subset of the primary client group, including the group member who made the initial contact. In developmental or long-term basic facilitation, the facilitator typically meets with the entire client group. The purposes of this stage are to continue to clarify the client's problem and the factors that will affect facilitation, to tentatively plan the agenda, and to agree on conditions for the first facilitated meeting.

The planning sessions are similar to the initial contact with the primary client in that the facilitator seeks to understand the client's problem and determines whether and how facilitation can help. Including members of the client group in addition to the initial contact provides different perspectives that aid in diagnosing the group's situation. It also enables the facilitator to watch the group in action—another rich source of diagnostic data. The facilitator seeks information similar to that in the initial contact with the primary client. However, in the planning sessions, the facilitator explores the questions and issues in more depth, and the group moves from identifying goals it wants to accomplish to developing an agenda to accomplish the goals. Sometimes, discussions during the planning stage result in identifying problems or goals different from those identified during the initial client contact.

Who Should Be Involved?

In basic facilitation, if the entire group is unable to plan the facilitation, a subset of the group needs to be selected. Underlying the question of who should be involved is the assumption that a group comprises members with different kinds of expertise, interests, and perspectives. In fact, a major reason work is performed in groups is to bring different kinds of expertise and perspectives to bear on a problem. **In groups comprising subgroups, the planning meetings should include representatives of each subgroup.** A subgroup includes any formal organizational entity that is a subset of the larger group (for example, different units within a department, or different political parties) as well as any group of members who see themselves as distinct in some way that affects the group's task. Formal and informal subgroups can be defined by race, age, sex, professional background, type of work performed, socioeconomic status, and include opinion groups that form around a particular issue.

The planning group should include members of the primary group who can represent formal and informal subgroups within the primary client group. Depending on the issues facing a group, informal subgroups may be more relevant than formal subgroups. For example, a board of education and its superintendent asked me to facilitate a discussion regarding the superintendent's performance after the board had voted 4-3 to reduce the superintendent's salary supplement. In this case, the formal subgroup representatives included the superintendent and the board chair. However, it was critical to involve two informal subgroups for planning—the groups voting for and against reducing the salary. Because the chair had voted to reduce the salary, an additional member was included who had influenced others to vote not to reduce the salary. Together, the three members represented the relevant subgroups and points of view reflected in the full group.

It is not always feasible to include representatives of all subgroups or points of view in the planning stage, particularly when that number would be large. However, failing to include a significant formal or informal subgroup representative can undermine the process, either later in the contracting stage or during the facilitation. A member excluded from the planning process may decide not to participate in the facilitated sessions or may disagree with the agenda when it is discussed with the full client group at the first meeting.

The planning group can also include nonprimary group members who serve either as staff members, in some advisory capacity, or even as the supervisor of the primary group. Where the group's discussion involves budgetary matters, a budget analyst can help the group plan its discussion to take full advantage of available information. Similarly, a personnel manager, planner, staff attorney, or other representative can be helpful, depending on the nature of the group's agenda.

In some cases, problems arise when the formal leader of the primary client group delegates the planning to others. For example, the secretary of a state agency had delegated the planning for a facilitated retreat to a deputy secretary and a planning manager, both of whom were members of the primary client group. After the initial contact with the planning manager, I had reluctantly agreed to plan the retreat with the planning manager and deputy director, with the condition that we would jointly meet with the secretary for the final planning session. In the first two planning meetings, the planning manager and deputy director emphasized that the secretary wanted the retreat to focus on long-term planning. However, in the final planning meeting, in which the deputy secretary, planning manager, and I presented the tentative plan to the secretary, the secretary emphasized the need to focus on team building, given the recent reorganization. As a result, the group needed to redesign the sessions.

The case raises the general question, Under what conditions can the leader of a primary client group delegate responsibility for planning the facilitation? The question engages the facilitator in the dilemma of choosing between direct access to the top manager and accepting the legitimacy of the organization's natural decision-making process. If the top manager delegates the planning, the facilitator is unable to directly understand her goals and expectations. Also, the top manager's role will likely require her to take certain personal risks, to which others cannot commit her. However, requiring the top manager to be involved in the planning process may be inconsistent with the organization's normal delegation process. Solutions to the dilemma lie in satisfying the interests that drove the decision to delegate in a way that also meets the facilitator's needs. For example, the top manager may be involved briefly in the planning process initially and then again near the end of the planning process. In any case, those to whom planning authority has been delegated need to have direct access to the top manager during the facilitated sessions and valid information about the organization's problems and goals, and they should participate in the facilitated sessions, to experience the effects of the planning.

Whether to Meet with the Group or Individuals Separately

Under what conditions should the facilitator begin diagnosis by talking to members individually instead of as a group? This question is relevant for basic and developmental facilitation. Embedded in the choice is another dilemma. Members are likely to provide more information in individual meetings, especially if the facilitator agrees to treat the sessions as confidential. However, if the conversations are to be confidential, the facilitator obtains useful diagnostic information that cannot be shared in interventions with the full group.

The facilitator who is allowed to share information from individual sessions runs the risk of taking responsibility for addressing group issues away from the group. In the extreme case, this may lead the facilitator to raise information that group members then deny they shared with the facilitator.

If the facilitator does not meet individually with group members, the group's progress is limited to what it can diagnose and discuss in the full group. The individual sessions can speed group progress by having the facilitator talk with individual members about how they can raise difficult issues that are important but threatening to mention.

A variation of the dilemma, which occurs in hierarchical groups and groups with conflicting subgroups, is whether to meet with each group individually before meeting with the full client group. Consider, for example, a hierarchical group in which the initial problem is a conflict between the manager and subordinates. If subordinates have little trust in the manager, they may withhold information in a group meeting with the manager that they would share if the manager were absent. Similarly, in a group that comprises doctors and nurses, nurses may be reluctant to share information in the presence of the doctors in the group, even if the nurses do not report to the doctors. In general, when power differences exist among subgroups, the less powerful subgroup is likely to be reluctant to discuss problems with the other subgroup, especially when the less powerful group has little trust in the more powerful group.

One way for the facilitator to manage the dilemma is to share it with the entire group and ask members to make a choice. While this lessens the risk for those who are reluctant to discuss problems in the full group, it does not remove it. A second approach for managing the dilemma is for the facilitator to make the decision, recognizing the various risks that the client group faces. Here the principle is that **the facilitator enables members to publicly share as much information as possible in a way that permits each member to make a free and informed choice about the risks of sharing the information.**

Stage Three: Tentative Contracting with the Primary Client

In stage three, the facilitator and client group develop and tentatively agree to a contract that describes what the parties expect from one another. Facilitators who have handled the previous contracting stages well will have already discussed many of the contract issues with the client. The purpose of this stage is to ensure that the facilitator and primary client group understand and are committed to the conditions that will govern their working relationship.

For several reasons, it helps to put the tentative contract in writing. First, the full client group often does not participate in the tentative contracting stage. In order to finalize the contract, the entire client group needs to agree with it. Putting the contract in writing enables the contracting subgroup to more accurately describe the tentative contract when discussing it with the full client group. Second, a written contract enables the facilitator and client group to more easily check, at a later date, whether their work has been consistent with their agreement. Finally, research shows that when individuals make their agreements public (for example, by writing them down), they are more likely to follow through on their agreements (Kiesler, 1971). One potential disadvantage of putting the contract in writing is that the client group (and especially members not involved in the tentative contracting) may view the tentative contract as rigid and unchangeable, which could harm the consulting relationship (Gellermann, Frankel, & Ladenson, 1990). The facilitator can mitigate the problem by stating clearly in the tentative contract that members are encouraged to review the contract and suggest modifications during the course of the working relationship. The facilitator should also regularly ask clients to discuss whether the current contract continues to meet their needs.

It should be clear that the primary purpose of the contract is not legal but relational. What is important is that the facilitator and client reach an understanding that meets both their needs, not that one party can collect damages if the other breaches the contract. Indeed, holding the client to a contract that no longer benefits the client is unethical (Gellermann, Frankel, & Ladenson, 1990).

Elements of the Tentative Contract

This section identifies a set of questions, the answers to which are the necessary elements of the contract. In addition to explaining each element, the contract should also explain the reasons for each element. This enables the reader to understand the logic underlying the agreement. Exhibit 3.3 lists the questions necessary for identifying elements of the contract. Issues to consider when contracting for each element appear in Resource A. Resources B and C provide samples of agreements for basic and developmental facilitation respectively.

Stage Four: Premeeting Conversation with Planning Representatives

In the fourth stage of contracting, the facilitator makes a last-minute check with the planning representatives to see whether anything has changed that might affect the contract or the facilitation. The conversation usually occurs shortly before the facilitation is to begin, when the facilitator gets to the site of the facilitation. For developmental or long-term basic facilitation, the conversation is relevant each time the group is about to meet, although the facilitator need not have it each time. Both conversations are based on the principle that **the facilitator regularly seeks to determine whether conditions that might affect the contract or the facilitation have changed.** A few general questions can determine

Exhibit 3.3. Questions for Developing an Effective Contract.

1. Who is the primary client and who will attend meetings?
    a. Will there be others who provide expert information?
    b. Will there be any other observers?
    c. Will news reporters attend?
    d. Do the participants include those necessary for identifying and solving the problems?
    e. Are any participants included who are not necessary for identifying and solving the problems?
2. What are the objectives of the meetings?
    a. Is the facilitation basic or developmental?
    b. Do the objectives meet the needs of all participants?
3. What are the agendas for the meetings?
    a. Do the agendas meet the needs of all participants?
    b. Do the agendas make effective use of the facilitator's skills and the presence of all participants?
4. Where and how long will the group meet?
    a. Do the location and facilities encourage full, uninterrupted attendance without distractions?
    b. Is the location considered a neutral site by all participants?
    c. Are the facilities informal enough to encourage open discussion yet formal enough to permit concentration on the work?
    d. Is the location consistent with the image the organization wants to project?
    e. Is the amount of time allocated sufficient to accomplish the objectives?
5. What are the roles of the different parties?
    a. Facilitator?
    b. Leader?
    c. Members?
6. What ground rules will the group follow?
    a. What ground rules do participants commit to follow in the meetings?
    b. How will (or will) the group make decisions?
    c. What limits, if any, will the facilitator and members put on confidentiality?
7. How will the group assess its progress?
    a. Will the group critique its meetings?
    b. What other methods will the group use to assess progress?
8. How will the facilitator's performance be assessed?
    a. Will the facilitator do a self-critique?
    b. Do members agree to give the facilitator feedback at the time of the behavior?
9. What are the facilitator's fees and other charges?
10. How long will the contract be in effect?
11. When and how is the contract changed?
    a. Will each party discuss changes in the agreement before unilaterally changing it?
    b. What does the facilitator require of the client before discontinuing the contract?
12. How and when will the tentative contract be conveyed to all parties?

whether the facilitator needs to probe further. These include, "Has anything happened since we last talked that might affect the facilitation?" "Is there anything else that would be helpful for me to know before we start the session?" or, "How are people feeling about the session?" If not everyone who is expected to attend is present, the facilitator can share that observation and ask whether someone is unable to attend.

The questions help facilitators determine whether they will need to change how they plan to intervene in the group or even whether to reach a new contract agreement. For example, in working with a group of school administrators and faculty who were trying to resolve a difficult conflict, I asked someone before a meeting if anything was new. I was informed that the principal—who had been a focal point of the conflict—had announced his resignation, effective at the end of the school year. Given this, I began the session by asking the group in what way his resignation affected our work together and whether we should change the contract.

The premeeting conversation also clarifies who will handle each of the initial meeting functions, including starting the meeting, introducing the facilitator, introducing other participants, and describing the events that led up to the meeting. If the planning group has decided that the facilitator will actively manage the process, the facilitator can ask the formal leader to begin the meeting. If the group comprises two or more subgroups and group leadership and power are highly conflictual issues, the facilitator can suggest that the facilitator begin the meeting. The facilitator should also state a preference for and seek the leader's preference for who is to introduce the facilitator. At this point, the person managing the group process can ask other participants (and observers) to introduce themselves. Finally, the facilitator should ask one or more members of the planning group to review the planning process so that all participants have the same basic information. The decisions may seem detailed and trivial, but the clarifications can help reduce the awkwardness that often characterizes the beginning of a facilitation.

Stage Five: Discussing the Tentative Contract with the Full Primary Client Group

In the fifth stage of contracting, the facilitator and the entire primary client group reach agreement on the contract. **Because the facilitator's client is the entire primary group, the contract is tentative until the entire group agrees to it.** This entails reviewing the tentative contract, explaining the interests that led to the elements of the contract, and deciding whether to modify the contract and, if so, how. In short-term basic facilitation, this typically takes place after clients and the facilitator have introduced themselves and reviewed the client-facilitator contacts that have led to the current meeting.

Because people view a written contract as less changeable than one conveyed orally, the facilitator needs to encourage members to identify parts of the contract that do not meet their needs. Psychologically, this stage is important because it represents the full client group's first chance to evaluate the facilitator. How the facilitator presents the tentative contract and responds to requests for modifying it sends a message to members about whether the facilitator will be concerned with all members' interests or just those in the planning group. If the facilitator has not accurately diagnosed the group's dynamics or if the planning group does not represent the range of members' interests, this stage may be difficult.

This stage is also the time to agree on elements of the contract that the planning group has purposely left for the entire group to discuss, including how members will handle confidentiality and how the group will make decisions.

Deciding What Ground Rules to Use

Finally, in this stage, group members decide what ground rules they will use during the facilitation (question six in Exhibit 3.3). The decision is critical because the ground rules that the group agrees to follow will affect the kinds of interventions the facilitator makes. Developing ground rules early influences the patterns of behavior that will continue throughout the group's work (Friedman, 1989). One choice the facilitator faces is whether to provide the group with a set of ground rules (see Chapter Four) that members can accept, modify, or reject or to have the group develop its own set. Groups are more committed to ground rules they have freely chosen, which may argue for having groups develop their own. However, if the facilitator plans to use the ground rules as a basis for interventions, providing the ground rules gives the group valid information about how the facilitator intends to help them. For basic facilitation, in which the client essentially asks the facilitator to manage the process, having the group develop ground rules may significantly reduce the time it has to accomplish its objectives. When conducting a single-session facilitation, the facilitator may present a subset of the ground rules, based on what the facilitator considers the needs of the group. Alternatively, the facilitator can provide a complete set of ground rules and ask members to select only those they consider useful (Spich & Keleman, 1985). When I have decided to present the ground rules to a group, I send copies of an article that describes the proposed ground rules to all group members, along with the tentative contract. The message is that the ground rules are an important part of the facilitation, and it allows members more time to make an informed choice about using them. (Readers may obtain copies of the article by contacting the Institute of Government. The address and phone number are listed in Resource B.)

In developmental facilitation, the group's ground rules can be used in four ways. First, group members can agree to use the ground rules only in their group conversations during facilitated sessions. In other words, the group will use the ground rules in meetings with the facilitator but not necessarily at other times. Second, the group can agree to use the ground rules in its facilitated meetings and when members interact with each other outside the meetings. Third, the group can decide to use the ground rules in the two previous situations and to adopt them when members work with others in the organization. Fourth, the group could agree to use the ground rules in interactions with those in the organization's environment (for example, clients and suppliers). It should be clear that in each succeeding option, group members commit to using the ground rules in a greater range of situations. The group should select an option consistent with its overall objectives. For example, if the group's objective is to improve functioning within the group, the second option is sufficient. However, if the group seeks also to improve its working relationships with other parts of the organization, the third option is more appropriate. Notice that no option binds nongroup members to using the ground rules. For a top management group to decide that all organizational members will use the ground rules would be inconsistent with the core values on which the ground rules are based.

Stage Six: Evaluating, Modifying, Completing, and Terminating the Contract

As the facilitation proceeds, the client and facilitator should continuously evaluate whether the contract serves their needs. When someone has doubts, the group should openly discuss them. While it helps to have set times for reevaluating the contract, this technique should not discourage the group from raising contract issues whenever they become relevant.

Deciding when a basic facilitation contract has been completed is relatively easy and can usually be identified before the actual facilitation begins. Many basic facilitation contracts, especially short-term ones, are designed around a specific date or set of dates on which the facilitator will work with the client. After the facilitator has worked with the client on these dates, the contract work has been completed. If the facilitator has contracted to help the group until it reaches decisions on some prespecified issues, the facilitator's work is complete when the group has made the decisions.

Deciding when a developmental facilitation contract has been completed is more difficult and can rarely be identified before the facilitation begins. Clients typically do not know enough about group process to specify in advance the level of skill they want to achieve. The group can make an informed choice only when the group understands what effective group process is and how its own process falls short. Consequently, the developmental facilitator must periodically help the group consider how much further it wants to improve its process skills.

At times, the facilitator or client wants to terminate a contract before the other party believes the agreed-upon work has been completed. The client may shift priorities or become dissatisfied with the facilitator's ability to help. The facilitator may believe the client is not sufficiently committed to the facilitation or may conclude that the facilitation is part of some charade. Or, the group has learned what it needs to learn and is simply reluctant to say goodbye and proceed on its own. When contracting with developmental clients, I ask that I be allowed to meet with the client group once if it decides to prematurely terminate the contract. (If I have decided to prematurely terminate the contract, I discuss my decision with the client.) The debriefing meeting helps me understand why the client is terminating the contract, provides me with feedback about my own behavior, and allows the client and me to publicly test some assumptions about each other. Although my purpose for meeting is not to restore the contract, I do not rule out that outcome.

Summary

This chapter discussed the stages that facilitators and their clients go through to develop an agreement about how they will work together and what they will accomplish. The stages are the initial contact, planning the facilitation, tentative contracting with the primary client, premeeting conversation with planning representatives, discussing the tentative contract with the full primary client group, and evaluating, modifying, completing, and terminating the contract.

The chapter emphasized that the contracting process establishes the foundation of the client-facilitator relationship and that contracting continues throughout the facilitation process. Ultimately, only the primary client group can contract with the facilitator. Ineffective contracting almost invariably results in problems later in the facilitation.

Chapter Four Diagnosis: Identifying Behaviors That Enhance or Hinder Group Effectiveness

Before deciding to intervene in a group, the facilitator must assess whether the group is functioning effectively. ***Diagnosis* is the process by which the facilitator observes a group's behavior, determines the nature of the behavior, and infers causal relationships consistent with the facilitator's model of group effectiveness.**

To diagnose, facilitators need two sets of knowledge and skills. First, they need to know what types of behaviors to look for. Facilitators know that while any behavior may be important for understanding the group's performance, certain behaviors represent important dynamics that influence the group's effectiveness. To do this, facilitators must have a model of effective groups in their heads that suggests which behaviors are important.

Second, facilitators need a process for diagnosis—a method for observing and making sense of behaviors, regardless of the specific behaviors involved. Diagnosis begins with observing behaviors and ends with identifying causes of behavior. When diagnosing causes of group behavior, facilitators often deal with concepts (such as control and trust) that cannot be observed directly but must be inferred. A useful process of diagnosis helps facilitators move from observation to inference in a way that minimizes distortions. This chapter presents a general model of diagnosis, identifies how a facilitator determines what to diagnose, and discusses problems and pitfalls in diagnosing behavior.

The need for a model of diagnosis to guide the facilitator's behavior is part of a fundamental principle that underlies this book: effective facilitators base their thoughts and actions on a model of effective groups and on models of diagnosis and intervention, all of which are internally consistent.

A General Diagnosis-Intervention Cycle

Facilitators help clients by repeating a cycle of behavior that includes diagnosis and intervention. **The cycle** (shown in Figure 4.1, with the diagnostic steps shaded) **has six steps, three for diagnosis followed by three for intervention.** This chapter briefly describes all six steps and then discusses the three diagnostic steps. The intervention steps are examined in the next six chapters.

The three diagnostic steps describe what goes on inside a facilitator's head (Schein, 1987). **First, the facilitator observes the behavior in the group, watching for certain behaviors and patterns but open to identifying other behaviors not immediately recognizable as significant.** For example, a simple behavior may be that each member speaks only after the supervisor in the group has spoken.

Second, the facilitator infers some meaning from the behavior. An inference is a conclusion reached about something unknown, based on some things that are known. When the facilitator observes that subordinates speak only after their supervisors, the facilitator may infer that subordinates are reluctant to contradict their supervisors.

Third, based on the observation and inference, the facilitator decides whether to intervene in the group. In practice, the facilitator often observes a behavior more than once before deciding to intervene in order to clarify the inference. Assume, for example, that after observing further, the facilitator notices that although subordinates wait until their respective supervisors have spoken,

Figure 4.1. Diagnosis-Intervention Cycle.

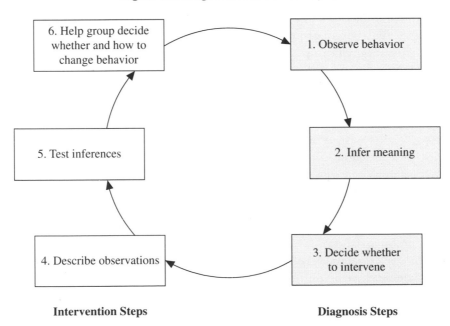

Intervention Steps   **Diagnosis Steps**

later in the meetings they often disagree with them. Consequently, the facilitator may change the inference from "subordinates are afraid to disagree with their boss" to "subordinates need to know their supervisors' opinions before offering their own."

Facilitators who decide to intervene enter the fourth step, describing their observations to the group. In this step, facilitators describe the behavior they have observed and ask group members whether they have observed the same behavior. **In the fifth step, the facilitator and group test the inference the facilitator has made and decide whether it is accurate. Assuming the group and facilitator agree, the facilitator and group enter the sixth and final step in which the facilitator helps group members decide whether and how to redesign their behavior to be more effective.** After the group has decided whether to change its behavior, the cycle begins again, and the facilitator observes whether the group has in fact changed its behavior in the manner it wanted.

The diagnostic steps describe the facilitator's thinking, and the intervention steps describe how facilitators share their thinking with the group. In fact, the diagnostic and intervention steps of the cycle are parallel. Steps one and four are parallel, as are steps two and five, and three and six.

The facilitator repeats the six-step cycle throughout the consultation with the group. In developmental facilitation, over time the group learns to conduct its own diagnosis and interventions, becoming less dependent on the facilitator. In basic facilitation, the group usually relies on the facilitator to diagnose and intervene.

The discussion that follows examines each of the three diagnostic steps in more detail. Because inferring meaning is tied so closely to observing behavior, at times the discussion refers to one when discussing the other.

Observing: The Types of Behaviors to Look for

What types of behaviors does a facilitator look for when observing a group? Chapter Two discussed the elements of effective group process, including how the group solves problems, makes decisions, manages conflict, and communicates. This section describes effective group-process behaviors in more detail to help guide the facilitator's observations. Because there are a huge number of behaviors, facilitators need a way to categorize them so they can search for fewer, more general types of behaviors. One way to narrow the list is to focus only on behaviors that affect the group's effectiveness. This section describes a number of behaviors by dividing them into three categories.

Functional, Dysfunctional, and Counteractive Behaviors

One way to categorize group process is by identifying whether a behavior contributes to, detracts from, or redirects the group toward effectiveness. Adapting the work of Dennis Gouran and Randy Hirokawa (1986), I call these *functional, dysfunctional,* and *counteractive behaviors* (Table 4.1). Functional behaviors maintain or enhance the group's effectiveness. For example, members often behave functionally when they seek to define a term (such as *respect*) that different group members have been using, seemingly to mean different things. In contrast, dysfunctional behaviors reduce the group's effectiveness. Dysfunctional behaviors include insulting members, failing to contribute relevant information to the discussion, and arriving late or unprepared for a meeting.

Finally, counteractive behaviors enhance the group's effectiveness by counteracting the effects of dysfunctional behavior. Oversimplifying, counteractive behaviors get the group back on the track after it has been derailed. Unlike functional behavior, one member's counteractive behavior can negate another's dysfunctional behavior. Because many groups have more dysfunctional than functional behavior, counteractive behavior is often the key to group effectiveness (Gouran & Hirokawa, 1986). Counteractive behaviors are similar to facilitators' interventions because they are designed to correct the group's ineffectiveness.

The following example illustrates the difference between functional and counteractive behavior. Assume that a quality improvement team has been trying to solve the problem of customers waiting too long to receive service. Having agreed on a definition of the problem and criteria for a solution, the group decides to move to the next step—brainstorming potential causes of the problem. After several members have each identified a potential cause, the following conversation occurs:

Bob: One reason may be that we don't have adequate coverage throughout the workday.

Table 4.1. Types of Behaviors.

Modes of Behavior	
Functional	Maintains or enhances the group's effectiveness

Dysfunctional	Reduces the group's effectiveness through
	  Acts of commission (for example, taking cheap shots)
	  Acts of omission (for example, withholding relevant information)

Counteractive	Enhances the group's effectiveness by negating dysfunctional behavior
Levels of Behavior	
Action	An individual comment or nonverbal gesture
Interaction	One person's comment followed by one or more persons' comments
Pattern	Meaningful behavior that occurs in larger chunks than actions or interactions—combinations of actions and/or interactions

Source: Adapted from Gouran & Hirokawa, 1986, p. 82.

Ted: [jumping ahead to proposing solutions] I'll tell you how to get good coverage—start docking people's pay if they miss part of their shift.

Sue: Yeah, I agree with Ted. Dock their pay or at least reprimand them.

Sam: Well, another reason that service is slow may be our computer system. The line workers don't have all the information they need on the system.

Ted: Well, I still think we should deal with people coming late and leaving early.

Pat: Ted and Sue, you're already talking about solutions, but the group was talking about possible causes. How about if we get back to talking about causes and hold the solutions for later?

The conversation begins with a functional behavior by Bob—identifying another cause. However, Sue and Ted exhibit dysfunctional behaviors—taking the group off track by proposing solutions prematurely. Sam's functional comment adds another potential cause, but Ted follows it by reiterating his solution. In contrast, Pat's counteractive behavior identifies Ted's and Sue's comments as off the track and asks them to return to the subject of discussion. The example illustrates that unlike functional behavior, counteractive behavior addresses the dysfunctional behavior in order to get members to act functionally.

It is useful to divide dysfunctional behaviors in terms of acts of commission and acts of omission. Insulting members is an example of a dysfunctional act of commission; withholding relevant information is an example of a dysfunctional act of omission. The distinction is important because when a group's ineffectiveness stems from dysfunctional acts of omission, the facilitator must observe *missing behaviors* in order to diagnose the group's problem. In general, it is more difficult to observe missing behaviors than exhibited behaviors because missing behavior does not cue the facilitator to analyze the behavior. Consequently, to identify acts of omission, facilitators need to constantly ask themselves, "What important behavior am I not observing?"

Levels of Behavior

When facilitators observe behavior in a group, they look for levels of meaningful behavior—meaningful in that the behavior either contributes to or detracts from group effectiveness. Often, one member's comment alone can be meaningful behavior. In this case, the facilitator can determine that it contributes to or detracts from group effectiveness by analyzing only the member's single comment, without considering its context. For example, a member's comment, "My idea is to offer the program, and I don't want to talk about problems doing it," is meaningful by itself because it represents a dysfunctional behavior—focusing on positions rather than the underlying reasons for the position. Similarly, a member's comment, "I think the work in the unit is distributed inequitably; what do the rest of you think?'' is meaningful by itself because it represents a functional behavior—focusing the discussion by inviting others to respond to the comment. When an individual comment (or nonverbal gesture) is meaningful by itself, that comment is called an *action* (Chilberg, 1989; Watzlawick, Bavelas, & Jackson, 1967).

More often, however, facilitators find that the meaning of a single comment is not fully known until they observe it in the context of other comments. Consequently, the next larger level of behavior is an *interaction*—one person's comment followed by one or more persons' comments. For example, a single interaction might comprise the following:

Jane: Jack, is it possible to get the work done by Friday if . . .

Bob: [interrupting] We're moving on to the next topic. Leslie, what's happening with the budget cutbacks?

The interaction is meaningful because Bob interrupts Jane and unilaterally changes the group's focus. Without observing Jane's and Bob's comments together it is not possible to see that Bob has interrupted and unilaterally changed the focus.

The term *pattern* (or *pattern of interactions*) is useful for describing meaningful behavior that occurs in chunks larger than actions or interactions. The simplest patterns to observe are recurring actions or interactions. Unlike recurring actions and interactions, more complex patterns are meaningful only at the pattern level of analysis. For example, the group leader may start discussing a topic by asking subordinates to make the decision. However, each time subordinates make a statement that supports a particular point of view, the leader defends an alternative view. As the subordinates are nearing a decision that supports a view the leader did not support, the leader tells the group not to decide until the next meeting. The pattern is meaningful because it shows an inconsistency between what the leader espouses (letting the group decide) and the leader's actions (delaying the group's decision). The pattern becomes clear only when the decision is about to be made. Such a pattern may take an hour or the length of a meeting to observe. This particular pattern is complex because it emerges over a period of time but is also simple because it represents dysfunctional behavior by only one person.

Patterns become more complex and more difficult to observe as they involve more people, involve more interactions among people, take more time to emerge, and comprise actions and interactions that alone do not indicate dysfunctional behavior. Some of the most difficult patterns to observe are group behaviors—patterns that involve all members. Technically, only individual people behave, not groups. However, *group behavior* refers to a combination of individual behaviors within the group that have meaning at the group level. For example, a group can reach consensus, meaning that each member has individually agreed to support a particular decision. Similarly, the pattern of "groupthink," (Janis, 1972) in which members do not realistically assess alternative courses of action, results when some members suppress their dissenting views because they believe that no one will agree. The groupthink pattern points out that patterns include patterns of thought as well as patterns of behavior.

In both the consensus and groupthink patterns, each member acts in a similar way. In other cases, the group pattern emerges from members who are acting in different ways. For example, in a rescue pattern, some group members do not perform the work expected of them and explain why they are unable to complete the work. Other group members discount the ability of these people to complete the work and, as a result, do it for them.

Facilitators can take steps to increase their ability to identify patterns. One approach is to become aware of behaviors or simple interactions that often mark the beginning of a pattern. For example, the groupthink pattern may begin with a suggestion by one member to which other members readily agree with minimal discussion. The simple interaction can serve as a mental marker for the facilitator to watch for the groupthink pattern. Over time, as facilitators become aware of different patterns, they can begin to identify the potential markers associated with them.

Although this chapter has discussed actions, interactions, and patterns of behavior separately, they occur simultaneously (Chilberg, 1989). This means that at any given time, the facilitator, if able to observe everything in the group, would see actions, some of which are embedded in interactions, some of which in turn are embedded in larger patterns. To make matters even more complicated, an action or interaction may mean one thing when observed in isolation and another when viewed as part of a pattern. By viewing the rescue pattern as a simple interaction, the facilitator might infer that the person offering to perform additional work is helping the group. However, by viewing the behavior as the larger rescue pattern, the facilitator can infer that by performing additional work, the member is colluding with others to avoid confronting a difficult issue.

To understand the notion that the facilitator must look at different levels of behavior to find meaningful behavior, consider the process of putting together a jigsaw puzzle. Imagine a jigsaw puzzle that, when completed, depicts a street scene with people, cars, and shops. When the person assembling the puzzle is faced with a box of individual pieces, some single pieces (an action) may be clearly identifiable as a person or a street light. In other cases, the assembler may have to fit together two pieces (an interaction) to obtain a distinguishable object such as a bus. In still other cases (a pattern), the assembler may need to fit together many pieces that look like bricks to figure out whether the view is of a cobblestone street or a building.

This discussion implies several things for how facilitators diagnose behavior. First, **because meaningful behavior occurs at different levels simultaneously, the facilitator must be able to simultaneously observe the different levels.** Second, **the facilitator must be able to recall the relevant behaviors that constitute a** pattern, not only to make ongoing diagnoses about complex patterns but also to describe the behaviors to the group when intervening. This means remembering dialogue throughout a discussion and even from one meeting to the next.

Third, because behaviors viewed as a pattern may have a different—even contradictory—meaning when viewed as an action or interaction, the facilitator must guard against premature diagnosis based only on lower levels of behavior. For example, a facilitator may observe that when solving a problem, members' individually engage in such functional behaviors as challenging assumptions and clarifying ambiguous words. Yet, the group makes a low-quality decision because it has failed to weigh its choices against the criteria it had earlier identified. This shows that a group's ability to make high-quality decisions rests not just on the individual actions and interactions but on the larger patterns as well (Hirokawa, 1988).

Finally, facilitators must consider the inferences they make from observations as working hypotheses that are open to change as additional observations warrant, not as unchangeable conclusions.

Basing Observations on the Contract and the Need for Help

The facilitator's contract with the group affects how the facilitator will observe certain behaviors. If the group sought help because members say they cannot resolve conflicts without bitter arguments, the facilitator should focus on behaviors related to the diagnosis to test whether the group's diagnosis is accurate. If the group sought help because it spends a lot of time discussing plans but never accomplishes them, the facilitator would focus on behavior related to that diagnosis. However, as the chapter on contracting discussed, the contract may specify particular behaviors that the client wants the facilitator to focus on, but it cannot limit what the facilitator can observe and diagnose. To act consistently with the core values, the facilitator must consider all valid information (that is, all behaviors) generated in the group, together with the facilitator's model of group effectiveness (see Figure 2.1) and the client's expressed needs.

Basing Observations on Ground Rules for Effective Groups

As Chapter Two discussed, groups develop a set of norms that tell members what kinds of behavior are expected and not expected of them. Unfortunately, because group norms are often unspoken, members may misinterpret them. This makes it more difficult to enforce the norms when members violate them. To reduce these problems, group members can explicitly agree to follow a set of ground rules.

Simply put, to the extent that the ground rules lead to effective behavior, the facilitator should focus on them when observing the group because the group has explicitly agreed to follow these rules. Consequently, facilitators can achieve significant improvements in a group's effectiveness by intervening on behaviors related to the ground rules.

The ground rules described here are principles for effective group process, even if the group does not fully understand or adopt them. Therefore, the facilitator uses them as a guide for observing members' behaviors and for intervening.

Ground Rules for Effective Groups

The sixteen ground rules (see Exhibit 4.1) are suitable for a group to the extent that it is responsible for solving problems, it deals with complex or nonroutine problems, each member is treated as making an important contribution, group decisions require the commitment of every member to be effectively implemented, the group meets regularly, and the group has sufficient time to solve problems. Examples include management teams and other regular work groups and task forces and special committees, including interorganizational groups. With some modifications, they also are appropriate for elected or appointed boards. The ground rules are based on the three core values of valid information, free and informed choice, and internal commitment. The ground rules also are supported by each other and work together. Together, the ground rules address the process problems that typically occur in groups. (Ground rules one, two, six, eight, nine, and ten are derived from the work of Chris Argyris and Don Schön [Argyris, 1982; Argyris & Schön, 1974]. Ground rule three is from the work of Fisher and Ury, 1983. Ground rules fifteen and sixteen, and modified versions of ground rules eleven, twelve, and thirteen, were jointly developed by Cortlandt Cammann and Roger Schwarz.)

Exhibit 4.1. Ground Rules for Effective Groups.

1. Test assumptions and inferences.
2. Share all relevant information.
3. Focus on interests, not positions.
4. Be specific—use examples.
5. Agree on what important words mean.
6. Explain the reasons behind one's statements, questions, and actions.
7. Disagree openly with any member of the group.
8. Make statements, then invite questions and comments.
9. Jointly design ways to test disagreements and solutions.
10. Discuss undiscussable issues.
11. Keep the discussion focused.
12. Do not take cheap shots or otherwise distract the group.
13. All members are expected to participate in all phases of the process.
14. Exchange relevant information with nongroup members.
15. Make decisions by consensus.
16. Do self-critiques.

Source: Adapted from Schwarz (1989).

1. Test Assumptions and Inferences

When people assume something, they consider it true without verifying it. When people infer something, they draw conclusions about what they do not know based on what they do know. Imagine, for example, that Bob, the group's chair, observes that Hank, although productive, has considerably more work than any other group member. To lighten Hank's work load, Bob begins transferring some of Hank's work to other members. One day, when Bob tells Hank he will no longer have to prepare a certain report, Hank replies, "Is there anything else I'm doing that you don't like?"

Bob had assumed Hank would know why he was trying to lighten Hank's work load, and Hank had incorrectly inferred that Bob was dissatisfied with his work. Furthermore, Bob did not test his assumption with Hank, and Hank did not test his inference with Bob; thus, neither could find out that he was incorrect. Consequently, it was only when Hank revealed his anger that Bob discovered his well-intentioned plan had backfired.

Testing assumptions and inferences enables members to get valid information to make informed choices. Before reacting to someone or making a decision based on something assumed or inferred, ascertain whether the assumption or inference is correct. In this case, Bob could have said, "Hank, I want to lighten your work load because I think you've got too much to do. I don't want you to misinterpret the work reassignment. I assume you know that I think the quality of your work is excellent. Do you know that?" Even if Bob did not test his assumption, Hank could have said, "When you started removing some of my duties, I inferred that you were dissatisfied with my performance. Am I correct?"

2. Share All Relevant Information

This ground rule means that each member tells the group all the information she or he has that will affect how the group solves a problem or makes a decision. Sharing information ensures that members have a common base of information. This includes sharing information that does not support one's preferred position. For example, a group is deciding whether to institute flexible working hours in the department. Sarah wants very much to have flexible working hours but thinks that it may require more careful coordination of scheduling. Sarah also knows that if others knew of the scheduling difficulty, they might not be as supportive of the idea. Here, sharing all relevant information means telling the group about the possibility of increased scheduling difficulties, although the information may reduce the chances that the group will choose to establish flexible hours. One indicator of whether members are sharing all relevant information is that they are sharing information that does not support their positions.

Group members' feelings are also relevant information to be shared. For example, an employee may want to tell a supervisor about how the supervisor's behavior creates problems. But the employee is concerned that the supervisor will use the employee's comments against him. In this case, sharing all relevant information would include the employee's saying, "I am worried that if I tell you this, you will use it against me. But I want to be honest with you, so I will tell you." Here, the employee shares three pieces of relevant information: concern about retribution, need for some assurance from the supervisor, and willingness to be vulnerable in order to solve a problem.

Exhibit 4.2 illustrates how members withhold relevant information. The top part of the figure shows a conversation between two group members (Paula and Ted) about the group's presentation to its board. The lower part of the figure shows the same conversation but also shows Paula's unexpressed thoughts and feelings during the conversation. Notice all the relevant information in Paula's

Exhibit 4.2. Sharing All Relevant Information.

The Conversation

Paula: How do you think your presentation to the board went last night?

Ted: I think it went OK, although there were some rough spots. Some board members can really get nit-picky.

Paula: We've got some really important reasons for doing it. Do you think they will fund the project now, or do we need to give them some more answers?

Ted: I think we're in OK shape. A couple board members came up to me afterward and said they appreciated the presentation. I think we should just wait and see.

Paula: Maybe, but I think we might want to give the members some more information.

Paula's Unexpressed Thoughts and Feelings	*The Conversation*
I thought it was a disaster and so did everyone I talked with.	*Paula:* How do you think your presentation to the board went last night?
Does he really believe it went OK, or he is just trying to put a good face on it?	*Ted:* I think it went OK, although there were some rough spots. Some of the board members can really get nit-picky.
Nit-picky! You couldn't answer some basic cost questions.	
I don't understand why you didn't emphasize why we wanted to do the project. The board won't fund a project if they can't get answers to some basic questions.	*Paula:* We've got some really important reasons for doing it. Do you think they will fund the project now, or do we need to give them some more answers?
I don't want to wait while this project dies on the vine. Besides, my reputation is at stake here too.	*Ted:* I think we're in OK shape. A couple of the board members came up to me afterward and said they appreciated the presentation. I think we should just wait and see.
I hope the board members don't think I'm responsible for your not having the answers to those questions.	*Paula:* Maybe, but I think we might want to give the members some more information.
Why didn't you use the information I gave you? I've got to get you to understand what you've done.	

Source: Adapted from Senge (1990, pp. 195–196). Based on the work of Argyris and Schön (1974).

unexpressed thoughts and feelings that she does not share with Ted. The point is not that Paula should share her unexpressed thoughts and feelings exactly as they appear in the left-hand column. To do so in that way would be inconsistent with many of the other ground rules. To be effective, Paula would share the relevant information by using the other ground rules (such as testing assumptions and inferences, and being specific—using examples).

3. Focus on Interests, Not Positions

To make decisions to which all members are internally committed, members must find a solution that meets everyone's interests. Interests are the needs, desires, and concerns that people have in regard to a given problem (Fisher & Ury, 1983). Solutions or positions are the ways that people meet their interests. In other words, people's interests lead them to support a particular solution or position.

An effective way for members to solve problems is to start by identifying their own interests (Fisher & Ury, 1983). Unfortunately, many groups start by talking about solutions or positions. For example, if the group is trying to solve the problem of when to meet, one member may start by saying, "I suggest we meet every other Monday at 7:30 A.M." Another may respond, "My position is that we should meet the second day of each month." Yet, their positions do not help the group identify each member's real needs, desires, and concerns. Here the person who suggested meeting every other Monday at 7:30 A.M. was interested in meeting early in the morning before some important customers would call. The person who wanted to meet the second day of each month was interested in meeting immediately after a relevant biweekly computer report became available. Each took a position that met his or her individual interests.

The problem with solving problems by focusing first on positions is that people's positions are often in conflict even when their interests are compatible. This occurs because people tend to offer their positions after they have provided for their own interests but before they have included the other members' interests. In the meeting example, each member's solution was rejected by the other because it failed to meet the other's interest. However, had each member been aware of the other's interest, either one may have been able to offer a solution that satisfied both.

To help the group focus on interests rather than positions, start by asking each member to list the criteria that must be met in order for that member to accept a solution. For example, if a group were to buy a car, one member might be interested in a car that can hold all six group members. Another might be interested in a car that uses fuel efficiently, while a third member might be interested in a car that has a good repair record. Notice that none of these interests specifies a particular make and model of car (position). If a member states a position (such as, "I want to buy a Chevy"), identify this as a position and then ask, "What interests do you have that lead you to favor that position?"

Eventually, when all members have stated their interests, members can begin to generate solutions or positions. In the car example, solutions would be the names of specific cars, such as a Ford Taurus or Dodge Caravan. When a member offers a solution, it helps to point out how that solution meets the interests on which the group agreed. In this way, the group increases the likelihood that there will be consensus on the solution.

4. Be Specific—Use Examples

Specific examples use directly observable behaviors to describe people, places, things, or events. Unlike general statements, specific examples generate valid information because they enable other members to determine independently whether the examples are valid. For example, if Vera makes the general statement to the group, "I think some of us are not doing their share of the work," other members cannot determine whether the statement is valid. Members cannot observe who "some of us" are; neither can they directly observe whether someone is "not doing their share of the work." In contrast, if Vera states specifically, "Selina and Joe, you did not complete and distribute your section of the report," other members can determine whether the statement is valid by directly observing whether Selina and Joe's section of the report is complete and whether they distributed it.

5. Agree On What Important Words Mean

This ground rule is an extension of "be specific—use examples." When members unintentionally agree or disagree with each other, it is often because the same word means different things to them. For example, a group decides to make decisions by consensus. However, to some members *consensus* means that a majority of people agree, while to others it means unanimous agreement. The first time the group makes a decision that has majority but not unanimous support, it will learn that it had not agreed on the meaning of consensus.

One way to determine whether all group members are using a word to mean the same thing is to ask them the first time the word is used. Say something like, "You used the word *consensus*. To me consensus means unanimous agreement and not majority agreement. Is that what consensus means to you?" Notice that describing what a word means helps also to describe what it does not mean.

6. Explain the Reasons Behind One's Statements, Questions, and Actions

This ground rule simply means that one person tells others why she or he is doing something. It is part of sharing all relevant information and identifying interests. For example, in asking a group for statistics on the number of days that people are late to work, one might say, "I am asking for this information because it will give me a better idea of how flexible working hours may have an effect on tardiness and absenteeism." Explaining one's reasoning helps people interpret one's behavior correctly and reduces the chances of people assuming or inferring things that may not be true. In this example, people may infer that the individual is considering some punitive action if that person did not explain the reasons for requesting the tardiness statistics.

7. Disagree Openly with Any Member of the Group

Disagreeing openly is consistent with the core value of valid information. Sometimes, the composition of the group makes it difficult for some members to disagree with others. For example, a member whose supervisor (or whose supervisor's supervisor) is also a member of the group may find it difficult to disagree with that person. Sometimes, groups are made up of subgroups, and members of one subgroup may be reluctant to disagree with each other in the presence of another subgroup's members. For example, managers may be reluctant to disagree with each other in front of employees. Watching members' nonverbal behaviors may provide cues about whether they are reluctant to disagree with other members. Of course, the cues are only inferences that must be tested with those group members.

8. Make Statements, Then Invite Questions and Comments

Making statements and then inviting questions and comments about them means expressing one's point of view (making sure to explain the reasons) and then asking others to respond, including whether they agree or disagree. For example, a group member might say, "I think it would help to give department heads their own budgets to work within, so that their accountability will be commensurate with their responsibility. But some of you may feel differently. I'd like to hear what each of you thinks about my idea, even if you disagree."

Inviting others to comment on one's statements encourages them to question and challenge the ideas and helps focus discussion as a dialogue rather than a series of monologues. The resulting discussion enables the group to determine the validity of the ideas and enables each member to make an informed choice. It may seem counterproductive to encourage disagreement, yet reaching a decision to which all members will be committed requires that members identify their disagreements and resolve them.

9. Jointly Design Ways to Test Disagreements and Solutions

Imagine that a group is discussing whether the organization responds quickly enough to customer complaints. Diane believes that customers are getting timely responses, but Kate disagrees. Normally in disagreements like this, each person tries to convince the other that she or he is wrong. Diane will offer all her evidence to support her position, and Kate will do the same for her position. Each may doubt the other's evidence, and neither will offer evidence to weaken her own position. Even when the disagreement is over, the "loser" is still likely to believe she is right.

If Diane and Kate jointly design a way to test their disagreement, it would work like this: once the two realized that they disagreed, and after they agreed on what the words *timely responses* meant, one would suggest that they work together to determine the true situation. To do so, each would have to be willing to accept the possibility that her information is inaccurate or incomplete. Then, they would jointly develop a method to test which facts are relevant. The method would include jointly agreeing on who to speak with, what questions to ask, what statistical data to consider relevant, and how to collect the data. For example, they might agree to speak with several employees, to talk with a sample of callers from recent weeks, and to review an agreed-upon number of written complaints. Diane and Kate might also agree to speak to each of these people together, so that both can hear the conversation. Whatever method they use, it is critical that both agree to it and agree to use the information that comes from it. Once Diane and Kate have collected their information, they should discuss it together and reach a joint decision about speed of response to customers.

Two important questions to ask when jointly testing disagreements are, "How could it be that we are both correct?" and "How could we each be seeing different parts of the same problem?" Often, members have different sets of facts because they are talking about different times, places, or people. In this example, both Diane's and Kate's information could have been correct but incomplete; some units could have responded to calls from customers in a timely fashion, while others did not.

By jointly resolving disagreements, members are more likely to be internally committed to the outcome because they freely agreed to the test.

10. Discuss Undiscussable Issues

Every group typically has undiscussable issues. These are issues that are relevant to the group's task but that members believe they cannot discuss openly in the group without some negative consequences. Some examples include members who are not performing adequately, members not trusting one another, and members reluctant to disagree with their superiors who are also group members. Unfortunately, because such issues often raise feelings of mistrust, inadequacy, and defensiveness, members usually deal with the issues either by not talking about them at all or by talking about them outside the group with people they trust. However, such issues are usually critical for the group to resolve, and the group's performance may suffer as long as they remain undiscussable.

In order for the group to share valid information and allow members to make free and informed choices, members need to make undiscussable issues discussable within the group. One way to achieve this is to raise the issue and acknowledge that it may be considered undiscussable: "I realize what I'm about to say may be considered an undiscussable issue, but I think we can be a more effective group if we deal with this issue." Group members also can explore their concerns about discussing such issues without actually discussing the specifics.

For example, a member might say, "I want to raise an important issue for the group, but I'm concerned that there may be reprisals toward me if I do. I want to talk about this before I decide whether to identify the undiscussable issue." If members can be assured that their fears will not be realized, they will be more willing to talk openly about previously undiscussable issues. Finally, once the group successfully discusses one undiscussable issue, members may find it easier to deal with others.

11. Keep the Discussion Focused

Focusing the discussion means ensuring that members are discussing relevant issues, everyone is focused on the same issue, and everyone fully understands the issue. Sometimes, a group spends time discussing issues that are irrelevant to its task. To get a group refocused on relevant issues, it helps to identify how the group got off the track: "We began this discussion talking about work loads, and now we are talking about photocopiers. I think we have gotten off the track; do others agree?"

At other times, group members are focused on different issues. To get everyone in the group focused on the same issue, it helps to identify the various issues that people have raised: "I think we are talking about different things. It sounds like Leslie and Debra are talking about the problem of coordinating different schedules, but Nancy and Hank are talking about how flex time will affect the amount of work we can accomplish. Do other people agree that we are talking about different things?" If other members agree, ask which topic would be best to discuss first.

One time when it is particularly crucial that members be focused on the same issue is when the group is defining the problem on which it will work. If various members believe they are solving different problems, the group will not accomplish its task.

Keeping the discussion focused also means discussing an issue until all members understand it. This ensures that every member will have the same information and will be able to make an informed choice. If even one person does not understand something, the group needs to discuss it until it is clear to everyone in the group.

12. Do Not Take Cheap Shots or Otherwise Distract the Group

At some time, almost everyone has been the target of a cheap shot—a witty or snide remark that insults someone. A cheap shot generally makes the target feel bad and does not help the group. In addition, there is a practical reason for not using them. Someone who has been the target of an insult usually spends some time thinking about the comment—wondering why the comment was made, being angry, or thinking about clever comebacks to use later in the meeting. In any event, the person usually is distracted from the group's conversation. A distracted person cannot participate in identifying and solving the problem being discussed. As a result, the person may later withhold consent.

When everyone's full participation is needed, members cannot afford to distract each other. In general, members should not engage in any behavior—such as side conversations or private jokes—that distracts the group from its task.

13. All Members Are Expected to Participate in All Phases of the Process

This ground rule means simply that each member's participation is essential for the group to work effectively. Because each member has a different position in the organization, each will likely have different experiences and different views about how to solve problems. In order for the group to benefit most from the different views, all must contribute to the extent that they have relevant information to share. Sometimes, this means simply stating why they agree or disagree with what others have said or that they have no interests that the group needs to consider when solving the problem.

14. Exchange Relevant Information with Nongroup Members

As discussed in the group-effectiveness model in Chapter Two, to be effective, a group must work well with people outside the group with whom the group members are interdependent. To make decisions based on valid information, groups often need to obtain information that resides outside the group. Working effectively with nongroup members includes continually sharing information with and seeking information from those whose work affects and is affected by the group. Consequently, the group must decide what information is relevant to share with various nongroup members and how to share it.

Because all the ground rules for group members are also effective when used with nongroup members, some groups may choose to add a related ground rule, which states, "Use the ground rules when working with nongroup members." The ground rules can increase effectiveness even when only one person knows how to use them. But because the ground rules are used *with* people, not *on* people, they become more useful as more people who are involved in a conversation understand and use them. This distinguishes the ground rules from manipulative tactics, which lose their effectiveness when the target person also knows the tactics.

Of course, nongroup members decide whether to use the ground rules with group members. Group members can help nongroup members make a more informed choice about whether to use the ground rules by describing the ground rules and explaining how they work.

15. Make Decisions by Consensus

Making decisions by consensus is at the heart of the ground rules. Consensus means that everyone in the group freely agrees with the decision and will support it. If even one person cannot agree with a proposed decision, the group does not have a consensus.

Consensus ensures that each member's choices will be free choices and that each will be internally committed to the choices. Consensus decision making equalizes the distribution of power in the group, because every member's concerns must be addressed and every member's support is required to reach a decision. For example, a member who needs to understand more about an issue can withhold consent until reaching an understanding. Reaching consensus usually takes more time than voting, because it is hard work to find a decision or solution that everyone supports. But because people are internally committed to them, decisions made by consensus usually take less time to implement successfully and encounter less resistance in the long run.

When the group thinks it is close to reaching consensus, one member should state the decision under consideration, and then each member should say whether he or she consents. This avoids the mistake of assuming that silence means consent. Voting is inconsistent with consensus decision making, but the group can take straw polls to see whether it is close to consensus and to see which members still have concerns about the proposal. Some groups, such as governing boards, have bylaws that require that decisions be made by voting, which may seem to exclude consensus. However, a group can attempt to reach consensus even if ultimately it must decide by vote.

Consensus should be used throughout the time a group is solving a problem, not just at the end when members are selecting the best alternative. Whenever the group is about to move to the next step of the problem-solving process, it should reach consensus to do so.

Some group decisions, however, may not require consensus. Throughout their work, groups make many logistical decisions, such as where and when to meet and when to take breaks. Groups can make logistical decisions without consensus so long as the decision does not affect the substantive consensus decisions that the group would make and so long as members ascertain whether anyone has strong negative feelings about the nonconsensus decision. However, for example, a group should not vote to meet at a certain time if that time excludes the attendance of a member with strong but minority opinions about the topic to be discussed.

Individuals are often reluctant to use this ground rule, because in their experiences groups rarely are able to reach consensus and because they fear that key decisions will not get made, perhaps creating a tyranny of the minority. However, many groups are unable to reach consensus because they do not use an effective set of ground rules; using the other ground rules increases the likelihood that a group will reach consensus. Also, recall from the beginning of this section that the ground rules are most appropriate when the full group must support the decision in order for it to be implemented effectively. Under this condition, the alternative to reaching consensus is to make a decision that may not be effectively implemented.

Using consensus meets the three criteria of group effectiveness discussed in Chapter Two. First, consensus increases the quality of a group's products or services by ensuring that decisions consider the valid information each member has shared. Second, consensus enhances group members' ability to work effectively together in the future by seeking solutions that everyone supports and by avoiding the divisiveness within groups that voting sometimes causes. Finally, consensus enables group members to meet their individual needs because it is designed to meet each member's interests.

16. Do Self-Critiques

For a group to become more effective over time, it must have some way to systematically incorporate its successes and learn from its mistakes. Self-critiques provide a way to do this. Before the end of each meeting, the group asks three questions: What ground rules did we use well? What ground rules do we need to improve on? Exactly what will we do differently next time?

For the critique to be helpful, members must be very specific and give examples (a ground rule) when answering each question. For example, John might say, "I think Debra helped the group focus on interests, not positions, when she asked Bob what interests led him to oppose flexible working hours. Do others agree?" A general comment, such as "I think we all could do a better job of staying focused," does not help the group identify exactly how the group lost its focus, and it assumes that other members agree that the group was not focused.

Giving someone negative feedback can be difficult, but it is easier if it is given in a way that is consistent with the ground rules, such as making a statement and then inviting people to disagree. It is easier to give negative feedback if members also keep in mind that the purpose of the self-critique is to improve the group's performance.

One way to conduct effective self-critiques while reducing the amount of negative feedback that members must give each other is for each member to identify ground rules that he or she has used well or poorly during the meeting. After each member has assessed his or her own performance, members can give each other feedback.

Because self-critiques can be uncomfortable and because groups are often pressed for time, groups sometimes do not conduct them. Ultimately, however, the only way a group can systematically improve its performance is to learn from its experiences—by doing self-critiques. In the short term, conducting the self-critique will increase the length of the meeting. In the long term, if the group learns from its self-critiques, its effectiveness will increase and it will take less time to make higher-quality decisions.

The principles of group effectiveness—which become ground rules when the group agrees to adhere to them—do not describe the only behaviors that facilitators should look for. Many other behaviors are relevant but beyond the scope of this chapter. (Additional readings are listed in Resource G.) However, the sixteen principles address much of the dysfunctional behavior common in groups.

Inferring from Behavior

The ability to think and talk about things stems in part from the ability to make inferences. An *inference* is a conclusion reached about something unknown on the basis of some things that are known (Hayakawa, 1972, p. 38). For example, someone who sees smoke in the distance infers there is a fire. The smoke is observed. But the fire is not observed; the person merely infers that it is there. When a person taps a pencil on the desk and says, "Go on, go on" in response to a subordinate's explanations, the inference may be that the boss is impatient. The impatience is not observed directly; it is inferred from the behaviors observed.

People must make inferences in order to function effectively. People need to make inferences when they need to make a decision and cannot get all the information they need. For example, if a group is trying to decide which task is more important to accomplish, members may have to infer what their manager thinks from the comments that person has made about each task if the manager has not specifically said which is more important.

Inferences also help save time by aggregating and meaningfully conveying a large number of behaviors. It can be more efficient to say, "She was very angry," than to describe the manager's behaviors: "In a loud voice she screamed, 'You've ruined the project.'" "She threw the report on the floor." "She left, slamming the door." Similarly, rather than saying, "It was 10:15 when I saw Frank enter his office and take off his trenchcoat. Frank is due at work at 9," people say, "Frank was late this morning."

Sometimes, inferences are used to identify the causes of behavior. When an auto mechanic announces, "Your car's timing is off" after listening to the engine and hearing complaints of engine hesitation, the mechanic has inferred the cause of a problem from its symptoms. Similarly, when facilitators suggest that the group is lacking focus after observing it fail to reach a decision in an hour, they are making a causal inference after observing different behaviors. **Facilitators must make causal inferences because groups can solve their process problems only after identifying their causes, and causes are often not directly observable.**

Sometimes, causal inferences are made about other people's motives. When someone says, "Dan has such a big ego, he always makes his department's presentations to the board," that person is attributing to Dan's big ego the cause of his always making the presentations.

Many inferences also involve value judgment, which is an expression of approval or disapproval (Hayakawa, 1972). If someone says, "Bob was disrespectful to Joan," that person is summarizing a large number of behaviors and stating implicit disapproval of Bob's behavior.

Yet, inferences can cause problems. The problem with inferences, however, is not that people make them but that people do not realize they make them or they realize they make them but still do not check with others to determine if they are true. Instead, they act as if they are true, which can create negative consequences if the inferences are wrong. For example, if a facilitator observes that one group member is making every other comment in the group and infers that the member is talking too much, an ineffective facilitator might say, "John, how about letting others share their thoughts?" If the facilitator has inferred incorrectly, other group members may respond, "No, John's not talking too much. He may be talking a lot, but we need to hear his information before we can make a decision." The effective facilitator would recognize that believing that John is talking too much is an inference (and a judgment) that should be checked with the other members of the group. For example, the facilitator might say to the group, "I've noticed that during about the last twenty minutes, John has made every other comment. I'm wondering whether people feel that his comments are relevant and whether others of you have been trying unsuccessfully to share your thoughts." The chapters on intervention discuss further how to test inferences.

Facilitators need to clearly distinguish between behavior they observe and the inferences they make from the behavior. In the last example, the facilitator needs to recognize that a member who speaks every other turn in a group may or may not be talking too much. The facilitator needs to recognize this so that in intervening, the facilitator can identify the inference as such and ask whether others interpret the behavior in the same way.

One area where the difference between behavior and inference becomes clear is emotions. An emotion is a state of feeling, which by definition is not a behavior. However, members often express their feelings through some behavior. A member who feels angry because other members have not responded to her questions may express her anger by sitting back in her chair, crossing her arms, tightening the muscles in her face, and furrowing her eyebrows. While the facilitator may quickly infer that the behaviors reflect anger, they may reflect some other feeling.

Why is it important to observe expressive behaviors and determine the emotions they reflect? First, while the expressive behaviors may not be dysfunctional, they may reflect reactions to other members' dysfunctional behavior. Identifying the meaning of the expressive behaviors can lead to determining whether other group members acted dysfunctionally. Second, while expressive behavior such as crossing one's arms may not be dysfunctional, it may cue the facilitator to look for the absence of a potentially functional behavior. In the example, the member who crossed her arms and sat back could choose to share relevant information by describing how another member's behavior led her to react. Sharing the information could help the members determine whether either person's behavior was dysfunctional.

An effective facilitator relies on observable behavior as much as possible and relies on inferences only when necessary. When facilitators need to make inferences to make a diagnosis, they make as low level an inference as possible (Argyris, 1985). Lower-level inferences are inferences that require adding relatively small amounts of unknown information to observable behavior in order to make the inference.

Figure 4.2 shows two sets of inferences that a facilitator could make, given the observable behavior (that is, Jeff's comment). For each inference, the assumption on which it is based is identified. One set makes positive inferences about Jeff's behavior; the other makes negative inferences. Notice that in moving to higher levels of inference, the statements become less connected with the original statement (that is, less concrete), less descriptive, and involve more value judgment. Because people make different inferences about the same observable behavior, as they move further away from the observable behavior, people are less likely to agree about their inferences. Indeed, as Figure 4.2 illustrates, facilitators can reach opposite conclusions about Jeff's behavior depending on which inferences they make.

Similarly, group members may make different inferences from the same observable behavior. Because group members' conversations about their conflicts

Figure 4.2. Two Ladders of Inference.

Negative Inferences	*Positive Inferences*
High-level Inferences	
Jeff did not respect his manager.	Jeff respected his manager.
Assumption: Publicly disagreeing and identifying a weakness in the manager's idea is disrespectful.	*Assumption:* Publicly disagreeing with his manager about the manager's values shows respect for sharing valid information and allowing informed choices.
↑ *Medium-level Inferences* ↑	
Jeff did not support his manager's idea.	Jeff differed with his manager's value of service to customers.
Assumption: Publicly disagreeing with the manager was not supporting his manager's idea.	*Assumption:* Jeff's manager does not value improving the speed of customer service.
↑ *Low-level Inferences* ↑	
Jeff identified a weakness in his manager's idea.	Jeff helped his manager see a negative outcome of his manager's idea.
Assumption: Increasing response time to customers is a weakness in the manager's idea.	*Assumption:* Increasing response time to customers is a negative outcome of the manager's idea.
↑ *Observable Behavior* ↑	
In the departmentwide meeting, Jeff said to his manager, "If my calculations are correct, your idea would increase our response time to customers by five days."	

Source: Adapted from Argyris, 1985.

often occur at high levels of inference, facilitators can help members clarify, if not reduce, the conflict by asking members to move to lower levels of inference in regard to observable behavior. As members do this, they share the logic of their inferences, which becomes open for discussion by the group.

In addition to illustrating the value of making lower-level inferences, the levels of inference figure suggests a second task for facilitators. When making inferences, facilitators need to clearly illustrate the directly observable behavior on which they base the inferences. The approach enables facilitators to explain how they reached a diagnosis, enabling group members to explore the facilitator's chain of logic.

Facilitators sometimes need to intervene on issues that require high levels of inference. Examples of high-level inference issues are trust, power and control, equity, and defensiveness. Such issues can have a significant effect on a group's effectiveness. **The approach to facilitation described in this book does not rule out diagnoses (or interventions) based on high-level inferences. Rather, the approach seeks to deal with issues at the lowest level of inference possible in order to avoid attributing more meaning to behaviors than is necessary.**

Embedded in high-level inferences are a nested set of lower-level inferences, as Figure 4.2 shows. Each successively higher-level inference adds more meaning and often more value judgment to the observed behavior. **Consequently, when facilitators do make diagnoses based on high-level inferences, they should test with the client group each successively higher level of inference, beginning with the level closest to the observable behavior.** This is important because changing group dynamics for high-level inference issues (such as increasing trust among group members) often involves group members' changing their behaviors. This requires that members clearly see how an abstract issue such as trust between members can be changed by changing behavior.

Deciding Whether to Intervene

Once facilitators have observed group behavior and inferred that it is dysfunctional (or functional or counteractive), they must decide whether to intervene. In practice, intervening means entering the group's conversation to help it become more effective. Deciding whether to intervene is the last diagnostic step in the diagnosis-intervention cycle (see Figure 4.1) and represents a transition between the diagnosis and intervention parts of the cycle. In this step, the facilitator must diagnose whether the potential intervention is based on reliable data, whether the group can benefit from the intervention, and whether other group members are likely to intervene on their own if the facilitator does not.

How does the facilitator decide when to intervene? A simple but incomplete answer is that the facilitator intervenes when a member of the group acts inconsistently with a ground rule that the group has agreed to follow or when the facilitator identifies some element of the group's process, structure, or organizational context that hinders its effectiveness. However, following this ap-

proach could lead the facilitator to intervene every minute, if only because following ground rules consistently requires much practice by groups. For groups
that have average to poor effectiveness, almost every member's comment may be
dysfunctional in some way. Theoretically, the facilitator could intervene every
time a member spoke, which obviously would prevent the group from ever accomplishing its tasks.

In deciding whether to intervene, the facilitator must balance the group's
need to get the job done with its need to learn how to work more effectively as
a group. In addition to preventing the group from accomplishing its substantive
tasks, spending too much time learning how to work effectively can overload the
group. People can process only a certain amount of new information in a given
time. If the facilitator overloads the group with interventions, members may learn
little. Consequently, the facilitator needs a set of criteria for deciding when to
intervene and when to remain silent.

Questions to Ask in Deciding Whether to Intervene

This section identifies questions (see Exhibit 4.3) and issues to help facilitators
decide when to intervene and when not to.

1. Have I observed the behavior enough to make a reliable diagnosis? Just
as it is less reliable to diagnose a disease from a single symptom, it is less reliable
to diagnose group behavior from a small number of actions. If a member interrupts another member once, it would be premature for the facilitator to infer that
interruption is a problem. If, however, the same member frequently interrupts
other members or certain members, the facilitator will have identified enough of
a pattern to ensure that the behavior persists over time and thus is reliable.

Waiting to intervene can have negative consequences. If facilitators wait
until their information is reliable enough to justify intervention, group members
may infer that the facilitator is not performing with vigilance. In addition, a
facilitator's early interventions show the group what it can expect from the fa-

Exhibit 4.3. Questions to Ask to Decide Whether to Intervene.

1. Have I observed the behavior enough to make a reliable diagnosis?
2. Have I contracted with the group to make this type of intervention?
3. If I do not intervene, will a group member intervene?
4. Will the group have time to process the intervention?
5. Does the group have sufficient experience and knowledge to use the intervention to
   improve its effectiveness?
6. Does the group have enough information (or can I give them enough information) to
   make a free and informed choice in regard to the intervention?
7. Is the group too overloaded to process the intervention?
8. Is the behavior central enough or important enough to intervene on?
9. If I do not intervene now, what is the probability that I can intervene later and still
   help the group avoid the negative consequences of its dysfunctional behavior?
10. Do I have the skills to intervene?

cilitator and can help the group quickly become aware of its behavior. The potential for problems can be reduced if facilitators state early in the facilitation why they may not intervene at times when others believe it would be appropriate.

2. *Have I contracted with the group to make this type of intervention?* The facilitator needs to make interventions that are consistent with the contract, but the facilitator also needs the freedom to use professional judgment to determine whether to raise an issue the group has not contracted to discuss. When facilitators believe that an intervention is necessary and that it is not consistent with the current contract, they can ask the group whether it is willing to recontract for the moment. When the facilitator observes issues that are equally important, the issues for which the group has contracted take priority. This situation is discussed further in Chapter Five in the section about depths of interventions.

3. *If I do not intervene, will a group member intervene?* Developmental facilitators' ultimate goal is to work themselves out of a job by having the group learn to manage its process. To do this, the facilitator must not intervene when the group is able to do so itself. Determining what the group can and cannot do at any point requires continual testing. It is reasonable to assume that the group will not be able to intervene in more difficult issues until it has intervened in simpler ones.

Not intervening can be a strategy for further diagnosis and group development. In developmental facilitation, the facilitator may decide not to intervene in order to determine whether members will intervene on their own. If a member does intervene, the facilitator learns that the group has developed its ability to diagnose and intervene and may be less dependent on the facilitator for resolving that type of issue. In fact, the facilitator must regularly decide not to intervene in order to help the group develop. Assuming that facilitators are more skilled than group members at observing the group's behavior, they are more likely to intervene before a group member. However, if facilitators always intervene immediately when they decide the issue is important, the group will never have the opportunity to develop its diagnostic and intervention ability. In short, the developmental facilitator must give the group the opportunity to fail in the short term in order to develop the ability to succeed in the long term.

4. *Will the group have time to process the intervention?* Without enough time to process an intervention, the facilitator frustrates the group and wastes its time. When the intervention raises undiscussable issues or other threatening feelings, the facilitator may elicit feelings of anxiety among members and may temporarily reduce the group's ability to function. Because the facilitator may not recognize important patterns of behavior until the end of a session nears, the facilitator may feel the need to intervene on the just-identified issues. The need may stem from a desire to help the group address an issue that has until now eluded them, or it may stem from the facilitator's need to show the group that she or he has identified an important group issue. In any case, as the meeting draws to a close, the facilitator should consider dropping the intervention, making it next time if possible, or if appropriate, noting a desire to discuss the issue

next time. In short, **a facilitator should not make an intervention if the group does not have the time to process it.**

5. Does the group have sufficient experience and knowledge to use the intervention to improve its effectiveness? Certain interventions (such as raising undiscussable issues) require that members take more risks than usual. Groups with sufficient experience and knowledge can respond to interventions that involve more personal risk and potential for defensive behavior without reducing group members' ability to work together in the future. For example, such a group would be able to discuss openly the effects of a member's poor performance without further inhibiting the group's ability to accomplish future tasks.

Ultimately, the members choose whether to pursue a facilitator's intervention. However, the facilitator decides whether to raise the issue, and just raising an issue can sometimes generate greater risk than members are willing or able to handle. Here, the facilitator may face the dilemma of either exposing the members to risks they are either unwilling or unable to take or unilaterally protecting them from issues that the facilitator believes they cannot discuss. The dilemma is tempered by the fact that groups often do not respond to interventions that involve more risk than they are ready to handle. The facilitator should also consider that unilaterally protecting the group in this way will require the facilitator to withhold relevant information, thereby violating one principle of group effectiveness.

To determine whether the group has enough experience and knowledge, the facilitator can examine the group's history and current status. Has the group handled other issues that involved similar levels of personal risk? What other issues has the group discussed during the current session? If the group has addressed only low-risk issues in the current session, members may find it difficult to address a relatively high-risk issue, even if they have done so in previous meetings. Facilitators working with basic groups are less likely to make the deeper interventions, because basic facilitation goals focus more on helping a group solve its substantive problems than on helping a group better understand and improve its process.

6. Does the group have enough information (or can I give them enough information) to make a free and informed choice in regard to the intervention? Sometimes, the facilitator's intervention requires the group to make a choice about how the facilitator should help them. For example, a facilitator might propose that a group examine its values and beliefs, either by beginning with some important decisions the members have made or by listing the values and beliefs they think they hold. However, if the group does not have enough information about what each of the alternatives would require from the group and how each would benefit the group, the group's decision to spend time on any of them will not be informed, and the quality of the decision may be poor. The situation often occurs at the beginning of the consulting relationship, when clients have only a vague idea of how the facilitator can help them. Here, the facilitator must find a way to provide the information necessary for the group to make an informed choice, temporarily make the choice unilaterally for the group, or ask the group to make a less-than-informed choice, noting that in each case the decision is open to change.

7. Is the group too overloaded to process the intervention? Individuals can process only so much information at one time. If, during one session, the facilitator has raised a large number of issues for the group to consider (or a few difficult ones), members may be too tired to integrate new interventions. This is especially true when the group has not yet resolved issues that were raised earlier in the session.

8. Is the behavior central enough or important enough to intervene on? Some interventions are more closely tied than others to helping the group increase its effectiveness. Given that facilitators cannot intervene on every dysfunctional behavior, they should choose those that are likely to have greater impact on the group's effectiveness. For example, consider a group that starts to generate alternatives to a problem before agreeing on the definition of the problem. During the conversation, a member makes a logically inconsistent statement. The facilitator should intervene on the first issue, because the larger group pattern of moving to a second subject before completing the first is likely to be more dysfunctional than the individual's logically inconsistent statement.

At any given time, the most useful interventions will not necessarily be those that are tied most closely to helping the group accomplish its task. As discussed in Chapter Two, an effective group not only must produce services and products that meet or exceed the standards of those who receive, use, and review them but its members must also work together in ways that maintain or enhance their ability to work together in the future, and that satisfy the personal needs of group members. Sometimes, the most useful interventions will be those that focus on group issues that relate more to the latter two criteria for effectiveness. Facilitators must continually keep in mind all three effectiveness criteria when deciding whether an issue is important enough to intervene on.

9. If I do not intervene now, what is the probability that I can intervene later and still help the group avoid the negative consequences of its dysfunctional behavior? Before deciding to pass up an opportunity to intervene, the facilitator should consider the probability of intervening later and still helping the group avoid the negative consequences of its dysfunctional behavior and the severity of the negative consequences. If the negative consequences are not likely to be severe, the facilitator can safely pass up the intervention. For example, members often interrupt each other, but this usually results only in longer, more disconnected meetings—a relatively mild consequence.

The facilitator need not always be concerned about missing an opportunity to intervene. **If a behavior or issue is important enough to intervene on, it will likely come up again in the group.** I refer to this as *the principle of repeating opportunities,* and it is especially true of dysfunctional behaviors. For example, a member who fails to test inferences on one issue is likely to fail to test inferences on other issues throughout the meeting. The principle of repeating opportunities also holds for a group's substantive decisions. For example, if a group makes a decision without getting consensus, the decision will probably be discussed again when there is insufficient support for implementing it.

The facilitator can still choose not to intervene if the consequences are likely to be severe; the facilitator will probably have another chance to intervene before the group faces the consequences. For example, if, early in their discussions, members of a recycling task force do not test their assumption that residents will fully support a recycling program, the program will suffer or fail if the assumption turns out to be false. Fortunately, before the members decide to implement the program, the facilitator will have many opportunities during the task force's discussions to help the members become aware that their assumption is untested.

The most harmful situation occurs when the consequences are likely to be severe and the facilitator is unlikely to have a second chance to intervene before the group faces the consequences. Consider, for example, a special committee formed to improve functioning in the human resources department and that reports directly to the chief executive officer (CEO) rather than to the head of human resources. The committee has quickly decided to send out a memo to all human resources employees recommending large-scale changes, without first consulting with the CEO. Here, the consequences of not consulting with the CEO are likely to be severe, and once the decision is made, the facilitator will have little chance to intervene before the memo is sent. The facilitator needs to intervene.

10. Do I have the skills to intervene? Some interventions, such as those that deal with members' defensive behavior, require significant facilitator skill. To be helpful, facilitators must intervene within the limits of their skills. This does not mean that facilitators should totally avoid intervening where they are not completely proficient. This would prevent the facilitator from taking reasonable risks in order to become more effective—a behavior the facilitator should be a model of for the group. However, facilitators should limit those risks to interventions that are close to their current level of skills.

Problems and Challenges in Diagnosing Behavior

This chapter has discussed how to observe behavior, infer meaning from the behavior, and decide whether to intervene. This section considers some challenges and problems that facilitators face that apply to all three diagnostic steps.

The Need to Continually Attend to the Group

One reason that facilitation is such mentally demanding work is that facilitators must continually be attending to the group during the entire time they are working with it. Consequently, a facilitator must diagnose behavior while simultaneously continuing to observe the group (Schön, 1983). Unless two facilitators are working together with a group, as discussed in Chapter Eleven, a facilitator cannot mentally take time out from the group to diagnose the group's behavior.

The Principle of Repeating Opportunities

In order to accurately diagnose, facilitators need to observe multiple behaviors simultaneously—a formidable task given the limited ability of human beings to process information. Because it is not possible to observe everything simultaneously, the facilitator is likely to miss some important behaviors or patterns that occur during a particular time period. Fortunately, as mentioned earlier in this chapter, group behavior is repetitive. If a member or the group has a certain problem, that problem will show up repeatedly. Consequently, the facilitator need not worry about missing a single critical behavior or pattern. **If the behavior is genuinely part of the group's process, the facilitator will have more than one opportunity to observe it.**

Being Comfortable with Ambiguity and Information Overload

At times facilitators are unable to make sense out of what they are observing in the group and may feel uncertain or confused. This is a natural feeling for even experienced facilitators, especially when they are just beginning to work with a group. The natural response to confusion is to try to impose some order. **The challenge for the facilitator is to become comfortable with ambiguity and not impose order prematurely by rushing to inferences and a diagnosis.** Diagnosing behavior prematurely increases the probability that the facilitator will miss important aspects of the group's behavior.

One reason the group's behavior seems ambiguous at times is that the facilitator is observing a complex pattern in the group, but the group has displayed only part of the pattern. Like mysteries that seem impossible to solve until the last pages of the book, the entire pattern must appear before the facilitator can interpret it. Sometimes, facilitators feel confused because they have missed the beginning of the pattern, much like walking into a movie theater after a film has begun. For example, a conflict between members just before the meeting begins may be played out in the meeting with the facilitator.

Apart from accepting that ambiguity and confusion are inevitable, the facilitator can try to make sense of the situation without imposing order prematurely. By generating alternative hypotheses about what is happening, the facilitator can observe behaviors that either confirm or disconfirm the alternative hypotheses. Of course, the facilitator can also share the ambiguity and confusion with group members and ask them to help diagnose the situation.

Misperception and Emotional Reaction

Facilitators are susceptible to the same perceptual and reasoning errors that they are helping their clients to overcome. Sometimes, facilitators react emotionally (and dysfunctionally) because they have misperceived the situation. The techniques described in this book for reducing perceptual errors and dysfunctional emotional reactions hold for facilitators as well as group members. To help clients avoid errors in logical thinking, facilitators must avoid the same errors (Gambrill, 1990). In both cases, the facilitator can first identify the source of the misperception or dysfunctional reaction. Several sources include different personal filters or biases, expectations based on past situations, and cultural values and beliefs (Schein, 1987).

Cultural differences include differences in race, gender, religion, socioeconomic status, ethnic group, and geographical region. For example, various cultures have different values and beliefs about sharing negative information. In certain cultures, giving others negative feedback about their performance is considered a way to show respect for that person; in other cultures, giving negative feedback is considered rude. Because effective facilitation is based on the former belief, facilitators who work in the cultures that see negative feedback as rude may misperceive clients' reactions when they initially provide only positive feedback to each other. Facilitators can reduce their cultural misperceptions by becoming aware of their own values and beliefs as well as those of the cultures in which they work. Also, two or more facilitators, each from a different culture that is represented in the client group, can work together as cofacilitators to the group. This approach is discussed in Chapter Eleven.

Dealing with misperceptions that stem from cultural diversity among group members can be particularly challenging work for several reasons. Members are often unaware of how their cultural values and beliefs affect their behavior in the group, and they are also typically unaware of how their values and beliefs differ from group members' who come from other cultures. Cultural values and beliefs are often deeply held, groups typically do not have much experience or skill in dealing with their cultural diversity, and the issue is often emotionally charged. Finally, group members' cultural values and beliefs, like any value or belief, cannot be observed directly. Rather, they are identified by making relatively high-level inferences from group members' behaviors. Consequently, to deal with issues associated with cultural diversity, a facilitator must make many interventions based on what are relatively high-level inferences that focus on deeply personal issues for group members who are likely to be relatively unskilled in addressing the issues.

For these reasons, facilitators need to be careful not to intervene on potentially explosive situations that they do not have the skills, time, or experience to process. As discussed in Chapter Three, when such issues are to be the subject of facilitation, the facilitator and client need to contract for deep-level interventions.

Facilitators' personal biases or filters lead them to misperceive by interpreting certain events in the same predetermined way. For example, facilitators who have a strong need to control situations may tend to interpret client disagreements with them as resistance rather than considering the possibility that the client has become independent enough to challenge the facilitator. In short, people do not always see things as they are; people tend to see things as people are. **Facilitators need to be aware of their systematic biases and personal issues (for example, needs for control or status, low self-esteem) to reduce the chance that these biases and personal issues will distort their group diagnoses.** Here too, working with a cofacilitator can reduce the problem.

Facilitators also develop expectations based on their work with previous clients. Consequently, a facilitator may prematurely diagnose a situation based on past experiences. Such misperceptions can occur easily when a facilitator works with one type of group (for example, boards of directors) for a long time and then begins working with another type (such as management teams) without recognizing the different nature of the groups. But the problem goes beyond recognizing differences between types of groups. Imagine that a facilitator has repeatedly encountered clients who, during the contracting stage, emphasize their total commitment and later on fail to have all their members present. At some point, the facilitator may come to expect that clients who claim to be totally committed will not follow through. As a result, the facilitator may treat this type of client group as if it has already failed to follow through on the commitment. What makes these situations complex is that the facilitator should learn two things from previous experiences: first, which early client behaviors are likely to predict later client behaviors, and second, how to prevent previous experiences from completely determining how the facilitator will react in a specific situation.

Because inferences often have an emotional component, facilitators are susceptible to inappropriate emotional reactions when they fail to accurately perceive a situation. To reduce the likelihood that this will happen, facilitators can become aware of the issues that are most likely to lead them to react emotionally and defensively. One way to do this is for facilitators to identify their deeply held values and beliefs. Second, facilitators can identify those aspects about themselves or others that they most dislike. Together, the values, beliefs, and the aspects facilitators most dislike represent areas where the facilitator is likely to misreact and become defensive. For example, a facilitator who values status might be insulted by a client who does not treat the facilitator with deference. Facilitators who become aware of these areas will be better able to monitor their reactions and minimize their impact on group diagnosis.

Facilitators sometimes get frustrated or angry when a client group or certain group members continually act ineffectively. If facilitators do not deal with the frustration, it can reduce their effectiveness. One way to deal with the frustration is to reframe the situation, that is, to think about it in a different way. When I am in this situation, I remind myself that my client group has sought my help because its members are less skilled in group process and interpersonal behavior than I am. Just as a teacher of disadvantaged students does not hold the disadvantages against the students, so I remember that most adults are never taught how to communicate or work effectively in groups and that I am choosing between holding my clients' ineffective behavior against them or using my skills to improve theirs. When I start to make attributions about whether certain members want to improve their skills, I recall one of my basic beliefs—that people do not get up in the morning intentionally trying to act ineffectively or make others' lives difficult. Instead, **people are faced with problems they try to solve, and they do the best they can with the skills they have.** To respond with frustration or anger would be to act like the physician who says to a patient, "I can't treat you. You're sick." If the group members' skills were effective, they would not have needed my help. While my reframing does not change the clients' behavior, it does change my reaction to it and therefore makes it easier for me to continue helping them become more effective.

Focusing Exclusively on Content

Focusing exclusively on the group's content instead of its process is a common problem that distracts facilitators from observing behavior and making inferences accurately. This situation can arise when the facilitator is especially interested in the content, is completely unfamiliar with the content, or feels overwhelmed by the group's process. For obvious reasons, facilitators with a special interest in the content may be distracted by it. Facilitators who are completely unfamiliar with the content can be drawn into it while attempting to help members examine their logic. Facilitators who feel overwhelmed by the group's process may seek comfort in the group's content, especially if it is familiar to the facilitator.

Effective facilitators do not ignore the content. They focus on it to help understand the process. In order to recall verbatim conversation, facilitators need to understand and pay attention to the content. However, they need to do so without attempting to solve the problem on which the group is working.

Expanding the Facilitator's Diagnostic and Intervention Tools

Facilitators' effectiveness is determined partly by the range of their diagnostic and intervention tools. The law of the instrument (Kaplan, 1964) essentially states that if the only tool available is a hammer, everything looks like a nail. The law is equally relevant to diagnosis and intervention and has several implications. As discussed in this chapter, facilitators can observe in groups a huge number of actions, interactions, and patterns that are relevant to the group's effectiveness. Similarly, there are a large number of interventions facilitators can make with a group, as the next six chapters discuss. The law of the instrument reasonably assumes that facilitators can diagnose only the kinds of behavior they have the ability to conceptualize and can make only those interventions they have the ability to make. Second, the law of the instrument implies that if facilitators' diagnostic or intervention tools are limited, facilitators will naturally construe the situation to fit the diagnostic and intervention tools they have. Consider, for example, a facilitator who has the ability to diagnose and intervene on cheap shots but not the ability to diagnose and intervene on undiscussable issues. The facilitator may continually identify the cheap shots to the group without ever identifying the undiscussable issue that may be generating them. To make the situation more difficult, within the limits of their diagnostic and intervention repertoires, facilitators have their favorite tools, which they may look for opportunities to use, even when other tools may be more appropriate. All of this, of course, reduces the effectiveness of facilitation and may harm the client. The challenge for facilitators is to develop the ability to diagnose the comprehensive set of behaviors related to group effectiveness and to learn to use a comprehensive set of interventions related to these behaviors.

Summary

This chapter discussed how to diagnose behavior in groups. The chapter introduced a six-step diagnosis-intervention cycle. The three diagnostic steps in the cycle are observing behavior, inferring meaning, and deciding whether to intervene. The chapter discussed several modes of behaviors (functional, dysfunctional, and counteractive) and several levels of behavior (actions, interactions, and patterns) that facilitators look for when observing behavior. The chapter described sixteen ground rules for effective groups, which can be used by facilitators and group members. The ground rules are important facilitator guides for observing group behavior and are addressed in more detail in the chapters on intervention. Because facilitators cannot intervene on all their observations and inferences, and because an important part of diagnosis is determining whether a diagnosis warrants intervention, the chapter discussed how to decide whether to intervene. Finally, the chapter considered some challenges and problems that facilitators face in accurately diagnosing group behavior.

To make the discussion in this chapter easier to follow, I discussed the diagnosis-intervention cycle as if the boundaries between diagnosis and intervention were clear and distinct. In practice, however, the boundaries are blurred and overlap. Facilitators' interventions are often designed to accurately diagnose the situation, such as when facilitators intervene to test their inference with the group. In short, facilitators diagnose in order to intervene, but they also intervene in order to diagnose.

Part Three Intervening

Effectively in Groups

Chapter Five # Things to Consider Before Stepping In

After facilitators have decided to intervene, they are faced with the basic question, What should I say and to whom should I say it? To answer this question, facilitators must first answer a series of questions including, What are the client's immediate concerns and interests? What is the client trying to accomplish? How much structure does the group need? How deep or personal should I make my intervention? What is the most important behavior to focus on?

This chapter and the next five that follow focus on how to intervene and address the question posed above. This chapter considers the questions that facilitators must first answer before deciding exactly what to say and to whom to say it.

Recall that to intervene means "to enter into an ongoing system of relationship" for the purpose of helping those in the system (Argyris, 1970, p. 15). In facilitation, **an intervention includes any statement, question, or nonverbal behavior made by a facilitator that is designed to help the group.**

Begin with the Client's Concerns and Interests

The chapter on contracting (Chapter Three) stated that a general principle underlying diagnosis and intervention is to **begin with the client's concerns.** Applying the principle means that the facilitator's choice of interventions is guided by the concerns of group members at the time. The principle assumes that if members are focused on a particular issue, they will not be able to attend fully to other issues raised by the facilitator until their issue is addressed. The facilitator responds directly to the client's manifest needs at the time, not according to the facilitator's agenda.

I experienced the consequences of failing to begin with the client's concerns when I was cofacilitating a committee of police department employees. I was the external facilitator and my cofacilitator was the internal facilitator. At the first meeting, my cofacilitator was about to explain to the committee all their objectives. (My cofacilitator was also the personnel director and was explaining the objectives in his role as personnel director.) Before he began, a committee member started to ask a question about the objectives. My cofacilitator interrupted, saying, "That's a good question; it brings us right to the objectives." My cofacilitator then explained the objectives, assuming that the member's question would be answered by the explanation. After my cofacilitator finished his explanation, he asked the member if his question had been answered. Looking away from my cofacilitator and with a frustrated look on his face, the member said, "No, but just go ahead anyway." Realizing something had gone wrong, my cofacilitator looked at me as if to say, "What should I do?" The member, who had actively participated until then, was silent for the next five minutes. By not allowing the member to ask his question initially, my cofacilitator had failed to begin with that member's concerns. As a result, his later attempt to answer the question was rebuffed.

Starting with the client's concerns and interests also means addressing a member's needs that may be different from the larger group's. It does not mean, however, that the group must drop the facilitator's intervention to discuss that member's concerns. Rather, it means allowing a member to briefly state the concern and then deciding (or having the group decide) how to proceed. In some cases, the group may decide that the concern should be addressed immediately. In other cases, the member will gladly return to the current agenda item if assured that the concern will be addressed before the meeting ends. Writing the concern on a separate piece of flip chart paper helps the group remember to address it and helps the member who raised it to focus on the current agenda item.

Intervening with attention to the client's interests and concerns becomes more difficult when members are unaware that they are not ready to follow the facilitator's intervention. A colleague and I served as cofacilitators and co-trainers of a group whose members were learning to facilitate groups. Having spent hundreds of hours together in intensive work, the group had become close-knit. Because members came from different organizations, some members often had not seen each other since the previous meeting. Each quarterly meeting began with members sharing their facilitation experiences and getting help from other members. On this occasion, as members arrived at the hotel meeting room, they greeted each other warmly and quickly tried to catch up on each other's lives. When everyone had arrived, they sat around the table, anticipating the beginning of the meeting. However, members were still engaged in small talk, and my colleague and I joined in. I waited several minutes, because I felt awkward about beginning the meeting. Finally, ignoring my feelings, I attempted to begin discussion by asking who wanted to start sharing a facilitation experience. Different members responded with comments, but no one volunteered, and members seemed uncomfortable with my intervention. It felt as if a group of close friends had suddenly become near strangers. Finally, my colleague said, "I'm feeling awkward. I feel like I want to relax and talk with people. I'm not ready to jump right in to sharing facilitation experiences. What are others feeling?" My colleague had captured what everyone was feeling but had been unable to express. The group quickly agreed to move to a more comfortable setting and spend some time relaxing and talking before tackling the first task.

The example illustrates several points. First, when the facilitator's intervention fails to address any of the members' current needs, the intervention will probably fail. Second, because members are sometimes unaware of their needs, facilitating effectively requires anticipating clients' needs at different points and verifying that they exist. It also requires diagnosing members' needs, sometimes from subtle cues, such as when members of a usually cohesive group act distant. Third, one source of diagnostic data is the facilitator's own feelings (Smith, 1990). Sometimes, facilitators themselves mirror the feelings and reactions that group members are experiencing (Alderfer, 1990). By being attuned to their feelings and tracing their origins, facilitators may be able to identify group members' needs that otherwise would go unaddressed. Finally, the example points out that spending time off task can actually increase a group's effectiveness. Chapter Two noted that an effective group does more than accomplish its task well; it works in a way that maintains group members' ability to work together in the future and that meets members' individual needs.

Is the Facilitation Basic or Developmental?

Another factor that influences how a facilitator intervenes is whether the facilitation is basic or developmental. Recall that in basic facilitation, the group seeks to accomplish some substantive task, while the facilitator helps to manage the group's process. In developmental facilitation, the group seeks to accomplish some substantive task and also learn to manage its process. In other words, in basic facilitation the facilitator helps the group temporarily improve its process in order to accomplish some substantive task. In developmental facilitation, the facilitator helps the group permanently improve its process.

Consequently, developmental interventions are often designed to help the group learn to diagnose and correct its problems. Depending on the group members' skills, the facilitator might say any of the following:

- "One of the group's ground rules is to focus on interests rather than positions. When you said, 'My opinion is X,' you stated a position, do you agree?" If the member agrees, the facilitator says, "Would you be willing to say what interests you have that are behind your position of wanting to lease the equipment?"

- "Bob, you just said, 'My opinion is we should lease the equipment rather than buy it.' I believe your statement is inconsistent with one of the ground rules. Do you see which one?"
- "What just happened?"

The second and third examples are designed to help members diagnose their own behavior. The first example is designed for either developmental clients who have no skill in diagnosing their own behavior or for basic clients. **One of the principles underlying developmental interventions is to intervene in a way that enables members to take as much responsibility as possible for diagnosing and redesigning their behavior. The corollary principle underlying basic facilitation is to intervene in a way that enables the members to remain focused primarily on the substantive task.**

Basic interventions also generally focus more on superficial dysfunctional behaviors than on the more complex dynamics that generate the ineffective behaviors. The distinction applies only to interventions directed at the "here-and-now" group process (that is, behaviors occurring in the group during facilitation) and not interventions necessary to solve the group's content problem. For example, in a group in which members take cheap shots at each other, the facilitator is likely to intervene by pointing out that members have acted inconsistently with their ground rule (no cheap shots). In developmental facilitation, however, the facilitator will also help the group explore the conflicts that lead to the cheap shots. For similar reasons, basic interventions are more likely to focus on actions than on interactions and patterns of behaviors. **Another principle that underlies developmental facilitation is to intervene in a way that identifies the root causes of dysfunctional behavior and solves the group's content problems. The principle underlying basic facilitation is to intervene to the extent that the group can temporarily increase its process effectiveness enough to solve the content problem.** Because developmental interventions focus more on the root causes of behavior, they are also deeper or more intensive.

Macro and Micro Interventions

Facilitator interventions vary according to how much they structure group members' behavior. Almost all interventions attempt to structure members' behavior to some degree. When a facilitator follows her statement by asking, "Sue, do you agree or disagree with me?" she attempts to structure only Sue's answer so that it responds to the question. When the facilitator suggests that the group develop a meeting agenda, however, the facilitator attempts to broadly structure the group's discussion for that entire meeting.

Interventions that are more *macro* (such as developing an agenda) provide greater structure; interventions that are more *micro* (such as the facilitator asking one member a question) provide less structure. Although macro and micro represent two ends of a continuum that measures structure, I will sometimes refer to them as absolutes for the sake of simplicity. For example, facilitators make a relatively macro intervention when they suggest that the group use a problem-solving model to discuss its problem. Other relatively macro interventions include establishing roles, ground rules, and expectations for a meeting, setting an agenda, and using an experiential exercise or self-knowledge instrument. (Experiential exercises and self-knowledge instruments are discussed in Resource D.) Macro interventions provide greater structure by limiting the range of appropriate actions that members may take while the macro intervention is in effect. For example, by agreeing to use a set of ground rules during a meeting, members limit themselves to certain behaviors throughout the meeting. In other words, macro interventions create structures that affect members' behaviors after the facilitator's intervention is over. Macro interventions also tend to create structure for the entire group. Establishing ground rules and developing an agenda, for example, apply to all group members.

In contrast, micro interventions provide relatively little structure. When the facilitator points out similarities among members' comments or asks members to define important words, the intervention limits the range of members' behaviors only in their immediate response to the facilitator's intervention. Whereas macro interventions tend to structure all members' behavior, micro interventions tend to structure individual members' behavior or a subgroup's behavior. When micro interventions do structure all group members' behavior, they do so for a relatively short time.

The facilitator must decide how macro or micro to make each intervention. **Interventions should provide the minimal amount of structure necessary for the group to accomplish its task.** Any additional structure unnecessarily constrains the group's ability to solve problems. Groups often resist unnecessary structure. As a facilitator for an employee-management committee, I once suggested that the group use a problem-solving model to work on its problem. The group agreed but abandoned the model after deciding it was too complex for its simple problem.

In abandoning the model, the group demonstrated that a facilitator's intervention does not automatically provide the intended structure for the members' behavior. Only if members accept the facilitator's intervention can it generate the intended structure. If members believe the facilitator is regularly attempting to create unnecessary structure, they may react negatively. Instead of creating the intended structure, the facilitator may generate a structure of resistance in the group or increase members' fear of risk. Ironically, the structure of resistance also constrains the group's behavior but in a way that can reduce the facilitator's effectiveness, depending on how the facilitator intervenes on the resistance.

Often, the facilitator must decide among several interventions. Interventions should provide the minimal amount of structure necessary for the group to accomplish its task. However, **when macro interventions are necessary, they should be made before micro interventions.** The approach often makes the micro interventions unnecessary. Imagine that the facilitator observes that a group has begun discussing issues that are completely off the agenda. At the same time, the facilitator observes that a group member has failed to test several inferences. If the facilitator intervenes first to get the group back on task (macro intervention), once the group is back on track, the untested inferences are irrelevant. However, if the facilitator intervened first on the untested inferences (micro interventions), the group would have spent time on an unnecessary issue. Note that macro and micro are relative terms. In this example, testing an inference is the more micro intervention, but could be more macro when compared to another intervention.

Finally, a macro intervention typically comprises at least several micro interventions. For example, the macro intervention for establishing ground rules includes a variety of more micro interventions. First, the facilitator gives a brief conceptual explanation about the value of ground rules. Next, the facilitator asks group members if they would like to use a set of ground rules. If the members say yes, the facilitator may ask the members if they would like to hear a list of ground rules the facilitator often uses, ask the group to develop their own ground rules, or both. After ground rules have been identified, the facilitator checks for consensus. Together, each of the individual micro interventions constitute the total macro intervention. For a facilitator to make an effective macro intervention, each of the component micro interventions must also be effective.

What Is the Appropriate Level of Behavior to Focus on?

Chapter Four discussed three levels of member behavior: actions, interactions, and patterns. When the facilitator's interventions focus on behavior, the facilitator sometimes could intervene at more than one level. This occurs when the facilitator identifies a pattern that results from actions and interactions, each of which also represents meaningful behavior.

How does the facilitator decide the level of intervention? **For developmental facilitation, the principle is to intervene at the level sufficient to identify the root causes of the problem.**

It is important to note that when facilitators intervene at the pattern level, they identify any actions and interactions that constitute the pattern. The individual actions and interactions provide the valid data on which the pattern is based. This enables the members to see how small dysfunctional actions can lead to larger dysfunctional consequences. It also shows members how functional interactions can occur within dysfunctional patterns.

For basic facilitation, the principle is to intervene at the lowest level necessary for the group to accomplish its substantive task during the facilitated meeting. This principle assumes that interventions at lower levels are less intrusive, are more easily understood, and are more likely to lead to positive changes in members' behaviors. When faced with a choice, the facilitator intervenes at the action rather than interaction level and at the interaction level rather than the pattern level. This is why basic group interventions focus so much on the ground rules, which generally prescribe actions and interactions. As Chapter Four mentioned, the principle also implies that basic facilitators will often not intervene at all on dysfunctional behaviors that would trigger intervention in developmental groups.

Sometimes, the facilitator could intervene at more than one level because meaningful but unrelated behavior is occurring simultaneously at different levels. In other words, the facilitator identifies a pattern while identifying other actions or interactions that do not contribute to the pattern.

However, there are exceptions to the principle of intervening at the lowest level. **When faced with different levels of behavior (actions, interactions, and patterns) that are equally appropriate for intervention and that include lower levels of behavior unrelated to the higher ones, greater priority should be given to intervening at the higher level of behavior.** Consider, for example, a group that is solving a problem about marketing its organization's services. If a facilitator observes that one group member is discussing the problem without being specific (an action) while simultaneously observing that the group repeatedly reaches decisions based on decision-making criteria other than those on which the group agreed (a pattern), the facilitator would intervene on the pattern. The principle is similar to the principle that states that when a macro intervention is necessary, it should be made before micro interventions are made.

The principle assumes that it is not always useful to intervene on several unrelated behaviors at the same time. Applying the principle makes efficient use of diagnostic data. Fortunately (for the facilitator), dysfunctional behavior is repetitive. However, because a pattern takes longer to emerge than an action or interaction, there may be fewer opportunities to intervene on a particular pattern. Still, if a behavior is worth intervening on, it will show up regularly. The facilitator can let the unrelated actions or interactions pass, knowing there will be ample opportunity to intervene on them if they are important.

How Deep Should the Intervention Be?

Interventions also vary according to their depth. In his article "Choosing the Depth of Organizational Intervention," Roger Harrison (1970) wrote that depth refers to

> how private, individual, and hidden are the issues and processes about which the consultant attempts directly to obtain information and which he seeks to influence. If the consultant seeks information about relatively public and observable aspects of behavior and relationship and if he tries to influence directly only those relatively surface characteristics and processes, we would then categorize this intervention strategy as being closer to the surface. If, on the other hand, the consultant seeks information about very deep and private perceptions, attitudes, or feelings and if he intervenes in a way which directly affects these processes, then we would classify his intervention strategy as one of considerable depth. (pp. 183–184)

Choosing the appropriate depth of intervention is critical because deeper interventions require more facilitator skill, more time, and more information from the group. Interventions that are inappropriately deep unnecessarily create personal risk for group members. Because members do not consider the interventions relevant, they do not accept them. Yet interventions that are inappropriately shallow fail to solve the group's problem, and facilitators often make them when they underestimate the process skills of group members.

Harrison used the depth of intervention concept to compare different strategies for organizational change, one of which includes group facilitation. The same concept can be applied within the group facilitation approach. Like other consultants, facilitators choose different macro interventions according to the client's presenting problem and the facilitator's initial diagnosis. For example, if members disagree about what the group should be accomplishing, the macro intervention may involve agreeing on group goals. If members agree on goals but have difficulty coordinating their actions, the macro intervention may involve establishing role expectations.

Interventions can be divided into five levels of depth (see Figure 5.1). Interventions at the first and most superficial level—the *structural-functional level*—focus on attitudes, values, beliefs, and perceptions about the roles and functions that members perform in the group, with little regard for the characteristics of the individuals who perform them. Consider a self-managing group that is just forming, where the intervention focuses on deciding whether to have a designated chair and where and how often the group should meet. While the tasks are not superficial, interventions related to them can be. Members can discuss the issue by focusing solely on the group's structure and roles, without referring to particular members of the group. Members' comments about having a chair are likely to reveal their attitudes about the value of centralizing authority and coordinating activities. However, these are not particularly private attitudes.

Interventions at the second level—the *performance-goal level*—focus on attitudes, values, beliefs, and perceptions about performance but in a way that focuses on goals rather than the processes by which individuals and groups achieve the goals. Examples include agreeing on goals and evaluating performance, as in the case of a board that evaluates its manager's performance. By focusing solely on results, members can avoid discussing the processes used to reach the goals or the personal characteristics of members that may affect reaching the goals, both of which are deeper levels.

Interventions at the third level—the *instrumental level*—focus on attitudes, values, beliefs, and perceptions about changing work behavior and work relationships, both of which are processes. At this level, members discuss what facilitates or inhibits the group's effective performance. They discuss how specific individuals should carry out their roles, including sharing information, coordinating activities, and making decisions. The group may discuss how one member's failure to share information makes it more difficult for other members to carry out their roles. Structural-functional interventions may focus on similar

Figure 5.1. Five Levels of Depth for Interventions.

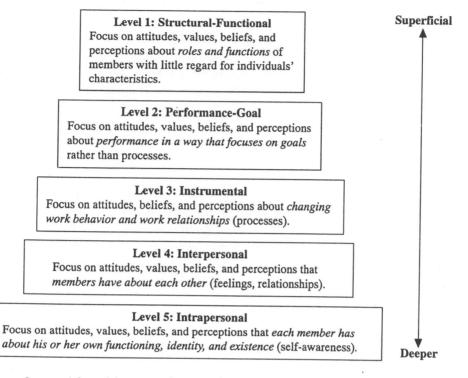

Level 1: Structural-Functional
Focus on attitudes, values, beliefs, and
perceptions about *roles and functions* of
members with little regard for individuals'
characteristics.

Level 2: Performance-Goal
Focus on attitudes, values, beliefs, and perceptions
about *performance in a way that focuses on goals*
rather than processes.

Level 3: Instrumental
Focus on attitudes, beliefs, and perceptions about *changing
work behavior and work relationships* (processes).

Level 4: Interpersonal
Focus on attitudes, values, beliefs, and perceptions that
members have about each other (feelings, relationships).

Level 5: Intrapersonal
Focus on attitudes, values, beliefs, and perceptions that *each member has
about his or her own functioning, identity, and existence* (self-awareness).

Superficial

Deeper

Source: Adapted from Harrison (1970).

issues. However, unlike structural-functional interventions, instrumental interventions focus on members' specific behaviors.

Interventions at the fourth level—the *interpersonal level*—focus on attitudes, values, beliefs, and perceptions that members have about each other. Examples include discussions about whether members feel accepted or rejected,
valued or discounted, and trusted or mistrusted by other members. Members
discuss feelings they have toward each other that they typically keep hidden,
partly because they have been socialized to believe that such feelings do not have
a place in organizations. The goal at this level is to help members express their
feelings honestly (and constructively) rather than to distort or suppress their
feelings.

At more superficial levels, members may also discuss their feelings, but this
is the first level that deals directly and intensively with the nature of human
relationships. Although the line between the instrumental and interpersonal levels can be fuzzy, the two levels have different focuses. Instrumental interventions
focus on some process designed to achieve a particular outcome; interpersonal
interventions focus directly on feelings, some of which may be related to the
group's processes.

Interventions at the fifth and deepest level—the *intrapersonal level*—focus

112 The Skilled Facilitator

on attitudes, values, beliefs, and perceptions that each member has about his or her own functioning, identity, and existence. For example, a member may reveal that despite her superior job performance and organizational success, she doubts her ability and feels like a fraud, fearing that someday someone will expose her. The goal at this intervention level is to help members increase and cope with their self-awareness. Such interventions tend to raise intense feelings about members' identities and about their relationships with others they are close to (Harrison, 1970). Members' responses to interventions at the fourth and fifth levels (such as whether someone feels mistrusted or feels like a fraud) can be difficult for other group members to independently validate, because the responses involve high-level inferences and attributions about one's own emotions.

While deeper-level interventions may seem inherently more emotionally charged, this is not necessarily true. Deeper-level interventions focus on attitudes, values, beliefs, and perceptions that are less accessible and visible to others, in-dependent of how strongly members hold them. However, lower-level issues may be more highly charged with emotion. For example, an employee-management group may have strong emotional battles that focus on a relatively superficial intervention, such as group goals. The conflict would be clearly visible by briefly observing the group's process.

Whereas macro and micro interventions vary according to how much they structure the group's behavior, interventions at different depths vary according to the privacy of the information that members reveal. At any given depth of intervention, the facilitator can make a more or less micro intervention. For example, at the interpersonal level, the facilitator can make a macro intervention by saying, "Given what each group member has said, I think it would be useful to spend the next hour or so discussing what members do that leads to low trust in the group. Do people agree?" Or, still at the interpersonal level, the facilitator can make a micro intervention by saying, "Heather, given what you just said, I'm inferring that you have lost trust in the group members? Am I inferring correctly?"

By choosing a particular depth of macro intervention, the facilitator and client simultaneously set the minimum depth at which the facilitator will need to make micro interventions. For example, if a group agrees to discuss what members should expect from each other, members must share their attitudes and perceptions about how other members are meeting and not meeting their expec-tations. It is not possible to effectively intervene on a instrumental issue if the facilitator's interventions can be no deeper than the structural-functional level. Therefore, the intervention carries with it a requirement that the facilitator in-tervene at least at the instrumental level. Consequently, during the contracting stage, the facilitator must help the group understand that choosing to discuss a certain topic (macro intervention) also means choosing to reveal a certain depth of values, beliefs, attitudes, and perceptions. This enables the group to make a free and informed choice about whether it wants to proceed.

Although selecting a macro intervention means selecting the minimum level of intervention, it does not mean that all micro interventions within it must occur at that minimum level. The facilitator's micro interventions may move through all five depths of intervention, as Figure 5.2 shows, although the group may expect micro interventions to remain at the level of the macro interventions.

Each micro intervention can be categorized in terms of the depth of response that the facilitator seeks to elicit from members. For example, within a structural-functional macro intervention, the facilitator could ask, "What would be the advantages and disadvantages of having a chair?" The micro intervention is also structural-functional. Members can easily answer the question, focusing solely on the group's structure and abstract relationships without ever referring to a particular individual in the group. However, if the facilitator asks, "What, if anything, have you not accomplished with the current structure that leads you to want to change it?" the facilitator makes a performance-goal-level intervention. Members' responses will focus on which goals have not been achieved. The facilitator may then ask, "Exactly what did members do in working with each other that led to not accomplishing the goals?" The instrumental intervention

Figure 5.2. Range of Depth of Micro Interventions.

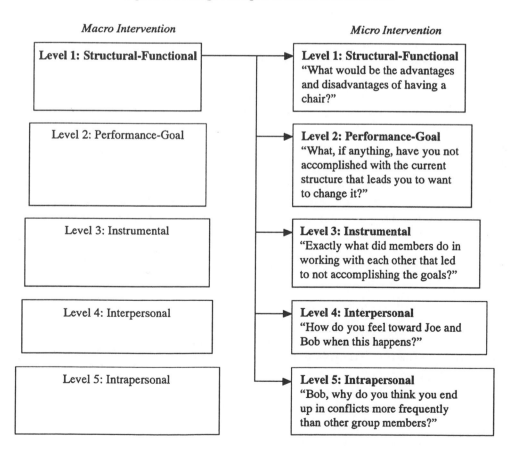

leads members to discuss the processes they engaged in that led to failure. They may say that Joe and Bob could not agree on what to say in a report and as a result, the report was late. If the facilitator then asks the group, "How do you feel toward Joe and Bob when this happens?" the intervention has moved to the interpersonal level. Members may respond by saying that they are now less likely to trust Bob and Joe when they are working together to complete a task for the group. Finally, the facilitator might say, "Bob, several times today, different members have given examples where a conflict with you reduced the group's performance. No one has described a conflict with another member in the group. Would you agree?" Assuming Bob says yes, the facilitator might ask, "Bob, why do you think you end up in conflicts more frequently than other group members?" With this last micro intervention, the facilitator has succeeded in moving through all five depths of intervention. Note that when the facilitator simply makes an observation, the intervention has no specific level of depth because it does not ask a member to reveal information at any particular level. The level of the intervention is open ended because the member determines the level of depth in responding.

The depth of the macro intervention influences the group's expectations about any micro interventions. The group may expect that the facilitator's micro interventions will be at a depth not much greater than the macro intervention. Therefore, the group may generally consider micro interventions increasingly less appropriate as they become increasingly deeper than the macro intervention.

I experienced this as a cofacilitator of a police department committee that was developing a process for selecting members for a task force. The group's task was largely structural-functional in depth. The committee was divided about whether to let the full department elect members directly to the task force or whether the committee should partially control the process so that "jarheads" (uncooperative, boisterous employees) would not be on the committee. Most members favored direct elections, arguing that they trusted the full department not to elect a jarhead, and even if the members did, that was the will of the majority. Turning to the member who strongly favored controlling the process, I asked, "Do you believe you can trust the full department not to elect a jarhead?" The member stared at the wall, avoiding all others' glances, seemingly uncomfortable with my question. After several seconds of silence, he responded, "You could say that." I believe that my question, which was necessary to test an important assumption, created discomfort for two related reasons. First, it moved the intervention from the structural-functional level to the interpersonal level. Second, it was particularly uncomfortable—and risky—for the one member who did not trust the full department, because he revealed a belief that was considered socially inappropriate by the group. The example points out that whether a deeper-level intervention is considered appropriate by a member depends on the member's concerns about the beliefs and values that that member reveals.

As the examples illustrate, facilitators can rapidly increase the depth of micro interventions. Recall that the depth of the intervention is measured by the depth of response that the facilitator elicits from members, not the facilitator's words. Therefore, facilitators must carefully word interventions so they are likely to elicit an appropriate depth of response. **Facilitators must constantly monitor themselves to ensure that they do not intervene at inappropriately deep levels.**

How does the facilitator decide when a micro intervention is too deep? Harrison (1970) has identified two criteria that serve as guides. First, **the facilitator should "intervene at a level no deeper than that required to produce enduring solutions to the problems at hand"** (Harrison, 1970, p. 181). Second, **the facilitator should intervene at a level no deeper than that at which the group can commit its energy and resources to solve its problems and create change.** The second principle essentially ensures that the group is internally committed to the intervention.

Unfortunately, the two principles may indicate different depths of intervention. Often, facilitators believe that they need to intervene at a level deeper than that at which the group is willing to commit its energy and resources. When the two principles generate different answers, which should the facilitator accept? Harrison has noted that some consultants have difficulty when the group chooses not to deal with interventions beyond a certain depth. The consultants try to push the group to work through what they perceive to be "resistance" to discussing uncomfortable issues. Such an approach is inconsistent with maintaining the group's free and informed choice and internal commitment, which are necessary for an effective intervention. While the approach may, at times, lead a group to make progress on its problem, progress may come at the expense of the facilitator's future effectiveness with the group. Other consultants take the opposite approach, dropping any interventions beyond a certain depth once the group has shown resistance. The opposite approaches are similar in that both make assumptions about the group's actions without testing them.

A third approach, which is consistent with the core values that guide group facilitation throughout this book, is to begin by explaining why the deeper interventions are important. For example, the interventions may be necessary to accurately diagnose the problem or to create some important change in process. When explaining this, the facilitator can ask members what concerns they have about the deeper-level interventions. Then, group members can determine how, if possible, to reduce their concerns enough for the facilitator to make the deeper interventions. For example, members may be concerned that their responses to deeper interventions will be used against them by others. The approach enables the facilitator to see whether the group can create conditions that make deeper interventions possible. The group's free and informed choice is thus preserved throughout.

If it is not possible to sufficiently alleviate the group's concerns, the facilitator and the group have two choices. First, they can choose to work on the problem at a shallower level, using more superficial interventions that are acceptable to the client. While this does not address the root causes of the problem, it may provide the group with some help. However, if the facilitator believes it is not possible to solve the problem by redefining it at a more shallow level, the only remaining choice is to stop working on that problem. Although it is not possible to prevent the situation from occurring, a thorough diagnosis during the contracting stage can reduce the likelihood of its occurrence.

Finally, facilitators must remember that facilitation is not therapy. For deep-level interventions to be appropriate, they must always be related to the three criteria for group effectiveness, discussed in Chapter Two. Further, while deep interventions may identify how an aspect of a group member's personality affects the group's functioning, it is not the role of group facilitation to help group members change their personality.

Which Members Should Be the Focus of the Intervention?

The facilitator must decide whether to address an intervention to an individual member, several members, or the entire group. The focus of the facilitator's intervention is determined by whether the facilitator is intervening on an action, interaction, or pattern of behavior.

The underlying principle is that **the facilitator should address those members who contribute to the action, interaction, or pattern of behavior identified in the diagnosis.** Because actions are single units of meaningful behavior by one member, focusing on an action leads to focusing on a single member. For example, if Sharon states a position rather than focusing on her interests, the facilitator addresses Sharon individually. Simultaneously focusing on several members' actions is appropriate when each has engaged in the same action within a short period of time.

Focusing on interactions (two or more members' actions that together create meaningful behavior) may require addressing both members or only one member. When one member interrupts another member, the facilitator need only address the interrupting member. However, if each member contributes some dysfunctional behavior, the facilitator describes how each member contributed to the interaction.

In developmental facilitation, effective behavior includes not only seeing that one's own actions are functional but also counteracting others' dysfunctional behavior (Gouran & Hirokawa, 1986). Consequently, if one member acts dysfunctionally toward another member, who recognizes but does not flag the dysfunctional behavior, the facilitator may also focus on that member's failure to flag the dysfunctional behavior. The intervention, illustrated in the dialogue that follows, occurs after focusing on the dysfunctional behavior:

Facilitator: Ted, when Al said, "I've got to handle the problem myself because Ted's department isn't willing to lend some people to the project," you realized he was making a false assumption. Is that right?

Ted: Yes.

Facilitator: What led you not to tell Ted he was making a false assumption?

Ted: I'm not sure. I don't like telling others they've made a mistake.

When focusing on patterns of behavior, the facilitator addresses all members who contributed to the pattern. First, the facilitator identifies the full pattern so group members understand the point of the intervention. Then, in the order in which they entered the pattern, the facilitator addresses each member's contribution. This allows the group to see how the pattern developed and also allows the facilitator to avoid premature conclusions.

Several points apply to all interventions, regardless of to whom they are addressed. First, the facilitator should also focus on members' functional and counteractive behaviors. Helping members identify their effective behaviors is also part of the facilitator's role. Second, when the facilitator identifies some action, interaction, or pattern in which all group members have been involved at some time, the facilitator may ask all group members what it is about the behavior that everyone seems to get caught in. If members frequently behave this way, the facilitator has probably identified an important issue.

Third, even when a behavior does not involve all members, the facilitator may address an entire developmental group. The facilitator may simply say, "Does anyone see what just happened?" This helps members practice their diagnostic skills and decreases their dependence on the facilitator.

Finally, interventions should identify who has behaved in what way. In short, the facilitator should name names. Some facilitators prefer to avoid naming names, instead saying, for example, "I notice that certain members tend to interrupt others and wonder whether this is getting in the way of communication" (Schein, 1987, p. 52). The consultants believe that naming names is a high-risk intervention because those named for dysfunctional behaviors may lose face. Others believe that by naming names, members focus on blaming rather than solving problems. While the assumptions may be correct, failing to name names is inconsistent with a core value of facilitation. Not sharing names means that the facilitator is providing data that members cannot independently validate. How can each member decide whether certain members tend to interrupt if the facilitator does not say who those members are? Also, the certain members cannot make an informed choice to change their behavior if the facilitator does not identify them. Avoiding names can lead to what is called *pluralistic ignorance*— each member agrees with the facilitator, but no member believes he or she was behaving dysfunctionally. Therefore, no member changes behavior.

Assuming that naming names does cause members to lose face, how should the facilitator deal with the problem? One way to reduce the likelihood of losing face is to avoid identifying dysfunctional behaviors unilaterally without testing the observations with the group. (Notice that the last intervention discussed does not check for members' agreement.) Still, if people lose face when they realize they are not as effective as they claim to be, testing interventions does not solve the problem.

How can members name names and not become defensive or focus on blaming? In developmental facilitation, one answer lies in helping members explore what leads them to become defensive (for example, lose face) even when they agree that their behavior is ineffective. Members then can figure out how to avoid becoming defensive when faced with their ineffective behavior. **Because defensive behavior prevents learning** (Argyris, 1990), **and learning is at the core of developmental facilitation, reducing defensive behavior is essential.**

The facilitator does not need to address particular members when the intervention is not designed to identify specific behaviors. This is true for interventions that are designed to get the entire group thinking about an issue. For example, the facilitator might say, "What are some ways to solve this problem?" However, the facilitator may still want to direct the intervention initially to a particular member. For example, the facilitator might say, "Doug, earlier, when the group was discussing causes of the problem, you mentioned that you had a solution. Would you like to start by sharing your solution, and if so, is this OK with everyone else?" Notice that the facilitator explains why the intervention is initially addressed to a specific member. Also notice that by asking the full group whether it is alright for Doug to begin, the facilitator avoids taking responsibility for the group.

When the facilitator is checking for consensus, the intervention can be made to the group in general, but ultimately each member must respond. This is consistent with the ground rule that all members are expected to participate at all stages of problem solving. The facilitator may handle this by asking for a show of hands or by asking each member for a response.

Here-and-Now Versus There-and-Then Behavior

When diagnosing and intervening, facilitators can focus on either here-and-now or there-and-then behaviors. Here-and-now behaviors are those that members exhibit while the group is discussing an issue. There-and-then behaviors are those that occur outside the facilitated session that become the subject of the group's discussion.

Consider, for example, an employee-management group that is discussing how to handle role conflicts in its department. Several members describe how a disagreement about who would handle a particular task led to the task's not being accomplished properly and to an unfavorable story in the local paper. As the members are describing the story, two other members are whispering to each other and glaring at the members telling the story. The account of the disagreement describes there-and-then behavior. The whispering and glaring while members are discussing the story are examples of here-and-now behavior. If the facilitator asks, "What did you do when you realized the task hadn't been done properly?" the facilitator is focusing on there-and-then behavior. If the facilitator says, "Lisa and Ken, I noticed you were whispering and glaring at Larry while he told the story," the focus is on here-and-now behavior. Whenever the group discusses a situation that occurred in the past, the facilitator can intervene on either type of behavior.

There are advantages and disadvantages to focusing on each kind of behavior. Here-and-now behavior provides the facilitator and group members with directly observable data about the group's behavior that can be validated immediately in the group. Members can immediately redesign their dysfunctional here-and-now behavior and improve the group's process. However, because interventions on here-and-now behaviors are by definition limited to behaviors that members exhibit during facilitation, such interventions cannot examine the many issues that group members face in their organizations but that do not arise during group facilitation.

In contrast, there-and-then behaviors provide the opportunity to examine the situations and issues that arise outside the group but not within it. Examining there-and-then behaviors helps members learn how to transfer the skills they develop within the group to their interactions with members of the larger organization and those outside the organization with whom members work. More generally, it helps members examine how they manage the boundary relationships between the group and its organizational context. As discussed in Chapter Two, managing the boundary relationships contributes to group effectiveness.

However, there-and-then behaviors cannot be validated in the group when they involve people who are not group members. Consequently, when discussing the situations, the group must clearly recognize when its analysis rests on untested inferences and assumptions about nongroup members. By role playing how they would act more effectively, the members become ready to correct their dysfunctional behavior with nongroup members, including testing their previously untested inferences and assumptions about them.

Alternatively, group members can overcome the barrier by asking nongroup members to participate in a facilitated session. This enlarges the here-and-now behavior to include interactions with nongroup members, and it helps members transfer learning to nongroup situations. It also increases the influence of the entire group facilitation project by enlarging the number of members involved in it.

Focusing on both types of behavior is necessary for developing an effective work group. Which one the facilitator focuses on at a given time is a judgment call. It depends on whether the facilitation is basic or developmental, the nature of the group's problems, and whether the group must solve a here-and-now problem in order to solve a there-and-then problem, or vice versa.

The developmental facilitator often makes deep interventions on here-and-now behaviors, which are not necessary for basic facilitation. The difference arises because the basic facilitator intervenes on here-and-now behavior solely to manage the process rather than to also help the group learn how to improve its process by reflecting on it.

Consider, for example, a group whose content task is to develop a flexible working-hours policy for the organization. During the meeting, members make comments about each other that suggest low levels of trust. Assuming the comments did not significantly undermine the group's ability to accomplish the task, in basic facilitation the facilitator would either not intervene on the trust issue or intervene at a superficial depth, perhaps by citing a relevant ground rule. However, in developmental facilitation, the facilitator would intervene on the trust issue, because the group's goal includes learning about its own behavior in addition to working on a content task.

When a developmental group faces intragroup and intergroup conflicts, members may be more comfortable discussing there-and-then situations than here-and-now situations, especially when the there-and-then situations enable members to discuss their conflicts with nongroup members who are not present. Although this can be useful, the level of the group's comfort should not be the criterion for determining the focus, especially if the group's preferred focus enables it to avoid facing its problems.

In developmental facilitation, moving back and forth between the two focuses helps members see the parallels between their problems with nongroup members in there-and-then situations and their dysfunctional behaviors in here-and-now situations. Members realize that their conflicts with nongroup members result from their own behavior too, rather than from the other parties' behaviors alone.

Timing and Sequencing Interventions

How soon should a facilitator intervene after identifying a member who is acting inconsistently with a ground rule? The advantage of intervening immediately after a ground rule has been violated is that the members will easily recall the conversation in which it occurred. However, the disadvantage of intervening immediately is that the other members have no opportunity to recognize and correct the behavior themselves. The disadvantage applies largely to developmental facilitation, in which over time the group must learn to correct its own behavior if it is to become less dependent on the facilitator.

When the facilitator believes that the group has the skills to recognize and correct a ground rule violation, the facilitator should give group members time to intervene first. If the facilitator believes the group does not have the skills, the facilitator should intervene soon after the inconsistent behavior. When facilitators first begin working with a group, they may choose to wait before intervening. This enables facilitators to diagnose the group's level of skill in using its ground rules.

Choosing from Among Several Interventions

When members have acted inconsistently with more than one ground rule, ideally the facilitator can make an intervention that simultaneously addresses all the relevant ground rules. However, sometimes it may take too long to address all the relevant ground rules, and the facilitator may need to choose one ground rule on which to focus. The facilitator can decide which ground rule to focus on by asking the questions discussed earlier in regard to the ground rule interventions.

Mindful of the principle of repetitive behavior discussed in Chapter Four, facilitators need not worry that they will forever lose the opportunity to intervene on an issue if they do not intervene the first time it arises. If facilitators decide to address one ground rule and not others that are being violated, they should make note of the other ground rules they chose not to address. The next time the other ground rules are violated, facilitators will be well prepared to address them.

Summary

This chapter discussed nine general factors that influence how facilitators intervene: the client's immediate concerns and interests, whether the facilitation is basic or developmental, the degree to which an intervention should structure the group's behavior (macro versus micro interventions), the level (that is, action, interaction, or pattern) of intervention required, how deep the intervention should be, whether the intervention should be addressed to an individual, a subgroup, or the entire group, whether to focus on the group's current behavior or on behavior that occurred in the past, how to time and sequence multiple interventions, and how to choose from among several interventions. Facilitators need to consider each factor, regardless of the specific interventions they are making.

Chapter Six How to Intervene

This chapter addresses the question, What should I say and to whom should I say it? First, it explores the different types of interventions that facilitators make. Next, the discussion returns to the diagnosis-intervention cycle introduced in Chapter Four, this time to examine the intervention steps and to consider how facilitators vary their interventions according to the skill levels of the group members. The chapter concludes by considering the need for facilitators to carefully choose their words when intervening.

General Types of Interventions

Throughout, the book has described how identifying member behaviors that are inconsistent with the ground rules is a major part of a facilitator's interventions. But this is just one type of intervention. This chapter considers the general types of interventions (shown in Exhibit 6.1), their purposes, and the forms they take. In practice, the types overlap and can be nested. That is, a given intervention may serve more than one purpose, and one type of intervention may have other types of interventions embedded in it.

1. Exploring. Exploratory interventions are designed to help the facilitator understand a situation by getting the basic facts, understanding how a series of events unfolded, or finding out how members think or feel about something. Examples include, "Please tell me what you think the problem is," "What do you want to accomplish?" or simply, "Say more about that."

2. Seeking specifics. One principle for effective group process is being specific—using examples. People are so used to talking in abstract terms that the

Exhibit 6.1. Types of Interventions.

1. Exploring

2. Seeking specifics

3. Emphasizing process

4. Diagnosing

5. Confronting and other feedback

6. Managing group process and structure

7. Making content suggestions

8. Teaching concepts and methods

9. Reframing

Source: Most interventions are adapted from Schein (1987, p. 163).

facilitator often needs to clarify exactly what they mean. Examples include, "What exactly did you say to him?" "Can you give me some examples of what you mean by 'not taking initiative'?" and "Who are 'they'?"

3. Emphasizing process. Because the facilitator helps groups improve their process, the facilitator must understand the processes underlying groups' problems. In making the intervention, the facilitator also explores and seeks specifics. Examples include, "Tell me what happened, step by step," "Tell me the exact conversation as best you remember it," and "What did you do then?"

4. Diagnosing. Diagnostic interventions move beyond simple exploration and help the group and facilitator analyze a situation. The intervention includes exploring members' interests; identifying the causes, symptoms, and consequences of a problem; pointing out similarities and differences among member's comments; and exploring members' theories and hypotheses about situations. Examples include, "What do you think are the causes of the problem?" and "What leads you to believe that processing clerks are unable to handle difficult calls from customers?"

Here it becomes clear that facilitators must not only diagnose to intervene, they must also intervene to diagnose. The interventions in this category are purely diagnostic. However, many other types of interventions have a diagnostic part embedded in them. For example, the general intervention cycle begins with facilitators checking to see if the group agrees with their diagnosis before they make a confronting intervention.

In a special form of diagnostic intervention, the developmental facilitator diagnoses the group's ability to diagnose or intervene on its own process. For example, rather than merely asking, "Do you see any pattern of dysfunctional behavior in this situation?" facilitators should explain that they are asking the question to determine whether the members can diagnose their process. By explaining the reasons for the intervention, facilitators clarify that they have their own diagnosis, which may be different from the client's diagnosis. It also enables the facilitator and client to check their diagnoses.

5. *Confronting and other feedback.* Confronting interventions require the group to reflect on some aspect of its behavior that the facilitator considers dysfunctional. The facilitator may point out inconsistencies between what the group espouses and what the group does or between the group's actions over time or with different people. Consequently, confronting interventions have a diagnostic step embedded in them to ensure that a facilitator's feedback is based on an accurate observation and inference. Identifying behaviors inconsistent with the group's ground rules is a confronting intervention. For example, a facilitator might say, "Lynn, a minute ago you said 'I just want to stop the project.' Do you remember that?" If Lynn remembers, the facilitator would continue, "Lynn, your statement focuses on your position without identifying your interest, which is inconsistent with the group's ground rules. Do you agree?"

Facilitators also need to help members see when they are beginning to act consistently with ground rules. Positive feedback helps solidify the group's learning.

6. *Managing group process and structure.* In these interventions, the facilitator helps the group determine what topic will be discussed, when, by whom, how, and for how long. In developmental facilitation, the facilitator and group jointly manage the process. In basic facilitation, the facilitator manages much of the process for the group, although ultimately the group jointly controls the process. Managing process comprises macro- and micro-level interventions, which include setting agendas, switching topics, recognizing people to speak, reducing interruptions, and monitoring time. Examples include, "How about if the group uses the problem-solving model to discuss this problem?" "I suggest that members first list all the expectations you have for each other. Then you can discuss each one. Does anyone have a problem with that approach?" and "You set aside twenty minutes to discuss this topic, and twenty minutes have passed. Do you want to continue or move on to another topic?"

7. *Making content suggestions.* In this intervention, the facilitator suggests ways the group can solve some substantive aspect of its problem. As discussed in Chapter One, the intervention is generally inconsistent with the facilitator's role. One exception may be when the group has tried but failed to identify solutions that meet all the members' interests. Here facilitators may suggest a solution, if they first receive the group's permission and immediately afterward ask whether the suggested solution meets all the members' interests. To reduce facilitators' substantive influence, their solutions should be based on members' previous attempted solutions.

For example: "Tawana, you said your interest behind sending a memo now was to let the department know what progress the group has made, correct? [continuing, assuming Tawana agrees] Ted, you said your interest behind not sending a memo now was to avoid having people falsely conclude that the group has made a decision, correct? [continuing, assuming Ted agrees] If the group sends out a memo stating very clearly that the memo reflects the group's current thinking, but that the group has not made any decision, would this meet everyone's interests?''

Technically, all content suggestions are inconsistent with the facilitator's role. However, some content suggestions are more inconsistent with the role than others. As discussed in Chapter One, when the content of a group's discussion involves how to manage process more effectively, the facilitator is implicitly partisan about the content. This happens because part of effective management is a behavioral process, and the facilitator's content expertise is managing behavioral processes. Consequently, content suggestions that are closely related to group or organizational process, and therefore closely related to the group's ground rules, are less inconsistent with the facilitator's role. The suggestion about sending a memo is an example. However, content suggestions that have no relation to group or organizational process are more inconsistent with the facilitator's role. An example is suggesting that a purchasing department buy rather than lease equipment.

Nevertheless, whenever facilitators make any content intervention, they take responsibility away from the group. If they make the intervention early in the facilitation, they increase the chance that the group will expect them to play this role. This in turn will make it more difficult for facilitators to leave this role.

8. Teaching concepts and methods. At times, the most appropriate intervention is to teach the group some concepts and methods it can use in solving its problems. Facilitators do this when they explain the principles for effective group process and ask the group whether it wants to adopt them as ground rules. Other examples include teaching a group to use a general problem-solving model, how to identify root causes of problems, and how to analyze forces for and against a proposed organizational change. Such interventions are entirely consistent with the facilitator's role if they focus on the group's process.

However, interventions that focus on the group's substantive issues are problematic. For example, I often facilitate management groups that want to increase the motivation of their employees or improve the services they offer the public. As an organizational psychologist, I know about concepts, methods, and research that would help the clients solve their substantive problems. Similarly, facilitators with other professional backgrounds have areas in which they are content experts. But sharing the information moves the facilitator from the facilitator role to the substantive expert role. Yet, withholding information seems inconsistent with the core value of sharing valid information. How can the facilitator resolve the dilemma?

To resolve the dilemma, remember that the facilitator role precludes providing expert information for two reasons. First, it makes the facilitator substantively nonneutral, which may lead members to doubt the facilitator's process neutrality as well. If this happens, members will lose trust in the facilitator. Second, the facilitator's substantive comments can strongly influence members if they perceive the facilitator as an expert (French & Raven, 1959). This may increase the group's dependence on the facilitator.

The dilemma can be resolved by creating conditions within the group such that members would not be inappropriately influenced by the facilitator's expert background and members and the facilitator could jointly test whether the facilitator's substantive nonneutrality was affecting the facilitator's process neutrality and, if it was, make changes to eliminate the effect. The conditions can be created but usually only in developmental facilitation. Developmental facilitation is designed to improve the group's process and allows time to create the conditions. Therefore, developmental facilitators may teach substantive concepts and methods as long as they share with the group the problems discussed here, develop with the group a way to examine and resolve the problems if they arise, and encourage the group to challenge its expert information.

9. Reframing. Reframing interventions help members change the meaning they ascribe to events. As the meaning of the events changes, people's responses and behaviors also change (Bandler & Grinder, 1982; Bateson, 1972). For example, group members are often reluctant to give each other negative feedback, because they say they care about members and do not want to hurt them. The facilitator helps members overcome the reluctance by helping them reframe what it means "to care." The facilitator suggests that really caring about members means *giving* others feedback about their behavior that can help them improve their professional effectiveness. Further, by *withholding* information, members hurt each other by precluding each other from making an informed choice about whether to change behavior.

A General Intervention Cycle

Chapter Four introduced a six-step general cycle for diagnosing and intervening in dysfunctional behavior. The cycle is useful when members have acted inconsistently with their ground rules or with other principles of effective group process. Figure 6.1 describes the entire cycle. Chapter Four discussed the diagnostic steps of the method. The discussion here focuses on the intervention steps, which are used after the facilitator has decided to intervene.

The three intervention steps mirror the three diagnostic steps. In step four, facilitators describe to the group what they observed in step one and test whether the group agrees with the observations. In step five, facilitators describe the inferences they made in step two and test whether group members agree with the inferences. Finally, in step six, facilitators help group members decide whether and how to redesign their behavior to be more effective. After the group has decided whether to change its behavior, the cycle begins again, and facilitators observe whether the group has in fact changed its behavior in the manner it wanted. Facilitators repeat the cycle whenever appropriate.

In basic facilitation, the group usually relies on the facilitator to diagnose and intervene. In developmental facilitation, over time the group learns to con-

Figure 6.1. Diagnosis-Intervention Cycle.

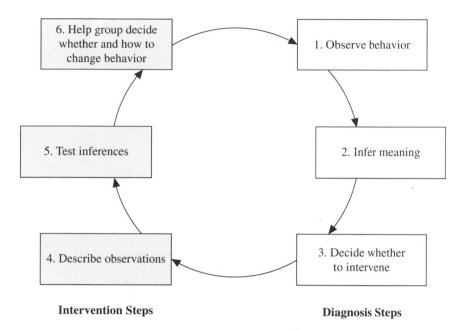

Intervention Steps   **Diagnosis Steps**

duct its own diagnoses and interventions, becoming less dependent on the facilitator.

The intervention half of the cycle is consistent with the core values of facilitation. As Figure 6.2 shows, each intervention step has two parts. In the second part, facilitators invite group members to agree or disagree (a principle of effective group process). By inviting members to agree or disagree about what the facilitator has observed and inferred, facilitators validate each step of their diagnosis. Facilitators move to the next intervention step only after the client and facilitator agree on the observations or inferences made in the current step. As a result, if members decide to change their behavior (step six), they have made an informed choice based on valid data. Step five is critical. If a group does not find the facilitator's observations valid, the group probably will not accept any inferences or suggestions for changing behavior that are based on those observations.

The intervention part of the cycle also uses several principles for effective group process. The second part of each step follows the principle "make statements, then invite questions and comments." Step four uses the principle "be specific—use examples." Step five uses the principle "publicly test assumptions and inferences." Finally, by going through steps four through six, the facilitator also uses the principle "explain the reasons behind one's statements, questions, and actions."

What follows is an example of a facilitator who is using the diagnosis-and-intervention cycle. A group of employees is discussing when to schedule future

Figure 6.2. Intervention Steps in the Diagnosis-Intervention Cycle.

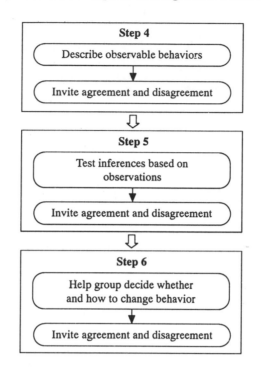

quality improvement meetings. The left-hand column shows the conversation, and the right-hand column provides notes about the conversation.

Conversation	*Notes*
Rufus: I think we should meet on Wednesdays. Most of us are on duty then, so the organization won't have to pay comp time or overtime for our meetings.	
Cynthia: That's fine, except some Wednesdays are technical training days for some of us. We can't meet every Wednesday or we'll mess up the departmental schedule.	Facilitator considers whether Cynthia's statement assumes the group will mess up the schedule if it meets every Wednesday *(diagnosis step two)*. The facilitator does not test whether Cynthia has made an assumption *(diagnosis step three)*.
Andrew: I wish the training was over. It's not done well, and it doesn't	Facilitator infers that Andrew is switching topic *(diagnosis step two)*.

help us do our jobs any better. Isn't there a better way to do technical training?

Donald: Yeah, we could bring in people who knew what they were talking about. Maybe we can ask the director to think about it.

Facilitator infers that Donald continues off topic *(diagnosis step two).*

Facilitator: A minute ago, the group was talking about when to schedule other quality improvement meetings. Then Andrew asked, "Is there a better way to do technical training?" and Donald suggested you could "bring in people who knew what they were talking about." Is that how the conversation went?

Facilitator describes observations and tests whether the group agrees *(intervention step four).*

Several people: Yeah.

Facilitator: One of your ground rules is to stay focused, to stay on track. I think Andrew's and Donald's comments about improving training are off track because they don't help the group decide when to meet. Andrew and Donald, do you agree or disagree?

Facilitator compares behavior to ground rule and infers that group is off track *(intervention step five).*

Facilitator checks for agreement with members who made off-track comments, explaining why the conversation is off track *(intervention step five).*

Andrew and Donald: Yeah, we're off track.

The two members agree.

Facilitator: Do the rest of you agree or disagree?

Facilitator checks for agreement with other members *(intervention step five).*

All: We agree.

Facilitator: What does the group want to do? Do you want to continue the conversation about when to meet or discuss the training?

Facilitator asks the group to decide whether to stay off track (switch topics) or go back to the previous topic *(intervention step six).*

Rufus: Let's finish deciding when to meet. At the end of the meeting, we can decide when to talk about technical training.

Facilitator: Does anyone have a problem with Rufus's suggestion to

Facilitator checks for consensus *(intervention step six).*

finish talking about when to meet
and to decide at the end of the meeting when to talk about technical
training?

All: No.

Facilitator: OK. Cynthia, you were   Facilitator asks member to continue
the last person to talk before the con-   where she left off.
versation went off track. Would you
repeat what you said?

Sharing Observations

Sharing observations means sharing directly observable behavior. One way to
think about directly observable behavior is as the information a video camera
(with sound) would record if it could simultaneously capture all group members'
verbal and nonverbal behavior. When facilitators share observations, they provide
group members with the valid information on which they based the inferences
that they will share with the group in the next intervention step.

The key in step four is sharing observations without making inferences or
attributions. Based on the conversation, Table 6.1 shows several statements facilitators can make to share their observations with the group and to test whether
the group agrees with them. Notice that the only way facilitators can share their
observations without making an inference or attribution is to repeat exactly the

Table 6.1. Sharing Observations at Different Levels of Inference.

Nature of Inference	Facilitator's Statement
High-Level Inference	
Infers that getting a group off track re-sults from not paying attention.	"Andrew isn't paying attention to the conversation."
Medium-Level Inference and Attribution	
Infers that not talking about training is off the track and attributes the cause to Andrew.	"Andrew got the conversation off track."
Low-Level Inference	
Infers that talking about training is not talking about scheduling.	"Andrew wasn't talking about scheduling."
Directly Observable Data	
Makes no inference.	"Andrew asked, 'Is there a better way to do technical training?' "

words they heard the group member use. Once facilitators add inferences or attributions, they move beyond observation to interpretation. To continue the earlier analogy, video cameras simply observe; they do not interpret.

Why is it important to share the observation without making an inference or attribution? Because, as Exhibit 6.2 shows, the facilitator's intervention follows a series of logical statements, and the directly observable behavior represents the first statement. If a group member disagrees with the facilitator's first statement, it is unlikely the member will agree with any conclusion the facilitator reaches based on the first statement.

In contrast, by saying, "Andrew got the conversation off track," the facilitator would be starting the intervention at the last step of logic. If Andrew responded, "I disagree," the facilitator would not know with which logical step Andrew disagreed that led him to disagree with the conclusion. To determine this, the facilitator would need to repeat each logical step and check for agreement. Beginning the intervention by sharing the directly observable behavior eliminates the need to do this.

Some facilitators often make their interventions in the form of a question (for example, Schein, 1987). The facilitator might begin an intervention by asking, "Andrew, do you think you're off track?" Edgar Schein states that the question format is generally more helpful "because it encourages, even forces, the client to maintain the initiative. . . . if the goal . . . is to help the client to solve his own problem, to own the responsibility, then the question is the best way to communicate that expectation" (p. 158).

The approach can be appropriate for groups that are becoming skilled at diagnosing their own behavior (the next major section discusses this issue). There are, however, several potential problems with the question format. First, it requires the facilitator to withhold relevant information. If the facilitator is thinking, "I observed X, which tells me Andrew is off track," but says to the group, "Do you think Andrew is off track?" the facilitator withholds personal observations. Without stating the observation, the facilitator cannot check whether the group agrees.

This leads to the second problem—the group can feel set up. Say the facilitator's group answers, "No, we don't think Andrew is off track," and the facilitator does not agree with the group's explanation. Unless the facilitator

**Exhibit 6.2. Logical Steps for Interventions
That Identify Behavior Inconsistent with Ground Rules.**

1. I observed member A say, "X."
2. The group has a ground rule that says when discussing an issue do Y.
3. Saying "X" is inconsistent with the ground rule Y because B.
4. Therefore, I conclude that Member A acted inconsistently with ground rule Y.

openly disagrees or drops the intervention, the facilitator must continue asking leading questions until the group figures out the "answer." Eventually, the group infers correctly that the facilitator is looking for the "right answer" but is unwilling to share it with the group. Feeling frustrated and set up by the facilitator, someone may say, "Don't play a guessing game with us. If you have something to tell us, just say it."

Finally, using the question format sends the message that the group must take responsibility for its observations but that facilitators do not have to take responsibility for their observations. This message is inconsistent with the group facilitation assumption that the facilitator is a model of effective behavior. There-fore, unless the group understands that the facilitator's question is designed to help the group learn to diagnose its own behavior, it is more effective to follow the conversation format. Here the facilitator repeats Andrew's words, checks for agreement, refers to a ground rule with which Andrew's words are inconsistent, checks for agreement, and then asks what the group wants to do about it.

Still, in developmental facilitation, it is important that over time the group take responsibility for its process.

Sometimes, it is useful for facilitators to begin step four by explaining the intervention they are about to make, before they share the directly observable behavior. The approach is useful when facilitators are about to describe a com-plex pattern that will require them to share and test a large number of behaviors. For example, the facilitator would say, "I've noticed a pattern of behavior in the group that I think makes it difficult for you to reach consensus. Let me share what I've observed, check it out with you, and see whether you agree." The statement gives members a context in which to understand each behavior that comprises the pattern that the facilitator will then describe and test with the group. Without a context, the facilitator would be describing and testing many behaviors, and group members would be wondering what the facilitator's point is.

Testing Inferences

In this intervention step, facilitators test the inference or inferences they made in step two of the diagnosis-intervention cycle. When intervening on behavior in-consistent with the ground rules, facilitators test their inference that what a member said or did represents behavior inconsistent with a ground rule.

Publicly testing inferences with the group prevents the facilitator from unilaterally acting on inferences that are inaccurate. Many research studies have found that after developing a hypothesis about what is happening in the group, people tend to seek data that is consistent with the hypothesis and avoid or discredit data that disconfirms the hypothesis (Nisbett & Ross, 1980). This leads people to self-fulfilling prophecies (Merton, 1957). In facilitation, facilitators could inadvertently misinterpret behavior in the group so that it supports their initial hypothesis (for example, Snyder & Swann, 1978).

I observed the tendency one day in a group facilitation workshop I taught. The facilitation students were watching videotapes of a group that was simulating various kinds of dysfunctional behavior. In the first videotape, the group leader's own ineffectiveness was an undiscussable issue, and the facilitation students accurately identified the problem from various behavioral cues. In the second videotape, several students also saw signs of group leader ineffectiveness, although none was there. In discussing the second videotape, one student mentioned that he was looking for places where the leader was acting ineffectively, as he had in the previous videotape. Having found the leader ineffective in the first videotape, he "found" ineffective behavior in the second videotape. Only after publicly testing his inference did he find that his data were missing.

As discussed in Chapter Four, **the facilitator makes the lowest level inferences needed for the intervention.** The same principle applies for testing inferences. Lower-level inferences require relatively small amounts of information to make the inference. In the example, the facilitator will have to infer that Andrew's comment was off track, because the ground rule is stated at the inferential level. If the facilitator intervenes only to help the group get back on track, the facilitator should not make any higher-level inference, such as "Andrew is controlling the conversation." The higher-level inference is unnecessary for the purpose of the intervention.

If, however, the facilitator intervenes because the inference is that Andrew is controlling the conversation in order to shift the conversation away from a particular subject, a different intervention is called for. The facilitator would present observable data that illustrate the attribution that Andrew attempted to switch the conversation when a particular subject was raised. If Andrew has led the group off track only once or twice in the meeting, the data are probably insufficient to support the high-level attribution.

When making attributions about members' motives or emotions, the facilitator should attribute them to the person without attributing them to the person's personality. For example, the facilitator should say, "David, given what you just said, I'm inferring the reason you do not want to give your consent is that you don't trust that Lucinda will help you complete the project. Is that correct?" rather than "You are not very trusting toward Lucinda" or "You aren't a very trusting person." The difference is important. The former statement is more closely related to the observable data. It makes an attribution about trusting behavior in a particular situation rather than overgeneralizing and implying that the person has a mistrustful personality. Also, attributing the behavior to a person's personality implies that it is unlikely to change, because aspects of personality are relatively stable. Consequently, the former statement is less likely to elicit defensive behavior.

As part of testing inferences, the facilitator may need to explain how a member's behavior is inconsistent with a particular ground rule or principle of group effectiveness. For example, supervisors who choose not to give subordinates increased autonomy, because they do not trust subordinates' judgment, may not understand how they are withholding relevant information by not telling the subordinates they do not trust their judgment. Here the facilitator would need to explain how withholding the information prevents the supervisor and subordinates from considering what the subordinates must do to earn the supervisor's trust. As group members become more familiar with the ground rules and principles for effective group process, they can better see how their actions are inconsistent with them.

Helping the Group Decide Whether and How to Change Behavior

The purpose of intervening is to help members act more effectively. However, intervention steps four and five only confirm that a group member agrees she or he has acted inconsistently (or consistently) with the ground rules. The last step helps the member decide whether and how to change behavior. The step has two parts: asking the member whether he or she wants to change behavior to be consistent with the ground rules, and if the member says yes, helping the member redesign her or his behavior. **The last intervention step ensures that group members maintain their free choice and responsibility for changing their behavior.** The facilitator's specific intervention will vary according to the ground rule that the member has violated and whether the facilitation is basic or developmental.

For most ground rules in developmental facilitation, the facilitator would begin the step by saying, "Do you want to try to restate that in a way that's consistent with the ground rules?" If the member agrees, the facilitator can continue, "Exactly how would you say it?"

For other ground rules, members act inconsistently with the ground rules by *not* saying something they should have said. Such ineffective behaviors are acts of omission rather than commission. Consider, for example, a member who had not tested an assumption. After the facilitator had made intervention steps four and five, the facilitator would say, "How would you test that assumption in a way that is consistent with the other ground rules?"

For still other ground rules, changing behavior may require the group to make a decision. An example is the dialogue in which members agreed that they had moved off the topic of discussion.

Sometimes, a member's redesigned statement is still inconsistent with the ground rules. In this situation, the facilitator repeats the cycle, sharing the observation, testing the inference, and asking the member whether she or he wants to try again. In this case, before sharing the observation, the facilitator should explain why the second intervention is necessary. This reduces the chance that the member will feel that the intervention has turned into a guessing game.

Notice that in developmental facilitation, the facilitator emphasizes the ground rules by saying, "How would you say that in a way that is consistent with the ground rules?" The emphasis is designed to get members used to thinking about their behavior in terms of the ground rules so that over time, members will internalize the facilitator's questions and will more frequently act consistently with the ground rules.

In basic facilitation, the facilitator uses essentially the same steps but may choose to place less explicit emphasis on the ground rules. If, for example, a member has stated a position without an interest, in step six the facilitator may say, "What is your interest behind wanting to postpone the hiring decision?" Here the facilitator's intervention (an exploring intervention) is designed to elicit the substantive reasons behind the member's position rather than to ask the member to restate the views using the ground rules. Because in basic facilitation the group is trying to solve a substantive problem without improving its group process, the intervention appropriately makes the facilitator responsible for managing the group's process.

Still, by using a more developmental approach in this step, a group using basic facilitation can quickly grasp some ground rules and begin using them to guide its behavior. To the extent members do this, the group can spend more time addressing substantive problems.

The discussion here has assumed that members are willing to redesign their statements to be consistent with the ground rules. But what if a member does not want to redesign a statement? **Although members have agreed at an intellectual or theoretical level to follow the ground rules, the discomfort of actually being confronted with their dysfunctional behavior and being asked whether they want to change it in front of other group members can be intense and unsettling.** If facilitators test for agreement at each intervention step, they can lessen the discomfort. But facilitators still need to be prepared to face reactions of members ranging from embarrassment and surprise to resentment, fear, anger, and denial. Chapter Ten discusses how facilitators can respond to such emotions. Ultimately, to preserve the group's free choice, the facilitator must respect members' decisions about whether they want to change their behavior.

Still, in developmental facilitation, the facilitator should first explore the group's interest behind its position. By doing so, the group may learn that some members are concerned about spending too much time on process or that members are frustrated by their inability to be consistent with the ground rules. Exploring these interests can help the facilitator and the group create the conditions necessary for members to be willing to spend time redesigning their behavior. **In practice, however, group members rarely choose not to redesign behavior that is inconsistent with the ground rules if the facilitator has validated his or her observations and inferences with the group.**

Collapsing Intervention Steps

The discussion here describes how a facilitator would use the three intervention steps in their full form. While each part of each step serves a purpose, sometimes the facilitator can collapse them and still intervene effectively.

There are several conditions when this can occur. First, in developmental facilitation, when a general agreement exists to redesign behavior (step six, part one), the facilitator need not ask each time whether the relevant member wants to redesign behavior. Instead, the facilitator can implement step six simply by saying, "How would you say that so it is consistent with the ground rules?" Second, in basic facilitation, where the goal is not to help members learn the ground rules, the facilitator may skip steps four and five completely, saying, for example, "What is your interest behind proposing that solution?" or "Do others agree with Ted's assumption that . . ." Third, facilitators can collapse the intervention when they want group members to take responsibility for diagnosing and redesigning their behavior. This occurs in developmental facilitation with a general agreement to do so. In a sense, facilitators do not so much collapse steps as shift responsibility for them to the group.

Still, collapsing steps always increases the risk that the intervention will be ineffective because it makes two assumptions. First, it assumes that members will understand the rationale for the facilitator's later steps without having seen the missing steps. Second, when the facilitator omits testing for agreement, the omission assumes that members will agree with the facilitator's observation or inference. When the assumptions are incorrect, collapsing steps will lead to an ineffective intervention.

Deciding when to collapse steps is a judgment call. But there are times when the risks clearly outweigh the benefits. Early in developmental facilitation, using the complete intervention cycle helps members learn all the steps. After members become familiar with the entire cycle, collapsing becomes less risky. Then members will know which steps have been omitted and can respond if they believe the missing steps need to be discussed. When a collapsed intervention creates problems, the facilitator should return to the full cycle. Because group members learn at different rates, facilitators should collapse an intervention only after they are sure that the individual to whom the intervention is addressed is familiar with the full cycle.

Using the full cycle can take time, especially if the intervention is complicated or if members disagree with the facilitator's diagnosis. However, the facilitator should not collapse steps simply because members feel the intervention cycle takes too long. To do so would increase the chances that the facilitator's intervention would be ineffective. Instead, the facilitator should explore the members' interests behind speeding up the process and test whether they see the value for each intervention step.

In any event, the facilitator should use the full cycle when the group is facing a difficult conflict. Conflicts often arise partly because people fail to publicly test their assumptions with each other. By using the full cycle, the facilitator avoids contributing to the problem.

Finally, because collapsing steps requires the facilitator to make untested assumptions, it is inconsistent with the principles for effective group process. Therefore, facilitators must decide if it is worth perhaps saving a little time to

Table 6.2. Interventions Based on Members' Skill Levels.

Intervention Steps	Examples
Level One: Beginner	

Used when members are not able to identify behavior that is inconsistent with the ground rules or to correct the behavior on their own

1. The facilitator asks the member a question in order to elicit a response that is consistent with the ground rules. But the *facilitator does not necessarily refer to the ground rules.*	*Member:* My opinion is that we should lease the equipment rather than buy it. *Facilitator:* Can you tell me what it is about leasing the equipment that makes that a better solution for you?

or

1. The *facilitator identifies the behavior* that is inconsistent with the ground rules. 2. The *facilitator helps the member redesign the behavior* so that it is consistent with the ground rules.	*Member:* My opinion is that we should lease the equipment rather than buy it. *Facilitator:* One of the group's ground rules is to focus on interests rather than positions. When you said, "My opinion is we should lease the equipment rather than buy it," you stated a position, do you agree? [if yes] Would you be willing to state your interests behind your position of wanting to lease the equipment?

Level Two: Intermediate

Used when members can identify behavior that is inconsistent with the ground rules but cannot yet correct the behavior on their own

1. The *facilitator asks the member to identify the behavior* that is inconsistent with the ground rules. 2. The *facilitator helps the member redesign the behavior* so that it is consistent with the ground rules.	*Member:* My opinion is that we should lease the equipment rather than buy it. *Facilitator:* You just said, "My opinion is we should lease the equipment rather than buy it." I believe your statement is inconsistent with one of the ground rules. Do you see which one? *Member:* Yeah, I stated a position, but I didn't explain why. *Facilitator:* I agree. Would you be willing to state your interests behind your position of wanting to lease the equipment?

Level Three: Advanced

Used when members can identify behavior that is inconsistent with the ground rules and can correct the behavior on their own; members may have to be asked directly or only cued to identify the relevant behavior

1. The *facilitator asks the member to identify the behavior* that is inconsistent with the ground rules. 2. The *facilitator asks the member to redesign the behavior* so that it is consistent with the ground rules.	*Member:* My opinion is that we should lease the equipment rather than buy it. *Facilitator:* You just said, "My opinion is we should lease the equipment rather than buy it." I believe your statement

Table 6.2. Interventions Based on Members' Skill Levels, Cont'd.

Intervention Steps	Examples
	is inconsistent with one of the ground rules. Do you see which one? *Member:* Yeah, I stated a position but I didn't explain why. *Facilitator:* I agree. Would you be willing to state it so that it is consistent with the ground rules?
	or
1. The *facilitator cues the group* to reflect on its behavior. 2. The *members take the initiative to identify the behavior* that is inconsistent with the ground rules *and to redesign it.*	*Member:* My opinion is that we should lease the equipment rather than buy it. *Facilitator:* What just happened? *Member:* I stated a position but I didn't explain why. [redesigning] The reason I favor leasing the equipment is that I'm concerned that the technology will change so fast that we will have obsolete equipment in three years if we buy it.

run the risk that members will learn, by watching the facilitator's actions, that assumptions do not always need to be tested.

Basing Interventions on Members' Skill Levels

As the previous section mentioned, facilitators vary their interventions according to group members' levels of skill in using the ground rules. Group members move through three levels of skill in terms of their ability to identify (diagnose) when they have acted inconsistently with a ground rule and correct (redesign) their behavior, as Table 6.2 shows.

At the beginner level (level one), members are not able to identify behavior inconsistent with the ground rules (or other effective group process) or to correct the behavior on their own. At the intermediate level (level two), group members can identify behavior inconsistent with the ground rules but cannot yet correct the behavior on their own. At the advanced level (level three), members can both identify and correct inconsistent behavior on their own. As the members of the group move from the first level to the third level, the facilitator can adjust the interventions so that the group takes more responsibility and becomes less dependent on the facilitator. To accomplish this, the facilitator asks the members to diagnose and/or correct their behavior if they are capable; the facilitator helps members diagnose and/or correct behavior only if they do not have the skills to do so.

Group members are likely to have different levels of diagnostic and intervention abilities. Therefore, facilitators' interventions will be more effective if they match the level of intervention to the skills of the relevant members. To avoid unnecessary dependency on the facilitator, the facilitator can regularly check whether a member can respond at a level higher than that at which the facilitator is intervening. For each level, Table 6.2 describes when each level should be used, the intervention steps, and an example of the intervention.

At the beginner level (level one), members cannot identify behavior that is inconsistent with the ground rules or correct the behavior on their own. At this level, a facilitator has two options for intervening. In the first option, the facilitator asks a question to elicit a response from the member that is consistent with the ground rules. The option is used typically only in basic facilitation where the facilitator is responsible for managing the process and the group is not trying to improve its process. Notice that the option is inconsistent with several ground rules (explain reasons, make statements, and then invite questions and comments). In the second option, the facilitator's intervention helps members identify how their behavior is inconsistent and the facilitator's statements and questions guide them in redesigning their behavior so that it is consistent with the ground rules.

At the intermediate level (level two), group members can identify behavior that is inconsistent with the ground rules but cannot yet correct the behavior on their own. The intervention enables the member (or group) to identify the inconsistent behavior.

At the advanced level (level three), group members can identify behavior that is inconsistent with the ground rules and can correct the behavior on their own. At this level, the facilitator has two options. In the first option, the facilitator asks members directly to identify the relevant behavior. In the second option, the facilitator simply focuses the group's attention on process by saying, "What just happened?" To clarify the intervention, facilitators can state that they are asking the group about what just happened to determine whether it can diagnose its behavior and that they will share their diagnosis as well.

Choosing Words Carefully

The specific words a facilitator uses are important; they are the fundamental elements of interventions. Small differences in the facilitator's choice of words can lead to large differences in meaning and in the group's reaction. If facilitators use language that states exactly what they mean—no more and no less—they will intervene more effectively.

This section identifies categories of words to use and to avoid. The guidelines, shown in Exhibit 6.3, increase the chance that the group interprets the facilitator's words as the facilitator meant for them to be interpreted, the facilitator acts consistently with the three core values, and the facilitator is considered content neutral.

Exhibit 6.3. Guidelines for Words to Use and Avoid.

1. Use words and phrases that have one meaning—the meaning one wants to convey.
2. Use descriptive words when they can be substituted for evaluative words.
3. Use proper nouns or other nouns rather than pronouns.
4. Use active voice unless the identity of the actors is not clear.
5. Use words that give equal recognition to all members and tasks.
6. Choose words that distinguish the facilitator from group members' roles.
7. Avoid imperatives; focus instead on cause and effect.
8. Avoid facilitator jargon.
9. Avoid humor that puts down or discounts members or that can be misinterpreted.

1. *Use words and phrases that have one meaning—the meaning one wants to convey.* Certain phrases carry more than one meaning. The facilitator may use a phrase intending to convey one particular meaning, but clients may interpret it to mean something else. For example, as part of a union-management cooperative effort, I served as the facilitator in a three-member training team that included a union and a management representative. At one point, employees were clarifying instructions we had given them as part of a training exercise. When an employee asked whether the exercise could be approached in several ways, the union representative on our training team said, "I don't care which way you do it." Later, the employee said he was annoyed that the union representative was not interested in answering the question. He interpreted the union representative's statement to mean "I'm not interested in your problem." However, the representative meant "I have no preference for how you conduct the exercise."

2. *Use descriptive words when they can be substituted for evaluative words.* Words that identify directly observable behaviors can be more easily validated than judgmental words. The ground rule "be specific—use examples" is based partly on this principle. It is easier for a group to agree whether a member failed to hand in a report by 5 P.M. than to agree whether the member was irresponsible.

Descriptive words are consistent with the facilitator's neutral role. Judgmental words contain some built-in evaluation, implying that the facilitator either approves or disapproves of a behavior or idea. For example, in facilitating a conflict between teachers and administrators, I intervened to summarize the two alternatives posed by members. I said, "You have identified two alternatives. The radical one is X. The other alternative is Y." As soon as the word *radical* left my lips, I realized I had made a mistake. By labeling one alternative with the adjective radical, I loaded it with all the political connotations with which that word has come to be associated. For some group members, radical probably had a positive connotation, while for others it was negative. In any case, by framing the alternative as radical, I added an unnecessary evaluative component. Had I intervened in a purely descriptive way, I would have said, "You described two alternatives. One is X. The other is Y."

Using judgmental verbs can have the same consequences. If, in summarizing an interaction between Sidney and the group, the facilitator says, "Sidney refused to participate," the implication is that Sidney's behavior was uncooperative. A descriptive alternative would be, "I did not see Sidney participate."

Sometimes, two words are synonyms but one is more judgmental than the other or is more easily misinterpreted. For example, in asking whether a group member knew about a situation, the facilitator could ask, "Were you unaware of the situation?" or "Were you ignorant of the situation?" Although *ignorant* means unaware, people often associate the word ignorant with *stupid*. Consequently, *unaware* is a better word to use.

3. *Use proper nouns or other nouns rather than pronouns.* Consider this interaction between the facilitator and José:

José: I talked with Peter about how to handle my conflict with Fred. Peter said he wasn't the kind of person who was particularly good at resolving conflicts and that I should try to solve the problem on my own. Or, I could work something out with Jack, Beth, or Nancy. Frankly, I don't think I can get help from any of them.

Facilitator: Do you think you can solve the conflict without him?

José: I don't have any choice.

Facilitator: Are you saying that you don't have the choice to talk with Fred about what's going on?

José: No, I wasn't talking about Fred.

Facilitator: When you approached Peter, didn't he say he wasn't good at handling conflicts?

José: No. Peter didn't say Fred wasn't good at handling conflict. He said *he* wasn't any good.

Facilitator: Oh, I misunderstood. I thought when you said, "Peter said he wasn't any good," "he" referred to Fred.

José: And when you asked me whether I could "solve the problem without him," I thought "him" meant Peter.

Facilitator: No, "him" meant Fred.

If the conversation seems confusing, it is. The confusion occurs largely because José and the facilitator unknowingly use the pronouns *he* and *him* to refer to different people. When pronoun confusions become complicated, they begin to sound like the famous Abbott and Costello routine "Who's on First?" By using individual's names or their distinctive titles, facilitators avoid confusion.

The pronouns *that* and *this* create similar confusion. Imagine a discussion in which a facilitator is helping a group move from positions to interests. Various members have each identified several positions. If the facilitator says, "Dan, would you be willing to explain what your interest was behind that?" *that* could refer to any of several positions that have been recently discussed. However, if the facilitator says, "Dan, would you be willing to explain what your interest was behind meeting with Andrea alone?" the ambiguity is reduced.

One exception to avoiding pronouns is the singular form of the word *you*. When the facilitator looks directly at a group member, and says, "Do you think X?" there is little ambiguity. Of course, saying, "Terry, do you think X?" further reduces ambiguity. However, using *you* to refer to a subset of the group can be confusing. Identifying the individual group members by name or by some appropriate label (for example, women or first-line supervisors) reduces the ambiguity.

4. *Use active voice unless the identity of the actors is not clear.* Active voice identifies who or what is taking the action; passive voice does not. "Sue decided to promote Glen" uses active voice. "It was decided to promote Glen" uses passive voice. When facilitators use active voice, they provide valid information to the group, reduce potential ambiguity, and act consistently with the belief that individuals should take responsibility for their actions.

However, the facilitator intentionally uses passive voice when the identity of the actor is not clear. Consider this interaction:

Ted: We've got a problem. Jan called the director and told him there was no way we could get the job done today.

Jan: No, I didn't call the director about that. When I spoke to him in the afternoon, he already knew we couldn't meet the deadline. Maybe Sue told him when she dropped off the plans. He mentioned that Sue had come by.

Sue: I didn't even see Hal when I dropped off the plan. I just left them on his desk.

Facilitator: When the director was told that the deadline couldn't be met, how did it create a problem?

Here several members disagree about who told the director that the group would not be able to meet a deadline. By using passive voice ("the director was told"), the facilitator is able to focus on how telling the director creates a problem without making assumptions about who told the director and thereby continuing the disagreement. If it is important to determine who told the director, the facilitator would need to return to the disagreement. Using passive voice to ignore conflicts or issues that need to be discussed is inappropriate.

5. *Use words that give equal recognition to all members and tasks.* Organizational members can be divided into various groups according to their position or title (for example, customer service representatives), functional area (for example, marketing department) work status (for example, full time, permanent), professional training (for example, psychologist, engineer, physician), sex, or race. Facilitated groups are rarely completely homogeneous. Even if all members are white male police officers, they may be different with respect to tenure (for example, old guard versus new guard) or belief about how to police (traditional versus community-oriented). The facilitator often has occasion to refer to subgroups, especially when there are conflicts among them.

Part of remaining neutral and credible with all subgroups entails referring to each subgroup in a way that maintains its identity and does not subordinate it to other groups. The principle is to **refer to each subgroup in terms that reflect its independent identity rather than in terms that use another subgroup as a point of reference.**

The principle is often violated when a majority of group members can be defined with one label. For example, in a group comprising mostly psychologists, with a minority of social workers and physicians, the facilitator may refer to the subgroups as "psychologists and nonpsychologists," especially if a conflict exists between psychologists on the one hand and social workers and physicians on the other. However, by making psychologists the subgroup of reference, the facilitator subtly recognizes psychologists at the expense of social workers and physicians. Used frequently, the reference subgroup may be seen as the high-status group. Depending on the context in which the facilitator uses the labels, members may think the facilitator favors or identifies with the psychologist subgroup. Typically, however, the reference subgroup is the group with the highest status or power, even if the subgroup does not represent a majority. By using independent names for each subgroup, the facilitator recognizes symbolically the importance of each subgroup.

Sexist language also fails to give equal recognition to members of both sexes. By sexist, I mean language that treats one sex differently than the other or that fosters stereotypes of social roles based on gender. Perhaps the most common way women are denied equal recognition through language is by using the supposedly generic words *he, him, man,* or *men* to designate both males and females. For example, the facilitator might ask the group, "If an employee disagrees with his performance appraisal, can he appeal it?" Although, as in this example, *he* is meant to refer to both sexes, studies have shown that *he* is rarely intended or understood to include *she* in spoken language (for example, Moulton, Robinson, & Elias, 1978).

Other language is sexist because it assumes that certain roles or jobs are held by a particular sex. Consider the terms *woman executive* and *woman fire fighter.* Using *woman* as an adjective either assumes that executives and fire fighters are men or implies that women executives and fire fighters are not real executives or fire fighters. Terms such as *male nurse* and *male model* create the same problems. Similarly, the term *working mothers* assumes either that mothers do not work (outside the home) or that being a mother is not work. The sexism becomes clearer when one realizes that there is no parallel term of *working fathers,* because fathers are assumed to work.

Some job titles are inherently sexist because they assume the job is performed by people of a particular gender. Examples include *mailman, girl Friday,* and *seamstress.* Nonsexist titles are gender neutral, such as *mail carrier* or *chore worker.*

A simple test to determine whether the phrase is sexist is to repeat the phrase, inserting the word for the opposite sex. For example, change *working mother* to *working father, woman executive* to *man executive,* or *girl Friday* to *boy Friday.* If the changed phrase is not in currency, or seems awkward or redundant, it is likely to be sexist.

Sexism is only one way in which language fails to treat different groups equally. Facilitators should also avoid language that treats any subgroup differently than its counterpart, whether the groups are divided on the basis of age, race, or any other variable.

6. *Choose words that distinguish the facilitator from group members' roles.* Facilitators' language should indicate that he or she is not a member of the group and are not involved in the substance of the group's decisions. A simple way to reinforce this is to refer to the group as *you* or *the group* rather than as *we* or *our group.* An exception occurs when the facilitator has a legitimate role in the group's process decisions, such as deciding how long to meet.

7. *Avoid imperatives; focus instead on cause and effect.* Imperatives such as "you must" or "you have to" discourage groups from making free and informed choices and put the facilitator in an expert role. An example is, "You must check out your assumption before acting on it. Do you agree?" Instead, focusing on the relationship between members' behaviors and their effects helps members see the consequences of their actions, without telling them they must change. For example, the facilitator might say, "When you acted on your assumption without checking it out, your action omitted valid information that reduced the group's ability to make a choice. Do you agree?"

8. *Avoid facilitator jargon.* This guideline is more relevant for basic facilitation. Terms such as *intervention, role conflict,* or *directly observable behavior* are shorthand that clients may not understand and that clients using basic facilitation have little need to learn. Facilitators should use everyday language instead of using jargon. In developmental facilitation, teaching the group the language of facilitation is an appropriate task in connection with teaching members to develop their own facilitation skills.

9. *Avoid humor that puts down or discounts members or that can be misinterpreted.* Humor can be a valuable tool for relieving tension in the group, emphasizing a point, and helping members to examine their behavior. However, certain types of humor can reduce the facilitator's effectiveness. Sarcastic humor about members' ineffective behavior can decrease their trust in the facilitator

because they are likely to interpret the humor as unsupportive. Ironic humor can create problems because it requires the listener to interpret the humorist's meaning as the reverse of the literal meaning of the words. The ironic statement "I can see there is a high level of trust in this group" means "there is *not* a high level of trust in this group." If members do not detect the irony, they will interpret the statement literally. Consequently, the members may begin to question the facilitator's diagnostic skills if they believe there is low trust in the group. Even if members do detect the irony, the facilitator has failed to be a model of explicit communication.

Summary

This chapter described nine types of interventions that facilitators make: exploring, seeking specifics, emphasizing process, diagnosing, confronting and other feedback, managing process and structure, making content suggestions, teaching concepts and methods, and reframing. Next it discussed the intervention steps of the diagnosis-intervention cycle: sharing observations, testing inferences, and helping the group decide whether and how to change its behavior. Sharing observations provides group members with the valid information on which the facilitator has based inferences. Testing inferences with group members ensures that the facilitator does not intervene on inferences that are inaccurate. Helping the group decide whether and how to change its behavior ensures that group members maintain free choice and responsibility for changing their behavior.

The chapter also considered how facilitators vary their interventions according to the skill levels of group members. Finally, the chapter offered guidelines for how facilitators can choose their words carefully, so they can communicate accurately as neutral third parties.

Chapter Seven Beginning and Ending Meetings

To be effective, facilitated groups need to perform certain tasks at the beginning and end of meetings. The tasks are critical because they provide for the general structure and process of the entire meeting and set the direction for the next meeting. To help the group perform the tasks (such as agreeing on an agenda and the roles people will play), the facilitator uses the type of macro intervention that involves managing structure and process. Some tasks may need to be performed at each meeting, others only intermittently, while still others are necessary only for the initial meeting. Who performs the task may depend on whether the facilitation is basic or developmental. This chapter describes the tasks and interventions that facilitators make to help groups perform them.

Preparing the Room

In basic facilitation, the facilitator usually arranges the seating and sets the room up before the meeting begins. In developmental facilitation, the group often takes responsibility for this task, especially after the initial meeting. The arrangements of seating and flip chart are part of the organizational context of the group—in this case, the immediate physical context—which affects the group's process. Four principles (shown in Exhibit 7.1) guide the arrangements.

1. *All participants and the facilitator should be able to see and hear each other.*

2. *The seating arrangement should enable members to focus on the flip chart (or other writing device) and the person or persons who will manage the group's process.* Focusing the participants' attention on the flip chart helps people stay on task. Focusing participants' attention on the person managing the

146

Exhibit 7.1. Principles for Seating Arrangements.

1. All participants and the facilitator should be able to see and hear each other.

2. The seating arrangements should enable members to focus on the flip chart (or other writing devices) and the facilitator.

3. Seating arrangements should distinguish participants from nonparticipants.

4. Seating arrangements should be spacious enough to meet the needs of the group but no larger.

group process makes it easier for that person to work. Facilitators usually sit in a location that physically distinguishes them from group members. Figure 7.1 shows seating arrangements for different sizes of groups (the F indicates the facilitator). For example, in medium-size groups, members often sit around a U-shaped table, with the person managing the group process standing or sitting at the opening of the U near a flip chart. In basic facilitation, this person is the facilitator. In very large groups, it is not possible to seat everyone so each person can see everyone else. A series of tables arranged in the chevron pattern shown in Figure 7.1 enables all members to see the facilitator and flip charts. In developmental facilitation, the facilitator may start out managing the group's process, but over time the role shifts to individual group members, or all group members simultaneously take responsibility for managing the process. When all group members take responsibility, a round, square, or rectangular table that does not distinguish a single leader reflects this decision.

Aside from designating a place for the facilitator and chair (if the chair will also be managing the process), participants should not be assigned specific seats. Applying the value of free choice and the principle of starting with the group's intents and concerns means enabling participants to sit where they feel comfortable. If all members of a divided group choose to sit with their subgroup members, that is their choice. (This can be useful diagnostic data for the facilitator.) If facilitators believe it would be helpful for members of the different subgroups to sit together, they can intervene by suggesting it explicitly and explaining their reasoning.

One exception to not assigning seats occurs with large groups. When conducting basic facilitation with groups larger than about forty members, the planning clients and facilitator sometimes assign participants to specific tables. They may group people either homogeneously or heterogeneously, depending on the purpose of the meeting and the type of activities that members at each table will perform. For example, each table might comprise representatives of the different functions in the organization. Assigning seating becomes necessary when groups are too large to organize themselves according to some criteria.

3. *Seating arrangements should distinguish participants from nonparticipants.* Groups often ask nonmembers to attend to provide information or just to observe. Seating the nongroup members separately from group members enables members to focus on one another without "psychological interruptions"

Figure 7.1. Seating Arrangements for Different Sizes of Groups.

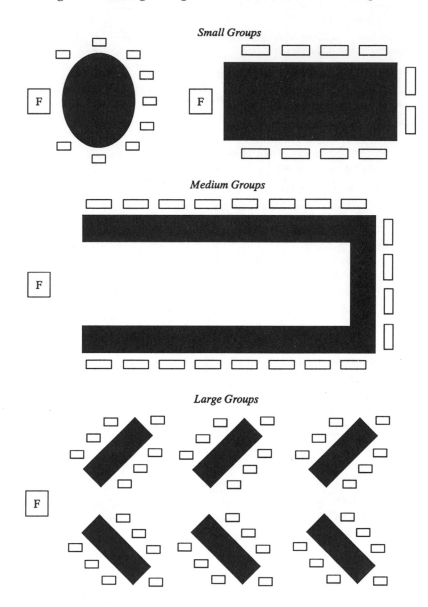

from nongroup members. It also makes it easier for the facilitator to attend to group members without being distracted.

4. *Seating arrangements should be spacious enough to meet the needs of the group, but no larger.* Facilitation involves bringing people together to work. Seating arrangements that leave empty spaces between participants create unnecessary psychological distance for members to bridge. Empty spaces also make it

more difficult for a facilitator to see at a glance whether everyone is present, for example, when checking for consensus.

Beginning the Meeting

After the room is arranged appropriately, the group can begin meeting. There are several macro interventions that facilitators make at the beginning of meetings (shown in Exhibit 7.2) that affect the structure and process of the entire meeting.

1. Make introductions. In small groups, only the facilitator may not know everyone in the room. In large groups, such as those that bring together individuals from different parts of a large organization or from different organizations, many people may be strangers. In any event, facilitators should introduce themselves and ask others to do the same. Beyond the individual's name, organization, and position, the information shared in the introductions will vary according to the group's history and its task. The facilitator may ask participants to include how long they have been an organizational or group member or to describe their jobs.

Icebreaker exercises enable people to introduce themselves. I attended a two-day meeting of organizational consultants and researchers in which everyone sketched out their professional histories on a piece of flip chart paper, taped them to their bodies, and milled around the room talking with each other about their backgrounds. Then participants formed a human network by standing next to those people with whom they had some connection. Remaining in the configuration, each member made introductory comments to the entire group and explained the connection to her or his neighbor. In thirty minutes, about fifty people were able to learn much more relevant information about each other than if each person had spoken individually to the entire group or members had formed pairs. The human network also enabled the entire group to see the various links within the group. The exercise was effective partly because it was based on the principle that **any experiential exercise should be consistent with the group's task.** Introductory exercises that are irrelevant to the group's task or inconsistent with the core values can quickly alienate the group from the facilitator.

Exhibit 7.2. Interventions at the Beginning and End of Meetings.

Beginning the Meeting

1. Make introductions.
2. Check for outcomes and concerns.
3. Agree on the agenda and time allocation.
4. Agree on the process, including ground rules.
5. Define roles.

Ending the Meeting

1. Review decisions and plans for action.
2. Schedule the next meeting and agenda.
3. Do a self-critique.

It may not be feasible for all members of large groups to introduce themselves. One alternative is for people to introduce each other in their small groups at their respective tables and for a representative at each table to summarize the table's introductory session. Another alternative is for members to seek out and introduce themselves to at least some individuals they do not recognize. Again, the specific introductory exercise should be based on the group's task and history. Introductions also are necessary whenever new members join the group.

2. *Check for outcomes and concerns.* Even when group members know the tentative agenda for a meeting, they often have different expectations about what the group should accomplish. Identifying expectations helps the facilitator and group address conflicting expectations and identify those that cannot be met, determine whether the tentative agenda is appropriate or needs changing, and take the steps necessary to meet the agreed-upon expectations.

The facilitator's intervention might sound like this: "I assume each of you came to this meeting expecting the group to accomplish certain things. Rather than guess what each of you expects, it would help to know what has to happen for each of you to leave the meeting feeling it was a success. This will help determine whether your expectations are compatible with one another and will help us take the steps necessary to meet the agreed-upon expectations. Is it OK if we go around the room and each person states his or her expectations?"

In addition to expectations, members have concerns about things that might happen that would prevent the meeting from being successful. In a group struggling with conflict, for example, members may be concerned that the conversation will break down into personal attacks, that the real issues will be glossed over, or that the group will come to a stalemate. Other groups may be concerned that certain members will dominate the conversation or not participate or that the group will get off the track and not solve the problem. Whatever the concerns, identifying them at the outset enables the facilitator and group members to pay special attention to the problems and intervene on them as soon as they arise. Such an intervention can be combined with the previous intervention or can follow it: "I also assume that each of you has some concerns about things that could happen or not happen during the meeting that would undermine the meeting's success. You may also have some ideas about how group members or I can deal with these things. Identifying your concerns about these things will help us watch out for them and, it is hoped, prevent them from becoming problems. Are people willing to share their concerns about these things and their ideas for preventing them from becoming a problem or reducing the problem? [if yes] Who wants to start?" When there is high conflict and low trust between subgroups, the subgroups may not be willing to share their concerns immediately with the other subgroups. In this case, the facilitator can ask the group to break out into subgroups and ask each subgroup to discuss the question among themselves and then share their responses with the other subgroups.

3. *Agree on the agenda and time allocation.* As part of the contracting process, participants should receive a tentative agenda before the first meeting.

For subsequent meetings, the tentative agenda should be established at the end of the previous meeting. In either situation, the tentative agenda should be posted and reviewed. Then the group needs to decide whether the tentative agenda remains appropriate, given the participants' expectations and concerns and any events that have occurred since the tentative agenda was developed.

The facilitator could intervene by saying, "Given your expectations and concerns, and anything that might have occurred since the tentative agenda was developed, does anyone think it would help to revise the agenda?" Once agreed on, the revised agenda should be posted on flip chart paper. This enables all members and the facilitator to refer to it throughout the meeting, especially when members get off track.

The group also needs to decide how much time to allot to each agenda item. The times should not be treated as deadlines that force the group to automatically move to the next agenda item. Rather, allotting time enables the facilitator and members to monitor the group's use of time and to point out how much time remains for a topic. If the group has not finished dealing with an item in the allotted time, the facilitator intervenes by asking whether the group wants to continue discussing the subject or move on.

The facilitator participates in the discussion of how much time to allot to each item, because this is a process issue. As process experts, facilitators tell the group how much time the group is likely to require to deal with each topic. The intervention is similar to those in the contracting process described in Chapter Three.

4. Agree on the process, including ground rules. The agenda represents agreement on the meeting's content, but the group still must decide what process to use for addressing each agenda item. At this point, the facilitator and group should agree on ground rules, a process described in Chapter Three. It is also the point at which members can agree on more macro processes, such as whether they will use a formal problem-solving model. Because different macro processes may be appropriate for different agenda items, the group can agree on these as it reaches each new agenda item.

5. Define roles. Related to the group process is the question of identifying who will assume each role. If the facilitator has managed the contracting process effectively, the group will have some understanding of the facilitator's role. In addition, when introducing themselves, facilitators may have briefly described their role. Now facilitators clarify their role and check for any questions or concerns. For example, in a basic facilitation, the facilitator might say,

> As facilitator, my role is to help you work together as effectively as possible to help you accomplish what you want to accomplish. To do that, I will help you follow the ground rules. When I think someone is acting inconsistently with the ground rules, I will point it out, see if you agree, and if you do, ask you if you're willing to make your point again using the ground rules. For example, if you

take a position, I will ask you if you are willing to state the interests behind your position. I will also help you keep on track and monitor your time, but whether you want to change the agenda or reallocate your time among agenda items is your decision. As your facilitator, I will be substantively neutral. That means I will not get involved in the content of your discussions. [(When appropriate I add:) As some of you may know, I have some expertise in some of the subject areas you will be working on, but it is not consistent with my role as facilitator to share that information. If, however, someone has a substantive question they want me to answer, and the group agrees that I should answer it, I will temporarily leave my facilitator role, answer it, and then return to my facilitator role.] If, at any time, you think I am acting inconsistently with what we have agreed is my role, please tell me immediately. Does anyone have any questions or concerns about my role?

Other roles that need to be defined include the formal group leader's, group members', nonmember participants', and observers.

Ending the Meeting

At the end of the meeting, the group should perform the following tasks:

1. Review decisions and plans for action. Reviewing decisions made during the meeting ensures that all members understand the decisions made. The facilitator can review the decisions or ask a member to do it. The facilitator states, "Let's be sure everyone understands what the group has agreed on. Will someone recap the decisions? If anyone hears something that they believe the group did not agree to, please say so."

Even if the group has not formally engaged in problem solving, it is likely to have made decisions that require some action. At the end of the meeting, planning ensures that members know who is responsible for each task and when it will be completed.

2. Schedule the next meeting and agenda. If the group plans to meet again, it is usually easier to schedule the next meeting while all members are already assembled rather than by contacting people individually. Similarly, building a tentative agenda for the next meeting is easier after members have reviewed the current meeting. The tentative agenda is reviewed and revised, as necessary, at the beginning of the next meeting.

3. Do a self-critique. Self-critiques enable a group to systematically learn from its mistakes and incorporate its successes in future meetings. Chapter Four explained self-critiques as a ground rule (or principle for effective group process). Although a self-critique can be used at any time during a meeting, it is typically employed at the end of the meeting.

The facilitator will have explained self-critiques in the beginning of the meeting, when discussing ground rules and agenda items. At this point, the facilitator can explain exactly how to conduct the self-critique.

The facilitator begins the self-critique by dividing a flip chart sheet into two vertical columns labeled *what we did well* and *what we need to improve on/ do differently next time*. The facilitator then asks members to reflect on the meeting and use the ground rules to identify specific examples of when they acted effectively (did well) and when they acted ineffectively (need to improve/do differently). Members can also identify more complex patterns that contributed to or hindered the group's effectiveness. Facilitators participate and encourage members to critique their behavior. In addition, members can evaluate how well they accomplished their substantive goals for the meeting.

Facilitators can help the group identify examples. They can ask members to review the ground rules and think of situations in which either they were used well or violated. They can ask members to think of a time they had a strong feeling or thought during the meeting but did not share it.

For the critique to be helpful, members must give specific examples, which is consistent with the ground rules. For example, John might say, "I think Debra helped the group focus on interests rather than positions when she asked Henry what interests led him to oppose flexible working hours. Do others agree?" A general comment like "I think we all could do a better job of staying focused" does not provide enough information for other members to decide whether the critique is valid. Nor does it help the group identify exactly how the group lost its focus or what to do differently. General statements also lead to a situation in which everyone agrees that the group could do a better job of staying focused, but no one believes she or he is responsible for getting the group off track.

Several variations are possible, depending on what kinds of critique skills members want to develop. The first variation gives members practice in taking responsibility for both their functional and dysfunctional behavior. Each person identifies something he or she did well and something he or she needs to improve on. A second variation helps a group in conflict see how other members contribute to the group's effectiveness. In this variation, each member identifies something another member did well.

A third variation helps members learn to give constructive negative feedback. Each person identifies something someone else needs to improve on, a technique that is useful for groups that tend to avoid or smooth over conflict. A final variation, which involves a combination of the others, is helpful when members are not willing to take the risks involved in the other variations or after members have begun with one of the other variations. Each member identifies something either any member did well or needs to improve on. The variation involves the least risk for members and also develops the fewest skills. In groups that begin with this variation, members usually identify things that other members did well. For all the variations, to maintain members' free choice, members can choose not to participate.

The variations work well for identifying individual actions. However, to identify interactions and more complex patterns, members need to identify how each member contributed to creating the dynamic.

Following the ground rule of "make statements, then invite questions and comments," each member should ask the other members of the group whether they agree or disagree with her or his self-critique statement. The group should attempt to reach consensus on the examples listed on the flip chart. For each item the group needs to improve on, it should also identify specifically how particular members will act differently. This will increase the likelihood that members will change their behavior. Here too, the group should strive for consensus. To increase the likelihood that the group will improve its process, it can begin each meeting by reviewing the part of the previous meeting's self-critique that listed what the group needs to improve on or do differently.

Sometimes, a self-critique generates a new understanding of something that occurred during the meeting or a new decision. For example, during a developmental self-critique with a top management group, one member said she did not raise an issue in the group because her supervisor (also a group member) had told her before the meeting it would be inappropriate. Members then discussed and reached a clear agreement about not preventing any issue from being raised in the group.

Facilitated meetings can be frustrating for groups that are not used to systematically discussing issues—especially process issues. The dialogue that follows shows how a member might express this frustration and how the facilitator can intervene:

Conversation	*Notes*
Member: I think we wasted time in the session.	
Facilitator: Can you say specifically what you mean by "wasted time"? Are you saying that these topics were not important to discuss in this group? Are you saying that the group could have discussed the topics more effectively? Or, are you saying something else?	Facilitator seeks to clarify meaning of important words.
Member: The topics were important to discuss, but I just feel that the discussion should not have taken so long.	
Facilitator: You said, "The discussion should not have taken so long." Is there anything the group or I could	Facilitator seeks to clarify meaning of important words and identify causes of "taking too long."

have done to use the time more effectively?

Member: No, not beyond the few small things that others mentioned. I can't think of anything. Everything we talked about was important.

Facilitator: Given that you don't think time was wasted, I'm wondering if you're frustrated because a process you think is important takes such a long time to solve the group's problems. Are you frustrated about this?

Facilitator tests inference.

Member: Yeah, I am. At this rate, it will take weeks to solve all our problems. That's a long time.

Facilitator: I agree that it will take weeks. Whether several weeks is a long time depends on how you look at the situation. I would agree that compared to how the group normally works, it's a long time to spend in problem-solving meetings. However, compared to the three years that the group has tried without success to solve these problems, several weeks is a relatively short period of time. Do you agree, or do you see it differently?

Facilitator reframes the meaning of "a long time" and checks for agreement or disagreement.

Member: I agree with everything you've said. I just don't know whether we can afford all that time in meetings.

Facilitator: That's an important question for the group to decide. Do you want to see if the group wants to discuss this issue?

Facilitator identifies group issue and checks for members' interest.

Self-critiques for basic and developmental facilitation are different. In developmental facilitation, group members take turns conducting the self-critique. Developmental self-critiques focus not only on ground rules but also on the underlying dynamics that lead a group to follow or not follow them. While self-critiques in basic facilitation focus on the ground rules, they also focus on how well the group accomplished its substantive goals.

Self-critiques are an excellent time for facilitators to get feedback about their performance. Unfortunately, group members are usually more willing to identify ways the facilitator has been helpful than ways the facilitator could have been more effective. Members are often reluctant to say something negative about facilitators because they have attempted to help the group and have high status. Basic facilitation group members also may have few comments because they are focused on the content of the group's discussion, not on its process. Even if members are focused on process, it is often difficult for them to comment on specific intervention techniques, because they have not developed an understanding of facilitation theory and practice.

The facilitator can help reduce the barriers to feedback. To minimize the chance of receiving only positive comments, facilitators might say, "While I am interested in knowing what you think I did that was helpful, my purpose for asking about my performance is not to fish for compliments but to learn how to facilitate better. So, I value comments about what you found less helpful." To underscore the point, facilitators can briefly identify something they learned from a self-critique with a previous group. They can also critique their own behavior in the group, identifying a specific time when they wished they had intervened differently, then asking other members to comment. This provides an example of the behavior facilitators would like from participants and demonstrates that their request is genuine. For example, in one group self-critique, I identified a specific time when I had let group members continue talking, although I thought they were off the task. When I asked members whether they agreed, several said they had hoped I would intervene sooner.

Finally, self-critiques often provide powerful diagnostic information about the group. They can help a facilitator assess how well group members understand their ground rules and whether certain behavior is functional or dysfunctional. Self-critiques also enable a facilitator to assess group members' levels of skill in an important area—giving feedback to other members.

Some group members may consider some tasks at the beginning and end of meetings (and the facilitator's related interventions) unnecessary and see them as cutting into the time the group has to accomplish its real work. However, the tasks are critical to the group's effectiveness because, as discussed in Chapter Two, they help the group accomplish its tasks in a way that maintains or enhances the group's ability to work together in the future. Facilitators can help members by explaining the need for the interventions, perhaps by describing the three criteria for group effectiveness (an intervention that involves teaching concepts). At the same time, facilitators can help members reframe the meaning of the time they spend on these tasks, which serve to maintain or enhance the group's functioning, so that members consider it an important part of their real work.

Summary

This chapter explored interventions that facilitators make to help groups perform critical tasks at the beginning and end of meetings. Before the meeting begins, seating arrangements are made. Tasks at the beginning of meetings include making introductions, checking for outcomes and concerns, agreeing on the agenda and time allocation, agreeing on the process, including ground rules, and defining roles. Tasks at the end of meetings include reviewing decisions and action plans, scheduling the next meeting and agenda, and conducting a self-critique.

Chapter Eight Helping the Group Solve Problems

Much of a group's work involves solving problems—identifying and closing the gap between some desired situation and the current situation. Examples of problem solving include a department that needs to improve service quality, a group that must reduce the cost of operations, an organization charged with developing a strategic plan, and a city council contemplating a shift from backyard to curbside garbage pickup. Groups that solve problems in a methodical way are more likely to develop higher-quality solutions. This chapter describes a general model that groups can use to identify and solve problems and discusses the interventions that facilitators make when helping the group use the model.

Because each problem-solving step requires certain actions, a problem-solving model helps facilitators predict the kinds of interventions they may need to make at each step. There are many different versions of problem-solving models. This discussion uses the model shown in Figure 8.1. Some of the problems that groups encounter are described for each step of the problem-solving model, as are some relevant interventions. Some interventions involve making specific statements, while others involve introducing a technique to help structure that step in the process.

One intervention that precedes the model is helping the group decide whether following the model in a formal manner is useful, given the nature of the problem. The model is more useful for more complex problems. For simple problems, following the model may take time and result in no better decision or greater acceptance than if the group used a less structured approach (Hirokawa & Gouran, 1989). The decision to use a structured problem-solving model lies

158

Figure 8.1. Problem-Solving Model.

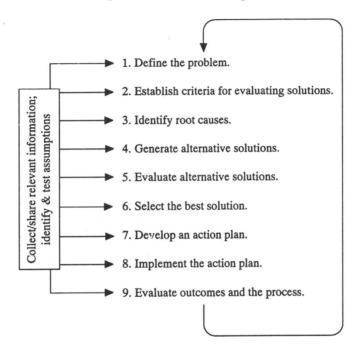

1. Define the problem.

2. Establish criteria for evaluating solutions.

3. Identify root causes.

4. Generate alternative solutions.

5. Evaluate alternative solutions.

6. Select the best solution.

7. Develop an action plan.

8. Implement the action plan.

9. Evaluate outcomes and the process.

Collect/share relevant information; identify & test assumptions

ultimately with the group. However, it is consistent with the facilitator's role to suggest whether using the model would be helpful.

Several intervention issues are relevant throughout the group's problem-solving process. First, a group discussion is more effective when all members focus on the same step at the same time. In contrast, if some members are trying to identify causes while others are already generating alternative solutions, the discussion is less effective. Therefore, checking to determine whether all group members are focused on the same problem-solving step is a fundamental intervention.

Second, a group generally is more effective when it follows the problem-solving steps in the proper order, beginning with identifying the problem and ending with evaluation. There are times, however, when a group may not follow the problem-solving model exactly in the order shown in Figure 8.1, such as when it needs to solve several problems simultaneously. Helping the group move through the problem-solving process in a practical manner is another fundamental intervention.

Third, the model does not have a separate step in which members collect or share information needed to solve the problem. Instead, as Figure 8.1 shows, the model recognizes that at any point in the process, members may need information from or may need to share information with nongroup members. Here the facilitator intervenes to make the group aware that it is making decisions without valid information. Similarly, the model does not have a separate step in which members identify their assumptions about solving the problems. Instead, the model recognizes that members make assumptions about how to define the problem, which criteria are appropriate, what the causes of the problem are, and so on. Here the facilitator helps members make their assumptions explicit so that they can test them, if possible, and so they can convey them to anyone who is reviewing or evaluating their work.

Failing to identify and test assumptions can reduce a group's ability to make valid decisions or even prevent it from finding any workable solution. For example, I once facilitated a retreat for a group of physicians who worked for a research hospital. The physicians were interested in adding a member to their group practice to reduce the waiting time for patients to get an appointment and to reduce the clinical work load on physicians already in the practice. The group made two assumptions: the demand for their services was so large that an additional physician would generate enough revenue to pay for the doctor's salary and that adding a physician would significantly reduce the waiting time for patients and the clinical work load of the other physicians. However, the two assumptions were mutually exclusive. If the first assumption was correct, once hired the new physician would become just as overloaded as the original group, and patient waiting time would remain the same. Without adding other assumptions or changing one of the two, the physicians could not solve their problem.

Step One: Define the Problem

Defining the problem is a critical but deceptively simple task. It has been said that a problem that is clearly identified is half solved. Without a clear definition, groups flounder. Group members often assume they know what problem they are trying to solve and that everyone agrees with the definition of the problem. Once a group has decided to follow a problem-solving model, the first intervention is likely to be helping the group recognize the need for clearly identifying the problem before moving on to other steps.

Defining the problem means identifying a gap between some desired situation and the current situation. For example, "infant mortality has reached 60 percent above the 'acceptable' rate," or "there has been a two-day lag beyond the guaranteed response time for customer service calls." A good problem definition implies or states explicitly not only the current situation but also the desired situation (for example, "acceptable infant mortality rate" or "no two-day lag beyond the guaranteed response time to customer service calls"). Here one intervention challenges the group to collect and use valid information to define the current situation instead of assuming that it already has the necessary valid information.

A second intervention involves helping the group agree on the desired situation. Often, this means having the group shift its focus from what it does not want to what it does want. This is necessary because the desired situation often is not the opposite of what the group does not want but some other alternative. Identifying the desired situation in large-scale organizational problems is easier when members have a shared vision of the organization and its mission to which they can refer. However, creating a shared vision and mission is, by itself, a major organizational intervention.

A good problem definition states only the current and desired situation and no more. An example of a good problem definition is "customers receive responses to billing error inquiries in four weeks, two weeks longer than acceptable." The statement implies no particular solutions and no potential causes. In contrast, the statement "clerks take ten days to check billing errors" unnecessarily narrows the definition in a way that implies that clerks are a primary cause of the problem. The problem statement "we need more qualified clerks" explicitly states part of the solution. Including the cause or solution in a problem definition diverts the group from exploring all the possibilities and increases the likelihood that the solution will not solve the real problem.

The more individuals have thought about a problem, the more likely it is they have begun to weigh causes and solutions. Consequently, it becomes more difficult to define the problem clearly. A facilitator can help the group identify the particular causes or solutions that members implicitly embed in their problem statements. This helps the group not only to develop a more satisfactory problem statement but also to make members aware of their current biases in thinking about the issue.

Finally, any given step of the model has a different meaning, depending on the nature of the group's task. For example, for a policy-making group, choosing among alternatives may mean deciding to restrict smoking in the workplace. Implementing the solution may mean directing a group of managers to put the policy in place. For the management group reporting to the policy group, choosing an alternative means selecting an effective set of procedures to implement the no-smoking policy. Implementing the solution involves carrying out the procedures.

The point for facilitators is that groups can use the full problem-solving model regardless of their task. The facilitator can help the group decide what steps such as "identify the problem" and "implement the solution" mean in the context of the group's task.

Step Two: Establish Criteria for Evaluating Solutions

Establishing criteria involves setting standards against which to evaluate alternative solutions. In other words, criteria define general characteristics that a solution should have, without describing a specific solution. To take a simple example, if a group were deciding to purchase a car for its use, some criteria might include "good gas mileage," "low-frequency repair record," and "large enough to accommodate all group members."

Establishing criteria is difficult because members sometimes cannot think about criteria without the context of a specific solution. Consequently, they may simply suggest specific solutions such as a Chrysler "Minivan" when asked to develop criteria. The facilitator can intervene by asking the member to describe what it is about the Chrysler "Minivan" that would make it a good solution. The intervention is similar to focusing members on interests rather than on positions.

One way to help members develop criteria is to ask them to complete sentences that naturally lead to identifying criteria. Some examples are, "The solution should be one that . . . ," "The solution should be one that does not . . . ," and "The solution should be implemented in a way that. . . ." The first example focuses on positive criteria, the second identifies negative unintended consequences, and the third identifies implementation criteria.

Problem solutions often generate additional problems because group members do not think systemically. Instead, they tend to evaluate alternatives that focus on how they will solve the identified problem, overlooking how the solution will fit with the rest of the organization. The facilitator can help the group think systemically by helping members identify criteria that focus on the fit between the solution and the larger organization. The intervention is based on the principle discussed in Chapter Three, that the facilitation should also consider the needs of the ultimate client group. Consider, for example, a group that is designing a merit pay system. One systemic criterion might be that the system must encourage excellent performance in a way that does not encourage competition among employees, which reduces the ability of the organization to provide excellent service.

Another intervention involves helping the group identify criteria that may conflict with each other. For example, in general a car large enough to accommodate eight group members may get relatively poor gas mileage. It is not necessary that the criteria be nonconflicting, only that members recognize potential conflicts and agree on ways to resolve them. One way that may reduce conflicts among criteria is to distinguish between criteria that the solution *must* meet and criteria that it would be *desirable* to meet.

Members will be reluctant to identify or to weight or rank criteria to the extent that it means exposing a hidden agenda. Here facilitators can make several interventions. First, they can try to reframe hidden agendas as legitimate concerns to discuss. This involves emphasizing that in consensus decision making, members are less likely to have their hidden interests met if they do not share them with the group. Second, facilitators can identify earlier comments by members that may reflect criteria of which they are unaware. For example, in a top management group, the facilitator might first point out that earlier, Rebecca had expressed concern that the manager had implemented a program without involving employees. The facilitator could then ask Rebecca whether employee involvement is a criterion she has for implementing the solution to the current problem.

Finally, the facilitator helps group members by challenging them to identify only those criteria that are needed or desired to solve the problem. Because each criterion places additional constraints on finding an acceptable solution, **each unnecessary criterion needlessly reduces the number of potential solutions.**

Step Three: Identify Root Causes

To solve problems so they remain solved, the group must identify root causes rather than symptoms. However, groups tend not to identify their own group as a cause of their problems. Instead, members tend to attribute the causes of problems to external events and to people other than themselves. When groups identify themselves as a cause, they usually identify only a subset of the group, not the entire group. All the biases increase the likelihood that the group will not identify some real causes of the problem. In this step, the facilitator helps the group examine a wide range of potential causes and challenges the group to move beyond symptoms to root causes.

Facilitators can use a number of macro interventions to structure discussion about root causes. One technique is often called a *fishbone diagram*—so named because it resembles the skeleton of a fish. The fishbone diagram (Figure 8.2) has a box at the left in which the problem definition is written. In the example, the problem definition is "reports of scattered garbage in yards and streets has increased by 50 percent above the standard in the last two months."

Figure 8.2. Fishbone Diagram.

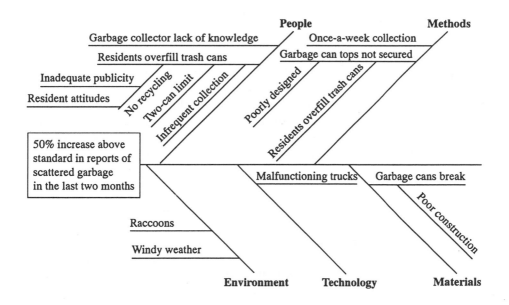

Five diagonal lines extend from the backbone, two above and three below. Each line has a label that represents a major category of potential causes. The categories may vary according to the nature of the problem statement, but together the major categories capture the domain of potential causes. The example uses the following five categories: people, methods, environment, technology, and materials.

Once the group has agreed on the comprehensive major categories, members brainstorm potential causes within each category. For example, one potential "people cause" of the increase in scattered garbage is that garbage collectors do not know how to transfer garbage to their large bins quickly without spills. Another potential cause is that residents fill their trash cans beyond capacity. In the environment category, two potential causes are increases in windy weather or increases in raccoon activity. In the technology category, the garbage trucks may be malfunctioning. The rules for brainstorming are simple and are shown in Exhibit 8.1. Brainstorming continues until the group has exhausted its ideas.

In the next step, the group brainstorms about the causes of the causes members have identified. As Figure 8.2 shows, residents may be overfilling their garbage cans because there is no recycling, because a policy limits the number of garbage cans to two per dwelling, or because garbage collection is infrequent. The process continues until the group has identified the root cause of each initial cause. For example, a recycling problem may stem from inadequate publicity about the program or by residents' attitudes about recycling. So that members can clearly read all the causes identified in a fishbone diagram, the facilitator can use separate pieces of flip chart paper for the different parts of the diagram. After potential root causes have been identified, the group may need to collect information to determine which, if any, of the causes are relevant.

To ensure that the group considers its role in the problem, the facilitator should ask directly, "In what ways might group members contribute to the causes of this problem?" In groups with conflicting subgroups, each subgroup is likely to identify the others' actions as contributing to the problem. By framing each potential cause as a hypothesis to be tested later, the facilitator can help the group identify conflict-related causes without the process becoming immediately mired in the conflict.

If the group has identified the problem statement satisfactorily, the fish-

Exhibit 8.1. Rules for Brainstorming.

---

1. Do not evaluate the ideas that members generate.

2. Include the wildest ideas possible.

3. Generate as many ideas as possible.

4. Combine and build upon ideas already generated.

Source: Osborn, 1953, pp. 300–301.

bone diagram builds naturally, simply by repeating the question, "What is a potential cause of the fifty percent increase above standard in reports of scattered garbage?" However, if the group has incorrectly defined the problem in terms of a solution, such as "give garbage collectors more training," members will have difficulty using the fishbone technique to generate causes and are likely to become frustrated. The difficulty occurs because it is logically impossible to find the causes of a solution. In other words, one cannot answer the question, "What is a potential cause of giving garbage collectors more training?"

If a major causal category has no entries, the group may have inadvertently defined the problem in a way that excludes that category. In such cases, facilitators may intervene by noting the group's difficulty, testing their observation, and suggesting that the group redefine the problem.

Sometimes, in brainstorming potential causes, group members identify similar causes under different categories. For example, in Figure 8.2, "residents overfill trash cans" is a *people* cause that is also a root of the *methods* cause "garbage can tops not secured." This occurs because a fishbone diagram artificially separates the causal categories, all of which are related in the real word. It is natural, for example, for a people cause to be the root of a methods cause. Rather than trying to avoid such causal redundancy, the facilitator should help the group see how the redundancies create important links among the causal categories. By doing this, the facilitator helps the group develop an integrated causal map of the problem it is trying to solve.

The purpose of the fishbone process is to brainstorm or make educated guesses about root causes. However, the group must then collect data to determine whether and to what extent each cause speculated is in fact a cause. When members have completed this step, they have agreed on a causal map of the problem that is based on valid information.

Sometimes, groups may find it easier to identify root causes (step three) before they develop criteria for evaluating solutions (step two). After members have identified root causes, however, they are naturally motivated to generate alternative solutions (step four), and may be less interested in developing criteria for evaluating solutions.

Step Four: Generate Alternative Solutions

Groups commonly suffer from two problems in step four. First, they combine generating alternatives with evaluating them. When one member suggests a solution, other members quickly offer reasons why it will not work. Second, groups have trouble identifying a substantial number of potential solutions. In part, this results from members who are prematurely evaluating each others' ideas. As a result, members become concerned that others will disparage them and so are reluctant to offer ideas. But members can also have difficulty generating ideas because they make assumptions that place unnecessary constraints on their own thinking about the solution. As with developing criteria, **every unnecessary assumption reduces the number of potential solutions.**

Several interventions can help the group avoid the pitfalls. First, at the beginning of the step, the facilitator can ask the group to brainstorm alternatives, using the rules in Exhibit 8.1. Members may, however, ask others to simply clarify their brainstormed solutions. Intervening quickly when a member has violated the brainstorming rules will help the group generate more ideas.

Second, the facilitator can help the group identify the assumptions underlying its alternative solutions and determine whether the assumptions are necessary. For example, underlying an entire set of proposed solutions might be the assumption that the solution must involve only those who are currently involved in the problem. If the assumption is unwarranted and discarded, members can generate new sets of solutions, unconstrained by the assumption. If the assumption is warranted, the assumption should be translated into an additional criterion for evaluating solutions.

Third, when the group has exhausted its ideas for solutions, the facilitator can encourage members to combine different aspects of previously generated solutions. Some solutions are likely to integrate the best aspects of various ideas and also are more likely to find consensus in the group.

One choice that members face is whether they should consider the criteria when generating alternative solutions. By considering the criteria, members are likely to generate fewer solutions, but those generated are more likely to conform to the criteria. However, by not considering the criteria, members may generate some workable solutions that are inconsistent with the identified criteria, thereby calling into question the necessity for some criteria. The latter approach takes more time but can serve as a check against arbitrary criteria. (Resource G identifies further readings for increasing the number of creative ideas.)

Step Five: Evaluate Alternative Solutions

In step five, the group weighs the alternative solutions against the previously established criteria. This can be done with various degrees of structure. In a highly structured approach, members can develop a matrix (see Figure 8.3), with each of the criteria listed on one axis and each alternative solution on the other. The criteria can be weighted if some are more important than others. For each solution, each member assigns a score to each criterion (for example, from one to ten, with ten the highest score); the score is based on the extent to which that solution meets that criterion. The group score for each alternative solution is determined by following these steps:

1. If the criteria are weighted, for each criterion multiply each member's score by the weight of the respective criterion.

Figure 8.3. Matrix for Evaluating Alternative Solutions.

	Criteria												Solution scores
Solutions	Criterion 1 × (weight)				Criterion 2 × (weight)				Criterion 3 × (weight)				
	Ann	Al	Jo	Lee	Ann	Al	Jo	Lee	Ann	Al	Jo	Lee	
Solution 1													
Solution 2													
Solution 3													
Solution 4													
Solution 5													

2. For each criterion, find the average of the members' scores by adding the results from step one and dividing by the number of members.
3. Add the results from step two for all the criteria.

Solutions that receive higher scores are considered more favorable by the group.

In a less structured approach, each group member gives an overall score to each alternative without scoring each criterion separately. The score for each alternative is determined by finding the average of the members' scores for that solution.

The facilitator needs to be careful when using evaluation matrices to help groups make decisions. Evaluation matrices are simply tools to help the group make better decisions. They should not be thought of as formulas that will automatically produce correct answers. Because the results of evaluation matrices are typically based on the average of members' scores, one or two members may drastically influence the group score by rating one solution very high or very low. Similarly, the solution with the highest score may be one that no member is committed to implementing. Therefore, evaluation matrices do not take the place of group discussion and the group's collective judgment.

In the evaluation step, the facilitator can help the group understand why members evaluate the same solution differently. If members have reached consensus on the criteria and are weighing the solutions against them, the intervention will focus on why members disagree about the extent to which a particular solution meets a given criterion. However, if the group has reached consensus on the criteria but is not weighing the solutions against them, the intervention will focus on the inconsistency. This occurs when a member is unknowingly applying additional criteria or has a hidden agenda.

Step Six: Select the Best Solution

Selecting the best decision requires that the group have some ground rule for making decisions, such as consensus or majority vote. Establishing this ground rule is part of the contracting process described in Chapter Three.

If the group is having difficulty making a consensus decision, the facilitator should identify when members are pressuring others to agree instead of allowing each member to make a free choice. The facilitator's interventions will focus on helping the group find an integrative decision by clarifying the specific issue of disagreement, clarifying interests, and then identifying ways to integrate similar interests and dovetail different interests. As a result of the interventions, the group may identify new solutions.

Step Seven: Develop an Action Plan

Developing an action plan increases the likelihood that the solution will be implemented effectively and on time. Here too, groups can choose from among a variety of types of action plans. Figure 8.4 shows an action-planning chart that identifies the steps needed to implement the solution, the objective to be achieved by completing each step, the date each step was assigned, when each step is be started, when each step is to be completed, the resources needed to complete the step, who is responsible for completing each step, and the current status of each step.

The facilitator can help the group avoid some common pitfalls that are typical for groups using these techniques. First, the group's energy and attention may wane during this step (and subsequent steps) if members view having agreed on a solution as the culmination of the problem-solving process. Like fans who leave a sporting event before it is over, members may lose interest if they believe that the outcome is no longer in doubt. By sharing this observation with the group, the facilitator can help the group refocus or decide to continue at a later date.

Second, the group may underestimate the time or other resources necessary to complete each task in the action plan. This may occur because members do not have valid information or because they have a fixed deadline for implementation. Although it is not the facilitator's role to identify realistic time frames for substantive decisions, the facilitator can intervene by asking members to consider how they arrived at the time frames. Finally, the group may assign tasks to individuals who are not present (and over whom they have no authority), without checking whether the individuals are available. Here, the facilitator can point out that the action plan is not final until the assignments have been agreed to.

Another facilitator intervention involves helping the group plan for unintended consequences. As a rational tool, action planning can create an illusion that the plan will be implemented exactly as it appears on the chart that members have created. In reality, however, groups often work on problems that are so complex that unintended consequences occur that require changing the implementation plan midstream. Group members may not be able to predict unintended consequences; however, the facilitator can help them develop an action plan that is flexible enough to be modified.

Figure 8.4. Action-Planning Chart.

Step	Objective	Date assigned	Start date	Completion date	Resources	Responsibility	Status

Step Eight: Implement the Action Plan

Much implementation typically takes place outside the facilitated group, which obviously prevents the facilitator from intervening directly. For implementation that occurs within the group, the facilitator's interventions depend on the nature of the group's process. The facilitator can help the group implement effectively by suggesting that project updates be added to each meeting's agenda so that the group has a regular way to check its progress. Similarly, the facilitator can help the group determine who has oversight responsibility for different parts of the action plan.

Step Nine: Evaluate Outcomes and the Process

Evaluation is probably the step most often underemphasized in problem-solving models—and some models do not even include this step. One reason groups do not conduct adequate evaluations is because they take additional time, which groups do not have. Another reason is that evaluation can be politically unpopular, especially if the group is punished as a result of identifying problems with its solution. Groups also forgo evaluation to avoid cognitive dissonance (Festinger, 1957), psychological discomfort that in this case arises when members are faced with data that challenge their beliefs about the effectiveness of the project. In a group in which all members are not internally committed to the solution, uncommitted members may push for evaluation, hoping to find data that will support their views. Those who are committed to the solution may be reluctant to evaluate, because they are concerned that negative evaluation results will reopen the entire issue.

All these concerns are understandable. However, some evaluation is essential for a group that values valid information. If the group does identify problems, it can decide whether to make changes to correct them.

Several interventions are associated with this step. First, the facilitator helps the group explore its reluctance to evaluate. After identifying the barriers, the group can decide whether it can reduce them sufficiently to conduct an evaluation. As part of the intervention, the facilitator may help the group reframe the meaning of evaluation from one of political or psychological threat to one in which members seek continuous improvement in their work. Second, the facilitator can help the group consider how comprehensive the evaluation should be. While some projects warrant sophisticated surveys and analyses of records, others need only brief conversations with key individuals. For example, the facilitator might begin by asking, "What is needed for you to know how well the solution is working, and if it is not working, why isn't it?" Finally, the facilitator can call the group's attention to evaluating the process by which the solution was implemented as well as the outcomes. Just as the problem-solving process affects the quality and acceptance of the group's decisions, the implementation process affects the quality and acceptance of the solution.

Summary

This chapter described a problem-solving model that groups can use to identify and solve problems. The steps in the model are identifying the problem, establishing criteria for evaluating solutions, identifying causes, generating alternative solutions, evaluating alternative solutions, selecting the best solution, developing an action plan, implementing the action plan, and evaluating outcomes and the process. The chapter also discussed interventions that facilitators make at each step to help a group use the model.

In general, the problem-solving model represents a group of relatively macro interventions that facilitators can make to help a group improve its effectiveness. Yet, group members can follow the problem-solving model steps and still act in ways that reduce the group's effectiveness.

Chapter Nine Helping the Group Follow Its Ground Rules

Regardless of the particular problems groups are trying to solve, they can increase their effectiveness by following the sixteen ground rules discussed in Chapter Four (Exhibit 4.1, page 75). Consequently, a major part of facilitators' work is helping group members follow the ground rules that the group has agreed to use. This chapter shows how facilitators apply the diagnostic-intervention cycle (Chapters Four and Six) to intervene on each ground rule, taking into account several of the factors discussed in Chapter Five.

Intervening on the ground rules is based on two principles. First, **people experience psychological discomfort (cognitive dissonance) when they become aware that they hold two or more thoughts that are logically inconsistent.** Second, **people are motivated to reduce the dissonance** (Festinger, 1957). In the case of ground rules, members experience dissonance when they realize they have acted in a manner that is inconsistent with what they have agreed is functional behavior.

To rationally reduce their dissonance, members have several options. First, they can change their behavior so it is more consistent with what they have agreed is functional behavior. The option leads members to improve group process. Second, they can change their belief that the ground rules represent functional behavior. This leads members to reconsider or reject the ground rules. This requires that members retract their explicit commitment to act consistently with the ground rules, which can create additional dissonance. Finally, members can add another belief that reduces the inconsistency between two other beliefs (Festinger, 1957). For example, a member could reason that she acted inconsistently with the ground rules because she believed the ground rules were not appropriate in that particular situation. To maintain the group members' free choice, the facilitator cannot force members to change their dysfunctional behavior.

By intervening when members act inconsistently with the ground rules, the facilitator's interventions are essentially sanctioned by the group. However, even if group members do not choose to adopt the full set of principles for effective group process, the facilitator may still use them to intervene. This is why it is important to distinguish ground rules from principles for group effectiveness. If a group explicitly agrees to follow some of the principles, the principles become the group's ground rules. However, regardless of how many ground rules the group decides to use—and even if the group decides to use none of them—the items remain principles for effective group process and can guide the facilitator's interventions. When a group has not explicitly agreed to follow the ground rules, the facilitator intervenes by using the three steps in the intervention cycle; however, the facilitator either does not refer specifically to the relevant ground rule or does so by describing it as a principle of group effectiveness and acknowledging that the group has not agreed to follow the principle.

While a group can make a free and informed choice to use none of the ground rules, it cannot require that a facilitator not intervene with the principles. To do so would prevent facilitators from using their expertise to help the group become more effective. However, the group is free to pursue or not pursue a facilitator's intervention.

As Chapter Four discussed, facilitators must decide whether to intervene when a member has acted inconsistently with the ground rules. Learning to use the ground rules is challenging work that takes time. When groups are just beginning to learn to use the ground rules, members' comments frequently are inconsistent with them. Yet, if the facilitator intervenes each time a member acts inconsistently with the ground rules, the group may spend little time on its substantive tasks, and members may quickly become frustrated. **A skilled facilitator balances the need to intervene on dysfunctional behavior with members' rate of learning and their need to accomplish substantive tasks.**

Interventions about behavior inconsistent with ground rules can be made at different depths and in accordance with different levels of the group's diagnostic and intervention skills (see Chapter Five for a discussion of depth of interventions). However, at a minimum, the interventions occur at the third level (instrumental), unless the facilitator intervenes in accordance with the first level of skill.

This chapter describes for each ground rule some typical diagnostic cues (observable behavior) for facilitator intervention and some verbatim examples of interventions. Readers may want to refer to the intervention steps in Figure 6.2 on page 128. Across ground rules, I vary the depth of intervention (Figure 5.1, page 111). The interventions vary according to the group members' skills (Table 6.2, page 137), but focus mostly on interventions aimed at the beginner level (level one), because they illustrate more completely the three intervention steps.

To complete an intervention on a ground rule, facilitators typically check for agreement after sharing their observations, inferences, and suggestions for change (see Figure 6.2 on page 128). Consequently, the course of the facilitator's intervention on a ground rule is contingent on the responses of the member (or members) who are the focus of the intervention. The examples include notes about the contingencies with the bracketed phrase [*if yes, continue*]. If, for example, the member agrees with the observations, the facilitator continues to share inferences based on those observations. Similarly, if the member agrees with the facilitator's inferences, the facilitator asks the member if the member would like to change the relevant behavior. In most of the examples, in order to focus on the specific ground rule, the assumption is that the member (or members) agree with the facilitator's observations, inferences, and suggestions for change. **If, however, the member disagrees with the facilitator's observations or inferences, the facilitator responds in a similar way, regardless of the ground rule intervened on; the facilitator, the member, and the rest of the group clarify their disagreement by sharing relevant information, testing their assumptions, agreeing on what important words mean, and by using any other relevant ground rules. If necessary, they jointly design a way to test their disagreement. After the group reaches agreement, the facilitator continues with the intervention steps to complete the diagnosis-intervention cycle.**

Test Assumptions and Inferences

Diagnostic Cues	*Intervention Examples*
A member's statement has important but (by definition, unspecified) implications.	"Ted, I need to test an inference. When the group was discussing using these ground rules with the director, you said, 'These ground rules are fine for the group but forget about using them with the director.' Am I accurate? [*If yes, continue.*] I'm inferring that you don't believe that if the group acted consistently with the ground rules, it would help it work more effectively with the director. Am I inferring correctly?" [*Beginner skill level, instrumental depth level.*]
"I'm assuming Sarah didn't invite me because she felt I wouldn't support her project."	"Linda, you said, 'I'm assuming Sarah didn't invite me because she felt I wouldn't support her project.' Rather than assume, would you be willing to check your assumption directly with Sarah?" [*Intermediate skill level, interpersonal depth level.*]

One or more members do something that seems significant but that the facilitator cannot make sense of.

[*Addressing the entire group*] "I'm wondering what people are thinking and feeling. For the last fifteen minutes, you have been discussing how you conduct performance appraisals in the organization. You agreed to discuss it after several of you—Carrie, Sam, and Ellen—said it was very important. Is that right? [*If yes, continue.*] And yet, as I look around the room, I notice that only Ellen and Ken have talked, while people on this side of the room are gazing out the window. Let me stop for a minute and see if others see the same thing. [*If yes, continue.*] I'm inferring something's going on, but I have no idea what. What accounts for your reactions?" [*Beginner skill level, open-ended depth level.*]

Facilitators help members test inferences they make about each other and also to test inferences facilitators make about group members. The latter sometimes consists simply of stating observed behavior and asking a person what it means. Other times, facilitators may state the behavior and share the inference they have made. At still other times, facilitators may state that they have several inferences they could make and ask the person to help identify which, if any, of the inferences is accurate. Finally, facilitators may share their observations and note that they have made no inference. Following the principle of sharing all relevant information, facilitators should, in testing inferences, share any inferences they have made.

Share All Relevant Information

Diagnostic Cues

Member takes one side of an issue rather than describing the advantages and disadvantages.

Intervention Examples

"You have given a number of reasons why it would not be a good idea to start the project. I have not heard you give any reasons why—if at all—it would be a good idea. Would you agree? [*If yes, continue.*] Do you see any reasons for starting the project?" [*Beginner skill level, performance depth level.*]

Focus on Interests, Not Positions

Diagnostic Cues	*Intervention Examples*
"My suggestion is X [*states solution*]."	"Bill, what is it about your suggestion that makes it a good solution?" [*Beginner skill level, performance depth level.*] "Bill, I think your statement is inconsistent with one of the ground rules. Do you see which one?" [*Beginner or intermediate skill level, depending on whether facilitator or Bill redesigns the behavior; performance depth level.*]
"I know this solution meets my interests, but it's still not acceptable to me."	"Jean, you said the solution meets your interests but is still not acceptable. Is that right? [*If yes, continue.*] And every other member has said the solution meets his or her interest. [*Checking with all members*] Do you agree? [*If yes, continue.*] I'm inferring that you have other interests you have not shared with the group. Am I correct?" [*Beginner skill level, open-ended depth level, depending on interest that Jean reveals.*]
A member has discussed interests in avoiding negative outcomes and has not discussed interests in creating positive outcomes.	"Bob, you said your interest is to have a budget process that does not lead people to 'play budget games.' Yes? [*If yes, continue.*] You have stated your interest in terms of something you do not want to happen, would you agree? [*If yes, continue.*] Can you also describe any interests you have in terms of what you *do* want to happen? That will make it easier for the group to devise a solution that not only avoids the negative outcomes of 'budget games' but also creates positive outcomes consistent with your interests. Can you say what those interests are?" [*Beginner skill level, open-ended depth level.*]

Members are having a difficult time identifying their interests.

"One way to identify your interests is to work backward from solutions. Think of your ideal solution for this problem. Now ask yourself, what aspects or qualities of the solution make it ideal? Let's go around the room and have each person say what those aspects or qualities are, OK?" [*Beginner skill level, open-ended depth level. This intervention also involves teaching concepts and methods.*]

Be Specific—Use Examples

Diagnostic Cues

Intervention Examples

Members make general statements such as, "There are times when . . . ," "Some people don't . . . ," and "This problem has come up before. . . ."

"Sue, when you say, 'They are making us look bad,' exactly who are 'they' and 'us'?" [*Beginner skill level, interpersonal depth level.*]

"Alan, you said, 'Some people have been talking too much.' One of the ground rules is to be specific and use examples. Unless you mention the members' names, the group cannot validate your observation. Do you agree? [*If yes, continue.*] Which members do you think were talking too much and when?" [*Beginner skill level (skipping step to check for agreement for observation), interpersonal depth level. The intervention includes a conceptual explanation of the reasons for being specific.*]

Agree On What Important Words Mean

Diagnostic Cues

Intervention Examples

Members are using different words to describe what seems to be the same event, person, and so on.

A word or phrase becomes central to a discussion.

"Each of you has used the word *minutes* to describe what should be summarized from the meetings. One of the ground rules is to agree on what important words mean. It would help to make sure that each of you is using the word minutes to mean the same thing or, if not, to agree on a meaning. How about if each of you says what you mean by minutes. It would also help to say what the word minutes does not mean to you." [*Beginner skill level (skipping first test for agreement), open-ended depth level, depending on the important words.*]

Explain the Reasons Behind
One's Statements, Questions, and Actions

Diagnostic Cues	*Intervention Examples*
"I just think we should do it the way I suggested."	"I understand what you want to do, but I don't understand why. One of the group's ground rules is to explain the reasons behind statements. What are your reasons for wanting to do it that way?" [*Beginner skill level, open-ended depth level.*]
Someone makes a statement that does not seem logical.	"I don't see how your second statement automatically follows from the first. You said, 'The group cannot currently accomplish the job,' yes? [*If yes, continue.*] And then you said, 'The group is incapable of doing the job, and it needs to be given to another group,' yes? [*If yes, continue.*] I don't see how your second statement necessarily follows from your first. Can you explain how it does?" [*Beginner skill level, performance depth level.*]
Someone makes two statements that seem inconsistent.	"I think you have said two things that are inconsistent and I want to see if you agree. Earlier you said, 'X.' Do you agree that is what you said? [*If yes, continue.*] And just now you said, 'Y.' Is that accurate? [*If yes, continue.*] The two statements seem inconsistent

to me because Z. If they do not seem inconsistent to you, would you explain how you see them as being consistent?" [*Beginner skill level, depth level depends on the substance of the two statements.*]

Disagree Openly with Any Member of the Group

Diagnostic Cues	*Intervention Examples*
When introducing the ground rules, the facilitator envisions that members could be reluctant to disagree with each other.	"One of our ground rules is to openly disagree with any member of the group. I believe it is natural and helpful for members to constructively disagree with each other. Open disagreement can lead to higher-quality decisions and greater support for the decisions. I also know from working with other groups that it can be difficult to disagree openly with other members, especially if they have more expertise, authority, or power than you. I raise this issue with you not because I have inferred that people are reluctant to disagree but because your group has members from all levels of the hierarchy who also report to each other. I realize you may be reluctant to answer, but does anyone have any concerns about disagreeing openly with anyone in the group? [*If yes, discuss the concerns; if no, continue.*] If at any time you do have concerns, they are appropriate to raise in the group." [*Beginner skill level, interpersonal depth level. This intervention combines conceptual explanation and reframing. It does not address dysfunctional behavior.*]
Members who have openly disagreed become quiet when another member, especially one of higher authority, states a position.	[*Addressing the full group*] "I want to describe a pattern I have observed and test an inference. Everyone was actively discussing and disagreeing with

each other about whether to contract out for the service until Ted said that he thought it should be done in house. After that, no one disagreed with Ted. Would you agree with my observation? [*If yes, continue.*] I also observed this earlier on the following issues: X, Y, Z. [*Check for agreement again.*] Because everyone in the group reports to Ted, one possible inference I make is that there is something about the supervisor-subordinate relationship between each of you and Ted that leads you to stop disagreeing after he has stated his point of view. My question is: is my inference accurate, and if not, what leads each of you to stop your discussion once Ted offers his opinion?" [*Beginner skill level, interpersonal or intrapersonal depth level.*]

Make Statements, Then Invite Questions and Comments

Diagnostic Cues	*Intervention Examples*
A member asks a question that seems to have a statement embedded in it.	"Robin, you just asked Gail, 'Do you really think that will work?' Yes? [*If yes, continue.*] I inferred from your tone that you were also making a statement—that you do not believe it will work. Am I right? [*If yes, continue.*] How would you restate it in order to be consistent with the ground rules?" [*Intermediate skill level, instrumental depth level.*]
	"Robin, do you see what you just said?" [*Robin describes her behavior as inconsistent with the ground rule and redesigns it.*] [*Advanced skill level, instrumental depth level.*]

The facilitator infers that a member made a statement so that others would respond to it, but the member did not directly ask others to respond. For example, "I think we should cancel the offer, but maybe I'm the only one."

Facilitator: Jim, how could you say that in a manner consistent with the ground rules to encourage people to respond?

Jim: I think we should cancel it, but I'm wondering if anyone else agrees. What do others think?

Facilitator: Yes. [*Advanced skill level, instrumental depth level.*]

Jointly Design Ways to Test Disagreements and Solutions

Diagnostic Cues	*Intervention Examples*
Members disagree about the facts of a situation.	"Chris and Ellen, do you agree that the two of you disagree about whether the program paid for itself? [*If yes, continue.*] How could you jointly design a way to test the areas of your disagreement?" [*Advanced skill level, performance depth level.*]
Members engaged in a disagreement assume that one of them is incorrect.	"Chris and Ellen, I am inferring from your statements that each of you is assuming that only one of you can be correct. Am I inferring correctly? [*If yes, continue.*] Another possibility is that each of you is partially correct because each of you is referring to something different: a different time period, a different part of the program, or some other difference. One way to test this is by being specific and using examples—another one of the group's ground rules. How about if we see whether each of you is referring to exactly the same thing?" [*Beginner skill level (without sharing directly observable behavior), open-ended depth level.*]

Discuss Undiscussable Issues

Diagnostic Cues

The group has not raised an issue that seems central to the problem the group is discussing. The issue may be merely undiscussed rather than undiscussable.

Intervention Examples

"I have not heard anyone raise the issue of whether the project can be completed within the deadline the group has set for itself. Has anyone raised this issue? [*If no, continue.*] This issue seems central to your decision, do you agree?" [*Beginner skill level, performance depth level.*]

The facilitator infers that members are withholding relevant information because it has been undiscussable in the group. Cues involve members who are discussing a problem in abstract terms, alluding to a situation without fully discussing it, answering the facilitator's specific questions in general terms, nervous laughter, silence, and members who are glancing knowingly at each other.

"I want to share some observations and raise what may be an undiscussable issue. The group has been discussing problems with providing service to clients. At least three of you—Bob, Pat, and Sandra—have mentioned that one problem is that some managers act inconsistently with what they espouse. Specifically, they tell their employees that they (the employees) have the autonomy to correct the client's problem on the spot, but when the employees do so, the managers reprimand them for not checking with them first. Is that right? [*If yes, continue.*] And on several occasions, Tom (the supervisor of some group members), you have agreed that could be a problem, but that you do not know any supervisors who acted that way. Is that right? [*If yes, continue.*] Tom, when you said that, I noticed Bob and Sandra rolling their eyes and glancing toward each other. [*To Bob and Sandra*] Would you agree? [*If yes, continue.*] From all of this, I'm inferring—and this is what I think may be an undiscussable issue—that the two of you (Bob and Sandra) believe that Tom is one of those supervisors he says he doesn't know of. Bob and Sandra, is my inference accurate?" [*Beginner skill level, interpersonal depth level.*]

Keep the Discussion Focused

Diagnostic Cues

The topic of conversation seems to switch without the group's explicitly agreeing to do so.

Intervention Examples

"I think the group has gone off track. I'll tell you why I think so and you tell me whether you agree or not. A minute ago, the group was talking about when to schedule other quality improvement meetings. Then Andy asked, 'Is there a better way to do technical training?' and Don suggested you could 'bring in people who knew what they were talking about.' Is that how the conversation went? [*If yes, continue.*] One of your ground rules is to stay focused, to stay on track. I think Andy's and Don's comments about improving training are off track because they don't help the group decide when to meet. Andy and Don, do you agree or disagree? [*If yes, continue.*] Do the rest of you agree or disagree? [*If yes, continue.*] What does the group want to do? Do you want to continue the conversation about when to meet or discuss the training? [*A few members say they want to return to original topic.*] Does anyone have a problem with Bob's suggestion to finish talking about when to meet and decide at the end of the meeting when to talk about technical training? [*If no, continue.*] OK, I'll put the issue of technical training on the flip chart to remind you to come back to it. Cynthia, you were the last person to talk before the conversation went off track. Would you repeat what you said?" [*Intermediate skill level, instrumental depth level.*]

"What just happened?" [*Advanced skill level, instrumental depth level.*]

"This is off the topic, but . . ."

"Bob, Sarah, and Julie, I have a question for you about getting off track. One of the group's ground rules is to stay focused, to stay on track. Just now Bob said, 'This is off the topic, but . . .' Have I quoted you accurately? [*If yes, continue.*] Sarah and Julie said the same thing earlier today. Sarah said it when she mentioned X, and Julie said it when she said 'Y.' Do you remember saying that? [*If yes, continue.*] My question is: What is it that leads you to know you are off track and then continue to take the discussion off track? I am asking this because by exploring the answer, you may figure out a way to change your behavior, if you want." [*Beginner skill level, intrapersonal depth level.*]

The group is on topic but is discussing several related issues simultaneously and, as a result, is not making progress.

"I hear three related issues being discussed simultaneously. First, Ellen has raised the issue of X. Ellen, have I captured it accurately? [*If yes, continue.*] Beth has raised the issue of Y. Right? [*If yes, continue.*] And Sam has raised the issue of Z. Right? [*If yes, continue.*] The issues are related but can be discussed one at a time. Do members agree? [*If yes, continue.*] Which one issue, if any, would be better to start with?" [*Beginner skill level, instrumental depth level.*]

Members have made related comments but have not identified the common issue.

"I think there is a common issue expressed in your comments. Let me identify it, and see if you agree or not. This issue is this: How do you work with a group of people with whom you are interdependent but over whom you have no formal authority.

Have I accurately described the issue?" [*Beginner skill level (skipping sharing observation step), instrumental depth level.*]

Members do not seem to see the ways in which their ideas are similar.

"Ted and Tom, I'm inferring from your comments to each other about ideas for redesigning the work flow as being 'totally unworkable' that you don't see that your ideas are similar in any way. Do you see any similarity? [*If no, continue.*] Let me tell you the similarity I see and get your reaction. I think your ideas are similar because they both X. Do you agree?" [*Beginner skill level (skipping testing observation), instrumental depth level.*]

Members do not seem to understand what others are saying.

"Jan, what I think Jill is saying is not that she wants to violate the law but that she cannot figure out how to both act within the law and act consistently with the organization's principles of effective management. Jill, is that what you are saying? [*If yes, continue.*] Jan, do you understand what Jill is saying?" [*Beginner skill level (skipping sharing observations), performance depth level.*]

Members are focused on topic but from a perspective that makes it difficult to solve the problem in a way that is consistent with its ground rules.

"You have been thinking about whom to invite in terms of *who will support* your project. Another way to think about it, more consistent with your ground rule of exchanging relevant information with nongroup members, is *whose support will you need* to implement the project, whether or not you believe those members support it. By inviting members whom you believe do not support you, you can find out why and see what interests you would need to meet to have them support the project. By taking this approach, you generate more relevant information, increase the chance of meeting others' interests, and therefore increase the chance that the project will be implemented successfully. What do you think about the approach I've described? Is it more consistent with your ground rules?" [*Beginner skill level, instrumental depth level. This intervention uses a conceptual explanation to help the group reframe its thinking.*]

The facilitator has been unable to get the group's attention because several conversations are occurring simultaneously (or members are yelling at each other).

"Time out. Several conversations are going on at once. Jan and Bob are talking to each other, Sam, Ruth, and Josh are talking, and Bob and Mary are taking lunch orders. One of our ground rules is to stay focused. How do you want to proceed?" [*Intermediate skill level (skipping test of observation), instrumental depth level.*]

The group seems to have discussed all the relevant issues and is repeating itself.

"I'm wondering whether the group is ready to make a decision. Several people have just repeated things that others have said before. For example, 'X.' Would you agree? [*If yes, continue.*] Does anyone have any other questions or comments or are you ready to move to the next step?" [*Beginner skill level, structural-functional depth level.*]

The group is about to exceed the amount of time it agreed to spend on a topic.

"You agreed to discuss this topic until ten-fifteen. It is now ten-fifteen. Do you want to continue this discussion, move on to another topic, or take some other approach?" [*Beginner skill level, performance depth level.*]

Don't Take Cheap Shots or Otherwise Distract the Group

Diagnostic Cues   *Intervention Examples*

A member has made what could be perceived as a cheap shot.

"Larry, I'm wondering if that was a cheap shot at Bob. Was it, Larry? [*If yes, continue.*] Larry, what was the point you were trying to make?" [*Beginner skill level, interpersonal depth level.*]

"Larry, I think your last statement was inconsistent with the ground rules." [*Larry identifies his cheap shot and redesigns his statement.*] [*Advanced skill level, interpersonal depth level.*]

All Members Are Expected to Participate in All Phases of the Process

Diagnostic Cues	*Intervention Examples*
One or more members have been silent for a period of time.	"Jennifer, Ted, and Sue, I haven't heard you say anything for the past twenty minutes. Am I correct? [*If yes, continue.*] One of the group's ground rules is for all members to participate in all phases of the process. Is there something any of you can add to the discussion?" [*Beginner skill level, instrumental depth level.*]
A member is having difficulty stating what he wants to say. For example, "Never mind. I don't know how to say it."	"Bill, don't worry about finding the exact words now. What is the basic point you want to make?" [*Beginner skill level, depth level depends on Bill's previous comment.*]
One member interrupts another.	"Bob, I think Ann wasn't finished talking when you started to speak. Am I right, Ann? [*If yes, and if Bob does not indicate that Ann should continue, the facilitator continues.*] Bob, would you be willing to let Ann finish?" [*Beginner skill level, instrumental depth level.*]

Exchange Relevant Information with Nongroup Members

Diagnostic Cues

The group has not discussed whether nongroup members have information that would help the group reach a better decision or whether the group has information appropriate to share with nongroup members.

Intervention Examples

"I see an inconsistency between your decisions and your ground rule about sharing appropriate information with nongroup members. Let me share my observations and see if you agree. You have just decided to make recommendations to the manager in a way that not only considers but meets the interests of all the parties involved. Right? [*If yes, continue.*] But you have also just decided not to share your discussions with any department employees until you have reached a decision, because you are concerned that employees will jump to invalid conclusions about what the group will do. Is that right? [*If yes, continue.*] The inconsistency I see is this: By not sharing the highlights of your discussions until you reach a decision, you withhold relevant information that department members could use to tell you whether you understood and were meeting their interests. Consequently, you decrease the chance that you will make decisions that *will* meet all parties' interests. Now, do you see your decisions as inconsistent with the ground rules and the goal you said you wanted to achieve?" [*Beginner skill level, instrumental depth level.*]

When a group meets with nongroup members to share appropriate information, the facilitator's interventions will vary according to whether a group member or nongroup member is the focus and nongroup members have the same contract with the facilitator as group members. For example, the group may have agreed to follow certain ground rules of which the nongroup members are unaware. Or, even if group and nongroup members have agreed to follow the ground rules, only group members may have agreed to developmental facilitation. Consequently, the facilitator's interventions with nongroup members are likely to remain at the first skill level and avoid the fourth and fifth depths of intervention. In any event, the facilitator needs to briefly contract with the non-group members regarding the facilitator's role in the meeting.

Make Decisions by Consensus

Diagnostic Cues	*Intervention Examples*
The group is about to check for consensus.	"Bob, before you check for consensus, would you restate exactly what you're asking people for consensus on?" [*Beginner skill level, depth level depends on subject of consensus.*]
"OK, it's decided. Let's move on."	"Dan, I didn't hear each person consent. Does everyone agree that X? Bob, Joan, Sue, Pam, Al, Andy?" [*Intermediate skill level, depth level depends on subject of consensus.*]
	"Dan, I didn't hear everyone give his or her consent, did you? [*If no, continue.*] How about checking for consensus?" [*Beginner skill level, depth level depends on subject of consensus.*]
	Facilitator: "Wait a second, Dan, I think you forgot something." *Dan:* "Oh right, consensus." [*proceeds to seek consensus from all members*] [*Advanced skill level, depth level depends on subject of consensus.*]
"OK, I'll agree. Do it that way if you want."	"Sue, you have given some reasons for not wanting to X, and now you say, 'I'll agree.' I'm wondering whether you are feeling pressured to agree. [*If no*] What has led you to change your mind? [*If yes*] What are you feeling pressured by?" [*Beginner skill level, interpersonal or intrapersonal depth level.*]

Do Self-Critiques

Diagnostic Cues	*Intervention Examples*
The group is starting the self-critique.	"Remember, the three questions for the self-critique are: What ground rules did individuals use well? What ground rules do individuals need to improve on? Exactly what will people do differently next time to improve? For each question, be specific—give examples." [*Beginner skill level, open-ended depth level. This intervention involves teaching concepts and methods.*]

Summary

This chapter described and gave examples of how facilitators intervene when group members act inconsistently with the ground rules. When making the interventions, facilitators take into account the skill level of members and how deep the intervention should be. The course of the facilitator's intervention on a ground rule is contingent on whether the member (or members) agree with the facilitator's observations and inferences. Consequently, if members disagree with the facilitator's observations or inferences, the facilitator and group members need to resolve the disagreement before continuing with the intervention steps.

As Chapter Six discussed, although members have agreed intellectually to follow the ground rules, and even if the facilitator tests for agreement at each intervention step, the actual discomfort of being confronted with dysfunctional behavior and being asked whether they want to change it in front of other group members can lead members to respond emotionally. Group members may also experience a range of emotions when dealing with previously undiscussable issues and issues they feel strongly about. Facilitators must be prepared to address these emotions.

Chapter Ten Dealing with Emotions

Facilitators help groups to solve difficult, conflict-ridden problems. While working on these problems, group members may sometimes become emotional. They may lash out in anger or frustration or withdraw in sadness or fear. Dealing with these emotions poses a particularly great challenge for groups and their facilitators. Skilled facilitators help members express their emotions in a way that contributes to rather than detracts from the group's effectiveness.

This chapter discusses how facilitators intervene on emotional behavior. It describes how emotions are generated and how people express them, and how facilitators intervene on behaviors that stem from negative and positive emotions, including emotional reactions toward facilitators.

Here, it is worth repeating an earlier point: **group facilitation is not therapy. The purpose of dealing with emotions that arise in group facilitation is to help the group become more effective at its work, not to change people's personalities or to focus on emotions for their own sake. To be appropriate, the facilitator's interventions on members' emotional behaviors must relate to the group's effectiveness.**

How Emotions Are Generated and Expressed

One way to begin is by considering, in an oversimplified way, how a person comes to express negative emotions (McConnell, 1986). (Recognizing that psychological research has not produced a consensus regarding how people experience emotions, this oversimplified explanation uses a cognitive perspective, which is consistent with the general orientation of the book.) A person is constantly exposed to various events, circumstances, and behaviors. A person cognitively evaluates the events, circumstances, and others' behaviors. The person who finds them threatening will experience a negative feeling and some physical arousal (for example, increased heart and breathing rate) or depression, which together create an emotion. Finally, a person will typically express the emotion in some form of behavior.

The facilitator helps the group identify, express, and discuss the emotions in a way that increases rather than decreases the group's effectiveness. To do this, the facilitator needs to know the factors (events, circumstances, and behaviors) that contribute to generating emotions in facilitation, the ways in which members express the emotions, and how to intervene on emotions that members express.

Factors That Contribute to Generating Negative Emotions

Knowing what factors contribute to negative emotions helps facilitators predict when a discussion is likely to become emotional. This gives facilitators extra time to plan any interventions they may need to make. To the extent that a facilitator can control these factors, the facilitator can even influence whether or how much a discussion becomes emotional.

Many factors contribute to generating negative emotions. Four major related factors are the content of the subject being discussed, the nature of the facilitator-client relationship, the depth of the facilitator's interventions, and how members think, which include the relationships among group members.

The Content of the Subject Being Discussed. The content of emotionally hot topics presents members with a threat of personal loss, such as losing social support, income, valued status symbols, familiar surroundings, opportunity to do interesting things, well-being (Sutton & Shurman, 1985), or control over some important part of their lives. Examples of emotionally hot topics can include performance appraisal, office relocations, employee titles, organizational restructuring, mergers, and "rightsizing." The threats of personal loss lead members to feel, for example, anxious, depressed, guilty, or embarrassed. Because people feel threatened by different things, the facilitator cannot always predict whether a topic will lead to negative emotions.

The Nature of the Facilitator-Client Relationship. The facilitator-client relationship requires the group to be both dependent on and independent of the facilitator. The group is dependent on the facilitator because, like any helping relationship, the facilitator helps the group accomplish something it cannot accomplish alone. But the group must also remain independent of the facilitator, because the facilitator cannot solve problems for the group.

Groups feel ambivalent about being simultaneously dependent on and independent of the facilitator. They value the facilitator's help, in some cases so much so that they want the facilitator to rescue them and solve their problems. For example, they may ask for the facilitator's advice on content issues or even ask the facilitator to make a content decision for the group. Effective facilitators do not allow groups to become inappropriately dependent on them. And yet, because their dependence is an acknowledgment at some level that they are not as competent as they want to be, they sometimes react by rejecting all of the facilitator's interventions.

The internal emotional tug-of-war can lead groups, especially developmental facilitation groups, to react emotionally to the facilitator, either because they are frustrated with having to depend on the facilitator, or because the facilitator will not allow the group to become overly dependent.

The Depth of the Facilitator's Interventions. Related to the nature of the facilitator-client relationship is the depth of the facilitator's interventions. As members respond to deeper-level interventions, they reveal information about themselves—their beliefs, values, opinions, and feelings—that is increasingly private. By revealing the information, they risk making themselves vulnerable. For example, a member may share the fact that his ineffective behavior with a boss is based on his belief that the boss cannot be trusted. Or, a member may reveal that her ineffective behavior results from believing that another member is not competent to do the job. Depending on what members reveal, they may fear a loss of support from peers, retribution by more powerful members, or loss of face. Consequently, members can be threatened by and react emotionally to interventions that ask them to reveal such information.

Facilitators help groups, especially developmental groups, identify inconsistencies between how they believe they act and how they act. Identifying the inconsistencies can have two effects on clients. On the one hand, it can create cognitive dissonance—the psychological discomfort that occurs when a person experiences two incompatible beliefs, attitudes, or other thoughts (Festinger, 1957). The experience can motivate members to reduce their cognitive dissonance by changing their behavior so it is consistent with how they believe they act. On the other hand, identifying inconsistencies can generate negative emotions. It can create frustration when members want to but are unable to reduce their inconsistencies. And, in a form of "kill the messenger," it can also lead to anger at the facilitator who identifies the inconsistencies.

How Members Think, Including Relationships Among Group Members. People who consider an experience threatening will experience some emotion. But because people think differently, two members can experience the same event, and one can consider it threatening while the other does not. For example, if two members are yelled at by a third member, one member may experience anger while the other does not. People experience the same event differently in part because some people have developed the ability to think in ways that reduce potentially dysfunctional effects of their negative emotions (Ellis & Harper, 1975).

To clarify, the suggestion here is not that negative emotions are inherently dysfunctional. Rather, members think and act dysfunctionally when they experience and act on their negative emotions prematurely, before testing the assumptions or inferences on which their emotions are based.

Members display different emotions toward each other in part because they have different experiences with each other. The nature of the experiences, combined with the way members think, affects the negative emotions that members experience.

The Group and Organizational Contexts. Chapter Two discussed how group and organizational cultures influence the way a group functions.

How Members Express Emotions

Members express their emotions in two ways—directly or indirectly. When members express their emotions directly, they describe what they are feeling. Examples include, "I am really angry at you" and "I fear that someone will get back at me if I'm honest."

Members express their emotions indirectly in two ways—verbally and nonverbally. Members can indirectly express their emotions verbally in many ways. Examples include raising or lowering one's voice, focusing repeatedly on a particular point or raising many unrelated points, immediately changing an opinion when pressured, and verbally attacking members or denying their actions. Nonverbal examples include glaring at or looking away from members, slouching in or perching on one's chair, folding or waving one's arms, tightening one's facial muscles, and sighing.

In both indirect methods, members transform their emotion so that the facilitator and other members cannot identify the emotion without asking or making an inference. Again, making untested inferences often creates dysfunctional consequences, and this situation is no exception. People—and even the same person—do not always express the same emotion in the same way. One person may express anger by becoming hostile, while another expresses anger by withdrawing from the conversation. Further, people may use the same behavior to express different emotions. One person's outburst may reflect anger, while another's outburst reflects anxiety. Consequently, the facilitator cannot reliably infer a member's emotions from that person's behavior.

Acting defensively is a common way that members indirectly express their emotions. Defensive behaviors are ways of trying to reduce anxiety or stress that involve denying or distorting reality (McConnell, 1986). Examples include denial, blaming others, withholding relevant information, and suppressing emotions. Defensive behavior is obviously inconsistent with the core values and ground rules for effective groups.

By identifying members' inconsistencies, the facilitator often shows members a part of reality they find threatening and that makes them anxious.

Consequently, members may act defensively toward the facilitator when they cannot accept their inconsistencies or the fact that, despite their efforts, they have been unable to reduce their inconsistencies.

Members express their emotions functionally by expressing them directly and in a manner consistent with the core values and ground rules. Whether a member acts functionally does not depend on how frequently or strongly the member expresses his emotions.

How members express their emotions is influenced by the culture and norms of the group and of the organization. As Chapter Two discussed, the culture of the organization and the resulting norms can strongly influence not only whether members raise emotionally hot issues but also how they raise them and how members react. Some organizations believe that discussing negative emotions is "touchy-feely" and unrelated to the group's performance. Consequently, members in these organizations feel pressure to avoid emotional discussions. In contrast, other organizations believe, as the research suggests (for example, Argyris, 1990), that unresolved issues of negative emotion—especially those that create defensive behavior—reduce the group's ability to maintain its working relationship and in turn reduces the group's ability to perform its task. Members in these organizations feel less or no pressure to avoid emotional discussions.

The group's own culture also influences whether and how members express emotions. Consider, for example, a client group comprising members from only one subgroup of the organization—a subgroup with a culture that values discussing emotional issues. The group is likely to discuss emotional issues, even if the discussion is not supported by the larger organizational culture.

Group members' skills also influence how they express their emotions. Because members must act consistently with the core values and ground rules to express their emotions functionally, members who are more skilled in the ground rules will, by definition, act more functionally. Understanding part of the culture of the organization and group helps the facilitator predict how a group is likely to express emotions.

Intervening on Negative Emotional Behaviors

To repeat an earlier point, the facilitator's role is to help the group identify, express, and discuss emotions in a way that increases rather than decreases the group's effectiveness. To do this, the facilitator can intervene by either helping members express their negative emotions functionally or by helping members reduce the potentially dysfunctional effects of negative emotions by learning to think differently. **In basic facilitation, the facilitator intervenes on negative emotional behavior only when it is expressed in a manner inconsistent with the values and ground rules. In developmental facilitation, the facilitator also intervenes on negative emotional behavior when it results from dysfunctional thinking, that is, thinking that reduces the long-term effectiveness of the group.**

Helping Members Express Negative Emotions Functionally

The facilitator helps groups express their emotions functionally by expressing them in a manner consistent with the core values and ground rules. In basic facilitation, the facilitator accomplishes this by helping members state their emotions, identifying comments that may upset other members, and rephrasing for members the way they have expressed their emotions. The example that follows shows a basic facilitator intervention with a group of department heads who are discussing potential budget cuts.

Dialogue	*Notes*
Dan: I don't think Bob needs all his people because he computerized his department. I think we can cut some staff in his area, meet the budget, and not reduce our productivity.	
Bob [*to Dan in a very loud voice*]: I'm sick and tired of hearing this line from you. You talk as if every other department has to justify its existence except yours. Well, we've got real good reasons for our staffing numbers. [*waving his finger at Dan*] You know that, but you're more concerned about your own little kingdom instead of the bigger picture. You're like a little kid.	Facilitator observes loud voice, pointing at Dan, and the phrase "I'm sick and tired," and infers emotion. Facilitator decides to intervene on the larger issue of Bob's anger rather than the cheap shot "you're like a little kid," which is part of the larger issue.
Facilitator: Bob, I'm wondering what you're thinking and feeling. A few minutes ago, the group was discussing what positions to cut and then Dan said, "I don't think Bob needs all his people because he computerized his department." Then you raised your voice, waved your finger at Dan, and told him you were "sick and tired of hearing this line." Have I accurately described what's happened?	Facilitator explains the reason for the intervention, describes the observable behavior, and checks for agreement.
Bob: Yeah, so?	
Facilitator: I don't want to make any inferences without checking them	Facilitator tests inference about Bob's anger and also explains why a test for

out, so let me ask you what may seem to be an obvious question. Are you angry about what Dan said?

Bob: You bet I am.

Facilitator: OK. What I don't understand exactly is what Dan said that made you angry. What were you thinking before you told Dan you were "sick and tired"? Can you say specifically?

Bob: Dan knows the whole point of computerizing the department wasn't to cut people. It was to cut our two-month backlog. There was never any intention of cutting people once the computer system was up. He's just trying to protect his own people—it's typical Dan.

Facilitator: So is it fair to say you're angry because you believe Dan knows this and that his comment is inconsistent with what he knows to be the reasons for computerizing?

Bob: Yes.

a seemingly obvious inference is necessary.

Facilitator asks Bob to describe his thoughts that generated his anger.

Facilitator clarifies the source of Bob's anger and checks for agreement.

In developmental facilitation, the facilitator can intervene to teach members how to express their emotions in a manner consistent with the core values and ground rules rather than have members rely on the facilitator to do this for them, as in basic facilitation. This intervention is illustrated as the example of the basic facilitation intervention continues. It also shows how developmental interventions can build on basic facilitation interventions.

Dialogue	*Notes*
Facilitator: So is it fair to say you're angry because you believe Dan knows this and that his comment is inconsistent with what he knows to be the reasons for computerizing? *Bob:* Yes.	Facilitator clarifies the source of Bob's anger and checks for agreement.

Facilitator: Listening to your comment to Dan, I do not think you shared that reason for your anger with Dan. Do you agree?

Facilitator identifies potential inconsistency with the ground rules.

Bob: Well, I told him that he knew the reasons for my staffing.

Facilitator: I agree that you told him he knew the reasons for your staffing. But I'm saying something different. I'm saying that you did not explain that you were angry because his comment to you did not reflect his knowledge about your staffing situation. Do you agree?

Facilitator clarifies where Dan and Bob agree and disagree and tests these points.

Bob: I see what you're saying. Yeah, I didn't point it out directly.

Facilitator: Yes. And I consider that inconsistent with the ground rules of "share all relevant information" and "explain the reasons behind statements." Do you see it as inconsistent?

Facilitator links behavior to being inconsistent with the ground rules.

Bob: I would agree.

Facilitator: How would you say it if you expressed your anger in a manner consistent with the ground rules?

Facilitator moves to the last intervention step of asking member to redesign behavior.

Bob: I'd say something like, "Dan, I'm real angry at you. You said that my department could be cut without any loss of productivity. But when we put in the computers, you agreed that we couldn't increase productivity unless we hired some additional people. Now you're saying something different than what you said before. Do you agree, Dan?" Assuming Dan agreed, I'd continue, "Well, that makes me angry."

Facilitator: I think that's consistent with the ground rules. Anyone see

Facilitator confirms Bob's statement and checks with the group for prob-

any problems with Bob's revised statement?

[*Members shake heads, say no.*]

Helping Members Reduce Dysfunctional Thinking

The basic and developmental interventions in the example help members express
their emotions but do not help members reduce their underlying defensive behavior, because neither intervention addresses the source of the defensive behavior.
Instead, the facilitator helps members bypass the defensive behavior rather than
"helping the group learn to [discuss these defensive behaviors] in order to get rid
of them" (Argyris, 1990, p. 102).

To address the underlying defensive behavior, the facilitator can help
members change the way they think about experiences so that they do not perceive them as threatening and therefore do not experience the negative emotions
that trigger the defensive behavior. Such developmental intervention involves
reframing at the deepest level and requires a highly skilled facilitator. Again, the
conversation begins by returning to an earlier part of the last example.

Dialogue	*Notes*
Facilitator: How would you say it if you expressed your anger in a manner consistent with the ground rules?	Facilitator moves to the last intervention step of asking the member to redesign behavior.
Bob: I'd say something like, "Dan, I'm real angry at you. You said that my department could be cut without any loss of productivity. But when we put in the computers you agreed that we couldn't increase productivity unless we hired some additional people. Now you're saying something different. That makes me angry."	
Facilitator: I think that expresses your anger in a way that is consistent with the ground rules. Anyone see any problems with Bob's revised statement?	Facilitator confirms Bob's statement and checks with group for problems facilitator may not have seen.
[*Members shake heads, say no.*]	
Facilitator: One other point. I'm wondering whether you are assuming that Dan knows his two statements	Facilitator begins to determine whether Bob contributed to his dysfunctional emotional reaction by making

are different. Assuming you're correct that Dan knew this, I can understand how you might feel angry. How do you know that Dan knows that the point of computerizing wasn't to cut people? Have you checked this out with Dan, or are you making an inference?

Bob: Everybody knew it. We talked about it in a lot of meetings.

Facilitator: Are you saying that you checked out your inference directly with Dan?

Facilitator clarifies Bob's response in terms of the facilitator's question.

Bob: No. I just think you would have had to have been totally out of the loop not to know it. You're right, I didn't test my inference with Dan.

Facilitator: Let me identify a pattern that led to your angry reaction and see if you believe it accurately represents what happened. Dan suggests that with the new computers, people in your department can be cut. You infer that Dan knows that wasn't the purpose of computerization, and you respond by getting silently angry at him. You attribute his actions to protecting his turf and then suggest that this is Dan's typical behavior. But you do not test your inference with Dan. Rather, you assume your inference is true and use your untested inference as the justification for your anger toward Dan. Have I accurately described what happened?

Facilitator shares observations and inferences and tests them with Bob.

Bob: I don't know if I would have said it so harshly.

Facilitator: When you say, "I don't know if I would have said it so harshly," are you saying that I haven't accurately described what happened?

Facilitator tests his inference about the meaning of the word *harshly*.

untested inferences about what Dan knew.

Bob: No, I agree with what you've described.

Facilitator: Then let's return to what happened. I would consider your thought process dysfunctional in that you think in a way that leads you to become angry with Dan without knowing whether your anger is justified. Do you agree that it's dysfunctional, or do you see it differently?

Bob: Yeah, I agree.

Facilitator: One thing the group can spend some time on is figuring out how members can reduce this type of dysfunctional thinking. I raise this because the group has had several occasions in which different members—Len, Amy, Bob, and Paul—have experienced similar negative consequences resulting from their dysfunctional thinking. I think this would help the group's ability to deal with some of the difficult issues the group has on its agenda, such as equitable work loads and coordination between departments. But the choice is the group's. Do you want to discuss reducing dysfunctional thinking, continue the conversation about cuts, or do something else?

Facilitator describes high-level inference (dysfunctional thinking) and tests it with Bob.

Facilitator identifies a pattern of behavior common to several group members. The facilitator then suggests the value of changing the dysfunctional pattern and asks the group to make the choice.

Dealing with Emotional Hot Buttons

Hot buttons refer to characteristics or situations that have a particularly strong meaning for an individual (either positive or negative) and that lead that person to respond dysfunctionally and defensively. Some people have their buttons pushed when they believe they are not afforded the respect, deference, or attention they believe they deserve. Other people have their hot buttons pushed when they believe others are questioning their ability, commitment, intelligence, or integrity. Still others have their buttons pushed when they believe they are being manipulated or otherwise controlled. Hot buttons often lead a person to react dysfunctionally when others act dysfunctionally. But because hot buttons lead to misperceiving others' remarks and actions, the person often responds dysfunctionally even when others have acted functionally.

A developmental facilitator can help members respond effectively by reducing the dysfunctional thinking that stems from their hot buttons. This involves first helping members identify their hot buttons and then helping members reframe their thinking about hot issues. For example, some members of groups I facilitate have difficulty responding effectively when people—especially those with less power or authority—yell or curse at them in anger. These people believe that yelling or cursing is a sign of disrespect for their official position or personal dignity. They also believe that letting a person yell or curse at them gives that person too much control. For all these reasons, they cannot tolerate yelling or cursing.

I help developmental client groups respond more effectively by helping them reframe how they think about yelling or cursing. First, I ask members to reframe how they think about the yeller's interests. For example, I often ask them to think of the yelling person not as being disrespectful but as having limited skills—not that the yeller is trying to make the member's lives miserable but is trying to solve a problem without the ability to do so. In other words, the person is not interested in yelling or cursing for its own sake. Yellers are doing the best they can with the skills they have, but they are not skilled enough to know how to manage a conflict without yelling or cursing.

Next, I ask members to consider reframing how they think about their own role. Because these people seek to manage conflict effectively, I ask them to think of themselves as being in the position of helping people who are less skilled at managing conflicts.

Finally, I ask members to consider adopting a response to the yeller and curser that is more consistent with the reframing of the yeller's interests and the member's role. For example, I suggest that, just as a physician does not say to a patient, "I can't treat you—you're sick," it would be inconsistent for the facilitator to respond dysfunctionally to the yeller, who does not have the ability to act functionally. Reframing at this deep level can reduce dysfunctional thinking, but it often takes many facilitation sessions and much skill to accomplish.

Because intervening on dysfunctional emotions can increase the threat members feel, the facilitator must make certain that interventions are consistent with the core values and ground rules. As discussed earlier in the chapter, to be appropriate, the facilitator's interventions on dysfunctionally expressed emotions must relate to the group's work effectiveness. Group facilitation is not therapy. **If facilitators intervene on emotions in a way that is unrelated to the group's accomplishing its task, they have left the facilitator role. The facilitator must also intervene on the emotional behavior (the directly observable data)—not on the emotions themselves, which can only be inferred. Finally, the facilitator must be certain that the member has made a free and informed choice to respond to the intervention.**

Dealing with Emotional Reactions to the Facilitator

When members express negative emotions toward the facilitator, the facilitator intervenes in a way similar to when members express negative emotions toward each other. The facilitator identifies the behavior, tests the inference, explores the cause of the negative emotions, and asks the members to decide whether they want to change their behavior.

Members may express negative emotions toward the facilitator either because the facilitator has acted ineffectively or because the members redirect their emotions about others toward the facilitator. Facilitators are partly responsible for negative reactions toward themselves that is caused by their ineffective behavior. In contrast, facilitators are not responsible for the negative reactions of members when facilitators have acted consistently with the core values and ground rules. This approach to facilitation is based on the assumption that **people who act consistently with the core values and ground rules act effectively and therefore are not responsible for others' ineffective behavior (such as defensive behavior) toward them.** Therefore, facilitators must determine whether they have contributed to the member's negative emotional behavior in order to shape the intervention accordingly.

To do this, the facilitator identifies the observed behavior and tests the inference that the member's negative emotions are directed at the facilitator. For example, the facilitator might say, "I'm inferring from your frown and head shaking that you're frustrated with me, am I correct?" If the member agrees, the facilitator starts to determine the cause of the frustration by asking the member to identify the facilitator's behavior that led to the member's reaction. Here the facilitator might say, "Can you tell me exactly what I said or did that led you to get frustrated with me?"

After the member describes the behavior, the facilitator and members can decide whether the facilitator in fact behaved as the member described and, if so, if that behavior was inconsistent with the core values and ground rules.

If facilitators have acted in a manner inconsistent with the core values or ground rules, they are likely to have contributed to the member's negative emotional reaction. In this case, facilitators acknowledge that they have acted ineffectively and, if possible, redesign their own behavior to be consistent with the core values and ground rules. For example, if a member is frustrated with a comment that the facilitator has just made, the facilitator can simply restate it. In some cases, however, facilitators cannot easily reduce the negative consequences of their own ineffective behavior. This is the case, for example, when a member is frustrated because a basic facilitator has repeatedly failed to identify when members have gotten off task. In basic facilitation, facilitators simply identify what they will do differently in the future. In developmental facilitation, facilitators can also ask the member what led the member not to say anything after seeing the group repeatedly go off task without being corrected. By pursuing this, facilitators are not trying to shirk their own responsibility. Rather, they are helping the group become more independent of the facilitator by exploring why members fail to intervene in the group when they believe it would be effective. For example, the facilitator might say, "Bob, if you noticed that several times the group was off task and I did not intervene, and you thought it would be helpful to intervene, what led you not to intervene?"

If, however, the facilitator has acted consistently with the core values and ground rules, the facilitator can explore with the member what led the member to react emotionally and dysfunctionally. For example, the facilitator may help the member determine whether the facilitator pushed one of the member's hot buttons. This intervention occurs at the third, fourth, and fifth depths.

Dealing with defensive behavior requires a lot of time, energy, and patience. Facilitators should attempt to explore an individual's defensiveness only when they and the group have the resources and when facilitators have the necessary skills.

Following Through on Interventions

Sometimes, interventions fail not because they are inappropriate or poorly timed but because the facilitator does not follow through. Facilitators may drop an intervention simply because they become frustrated when members remain silent or do not respond directly to questions. Faced with restating the intervention again or dropping it, the facilitator chooses the latter. However, sometimes the facilitator backs off because the member responds angrily, tearfully, or defensively.

Failing to follow through on interventions creates problems for the facilitator and the group because not following through implicitly supports the member's dysfunctional behavior. For example, backing off because a member responds angrily, defensively, or with tears, conveys to that member (and others) that such responses can successfully control the group and the facilitator by stopping others from raising an issue with that member. Even if the member did not intend to stop discussion, the facilitator's response makes it clear that members can use emotional responses to unilaterally control the group. **Failing to follow through on interventions may also lead members to infer that the group's ground rules—on which the facilitator's interventions are based—are not effective in difficult situations.** If members reach this conclusion, they may legitimately doubt the facilitator's ability to help them.

When I ask facilitators why they do not follow through on emotionally difficult interventions they consider appropriate, they often explain that the member or entire group would be embarrassed and could not handle it. The explanation is an untested inference that discounts the member's ability. The facilitators could have quickly tested their inference with the client but did not. After further discussion, the facilitators often explain that they back off because they are also uncomfortable when pursuing such interventions. Like their clients, they may lack the confidence that they can turn an emotionally negative situation into a constructive one.

To effectively follow through on interventions, **the facilitator should pursue with the member issues of conflict, discomfort, and frustration rather than move away from them. When clients do not respond directly to an initial intervention or when they respond dysfunctionally, the facilitator should follow up, not by simply restating the intervention (or withdrawing) but by making a meta-intervention.**

A meta-intervention is an intervention that refers to a previous intervention. Meta-interventions enable the facilitator and group to talk about interventions. Consider, for example, a member who remains silent when the facilitator intervenes by asking the member to identify her interests. The facilitator may respond with the general meta-intervention, "Jill, when I asked you what your interests were, you remained silent, yes? [if yes] Can you say what led you not to answer my question?" The meta-intervention enables Jill and the facilitator to identify why the initial intervention failed. Once the cause is identified and addressed, the facilitator can return to the initial intervention.

Why do members not respond directly to a facilitator's interventions the first time? Sometimes, members do not respond at all simply because they have not heard the facilitator. Other times, members have heard what the facilitator said but have not understood what the facilitator meant and do not ask the facilitator.

Often, members believe they are answering the facilitator's question, although the facilitator does not think so. In this case, the facilitator's meta-intervention might be, "Bob, when I asked what your interests were in combining the two departments, you said that people have been concerned about the high turnover in these departments. Is that what you said? [If yes] I don't understand how what you said identifies your interests. Can you tell me?" Notice that the meta-intervention does not assume that the member is not addressing the facilitator's initial intervention.

Sometimes, members respond indirectly to avoid discussing a difficult or undiscussable issue. If facilitators have observed behavior that lead to an inference that this is the case, they should share the inference with the members and test it.

At other times, members do not respond directly because they are preoccupied with something else that has happened in the group—usually something they consider negative. For example, the member might be concerned that other members are controlling the meeting or that his department is being scapegoated. Given the principle of starting with the member's concerns and interests, the member is likely to have difficulty responding to any facilitator intervention that does not address the topic with which the member is preoccupied. Here too, if facilitators have data to support it, they should test the inference that the member is preoccupied. If the member is preoccupied with a previous group issue, group members can decide whether to discuss it or continue their conversation. Even if the group decides to temporarily postpone discussing that member's issue, recognizing it and agreeing on a time to discuss it often enables the member to reduce or eliminate the preoccupation.

To make an appropriate meta-intervention, facilitators need to test the inference to determine why the member has not responded directly to the initial intervention. Like talking louder to someone who speaks a different language, simply amplifying the same intervention is unlikely to work when the member has heard the facilitator's initial intervention.

Following through on interventions can raise issues that are difficult for the group to address and that require deeper interventions. For example, a meta-intervention may prompt members to discuss how they disagree with the goals of a program or how they question other members' performance. The facilitator should not be concerned if the group abandons the initial intervention to pursue the issue uncovered by the meta-intervention. In fact, the facilitator should consider this a success. Meta-intervention issues often help the group move beyond discussing symptoms to exploring underlying problems and causes. Consequently, a successful meta-intervention can help the group solve a problem so that it stays solved.

Finally, when is it appropriate not to follow through on an intervention? The answer lies in the core values of valid information and free and informed choice. **The facilitator should not follow through if, after explaining the reasons for making the intervention and explaining the potential outcomes of the member's choice, the member chooses not to pursue the facilitator's intervention.**

Intervening on Positive Emotional Behaviors

This chapter has focused on dealing with negative emotions, largely because they are typically more challenging for the group and the facilitator. Yet, helping members learn to functionally express their positive emotions is equally important. Facilitators help group members accomplish this in several ways.

Facilitators support group members by providing positive feedback when they have acted consistently with the core values and ground rules. For example, a facilitator may say, "Alan and Melissa, you did a nice job of focusing on interests just now when discussing the conflict over publication deadlines. What do others think?" Positive feedback is particularly important when members are just beginning to learn how to use the core values and ground rules.

Facilitators can also help group members positively reframe the meaning of their experiences when members feel frustrated or disappointed because they rarely act consistently with the core values and ground rules they espouse. Facilitators can remind members that learning to act consistently with the core values and ground rules is difficult work that takes a long time. They can also help put the members' frustrations in perspective by helping them understand that although group members may have much to learn, they have also made progress and should acknowledge it as such. When providing positive support, facilitators should be careful that their comments are based on valid information and that they do not simply become cheerleaders for their groups, giving inappropriately positive feedback, which discounts the group's ability to evaluate its own performance.

Being a facilitator does not mean being stoic or humorless. When members say and do things that are genuinely funny, facilitators laugh accordingly. The challenge for facilitators, however, is to make sure that they do not join the group in laughing when the humor is inconsistent with the core values and ground rules, such as laughing at a joke that is also a cheap shot at a group member. This reduces the facilitator's credibility.

Just as groups are less effective when they cannot functionally express negative emotions, groups are also less effective when they cannot functionally express positive emotions such as happiness, pride, or passion. Withholding positive feelings is a form of withholding relevant information. Yet some groups have group or organizational cultures that do not value or believe in the expression of positive emotions. A number of years ago, as a member of such a group, I heard the chair announce that one member had just received a prestigious award, an award that members agreed the recipient deserved and were delighted he had received. Yet, when the announcement was made, no one applauded or cheered. In fact, no one said anything. My untested inference was that members felt awkward in openly expressing their positive feelings about another member.

Diagnosing such a situation is difficult because, as Chapter Four noted, it requires that the facilitator observe the absence of some functional pattern of behavior. Intervening in such a situation is also challenging, because the interventions occur at deep levels (four or five) and members may see the expression of positive emotions as unrelated to the group's effectiveness. For these reasons, they may consider the facilitator's interventions inappropriate. Because the expression of positive emotions is less central to the primary task of basic facilitation, the interventions are typically limited to developmental facilitation.

The facilitator intervenes by using the steps in the intervention cycle. For example, a facilitator might say, "I've noticed a pattern of behavior in your meetings that I'd like to share and get your reaction to. In the last two meetings, you have discussed items such as your having received the annual award for outstanding service quality and your winning the largest contract in the organization's history. Do you remember these discussions? [if yes, continue] In none of these discussions did I observe what I would call any expression of positive feelings. For example, no one expressed good feelings or pride about these events. Do you agree with my observations? [if yes, continue] Yet in these situations I would consider it functional, even natural, to show your positive feelings, which is relevant information. I'm not sure what to infer from this. Do members consider these situations appropriate for expressing positive feelings? If so, what leads you to not do so?" Facilitators can also use the intervention to identify the absence of what could be considered functional negative emotional behaviors.

When members do express positive emotions, they can be misinterpreted. Facilitators help reduce misinterpretation by helping members clarify the meaning of their expressions. Members can easily misinterpret positive emotional behavior when it seems inappropriate for the situation. Consider, for example, a situation in which a member is describing how stressed she feels about the increase in demands on her time. She explains that if she does not make some changes to get more control over how she spends her time, she will not accomplish her long-term goals for the group. While she is sharing this, a more senior group member starts to smile. As the junior member becomes more frustrated, the senior member's smile grows. The junior member sees the senior member smiling. At this point, the facilitator intervenes. "Daniel, as Rachel has been sharing her frustrations, you've been smiling. Would you be willing to share what you are thinking or feeling?" Daniel responds, "I'm smiling because, in a way, I'm happy for Rachel. I know she has felt stressed out for a long time, but this is the first time I've seen a resolve on her part to make some changes that will improve things for her. It's great to see that."

At other times, members use positive emotional behaviors to mask their negative feelings. Consider, for example, a member who is frustrated with another member who constantly interrupts and takes cheap shots. The frustrated member may react by acting especially friendly or gracious toward that member, but not by stating frustration. The dysfunctional use of positive emotional behavior can be difficult to diagnose. However, the facilitator may be able to identify the behavior by observing whether a member's expressed positive emotional behavior seems extreme for the situation, forced, or does not match other nonverbal behavior.

Sometimes, group members' positive emotions can reduce the group's effectiveness, even when members express the positive emotions functionally. For example, groups sometimes feel euphoric when they have reached consensus after working hard to resolve a difficult conflict, especially when members did not expect that they could reach consensus. Fearing that their euphoria may be shattered if they continue working, the group may fail to wrap up some loose ends, such as how or when the solution will be implemented. The facilitator can help group members by recognizing their hard-earned positive feelings and help the group deal with the loose ends and the underlying fears by addressing them.

Finally, when done well, self-critiques enable members to discuss the positive and negative emotions that they experienced during the meeting. By reflecting on the meeting, members may recognize feelings they had but that they were unaware of at the time. To get directly at such emotions, the facilitator can add a three-part question to the self-critique: How did you feel throughout the meeting, what led you to feel that way, and how, if at all, did you express the feelings? Adding the questions links members' emotions with the process of improving their group's effectiveness.

Making Mistakes and Asking the Group for Help

Facilitators make mistakes. Despite their training and constant self-monitoring, they sometimes act inconsistently with the core values and ground rules. For example, facilitators may have failed to test their assumptions about an ambiguous contract, unilaterally cut off the group's discussion, or failed to follow through on an intervention.

However, facilitators should be able to quickly recognize their dysfunctional behavior and correct it. **Sharing relevant information means that a facilitator tells her clients when and how she has acted dysfunctionally.** (Facilitators must decide whether their mistakes are relevant information to share, depending on whether the facilitation is basic or developmental.) Sharing helps members better understand the core values and ground rules, as well as the conditions that lead even skilled people to violate them. Facilitators may also ask members whether they recognized the mistake and what negative consequences they saw. In doing so, facilitators use their own ineffective behavior to help the group members learn, and, paradoxically, to be models of effective behavior.

Facilitators are not omniscient. At times, facilitators probably will be stumped. Their intuition may tell them that something is wrong, but they will not be able to identify any group behavior to make a diagnosis. Or, having identified the problem, they may be uncertain about how to intervene.

In such cases, facilitators should consider directly asking the group for help. For example, a facilitator might say, "I'm stumped. I think the group is having a problem, but I can't figure out what it is, and I also can't point to any behavior that leads me to conclude this. Does anyone else see a problem?" By asking the group for help, the facilitator makes explicit and discussable what everyone already knows: that the facilitator is human and has limits and that ultimately the group must help manage its process.

Summary

This chapter considered how emotions are generated and expressed and how facilitators intervene on negative and positive emotional behaviors. Several major principles guided the discussion. First, group facilitation is not therapy. The purpose of dealing with emotions that arise in group facilitation is to help the group become more effective *at its work,* not to change people's personalities or to focus on emotions for their own sake. To be appropriate, the facilitator's interventions on members' emotional behaviors must relate to the group's work effectiveness. Second, effective groups do not suppress their negative or positive emotional behaviors; they learn to express them functionally by expressing them directly and in a manner consistent with the core values and ground rules. Finally, effectively intervening on emotional behavior often involves deep-level interventions and often requires the facilitator to follow through when members do not respond to the initial intervention. At the same time, however, the facilitator must always preserve group members' free and informed choice to not respond to the intervention.

Chapter Eleven # Working with Another Facilitator

Facilitating groups is mentally challenging work. It requires simultaneously paying attention to content and process, verbal and nonverbal behavior, those who are speaking and those who are not, and comparing what is apparently happening in a group to what has happened in the past and what will likely happen in the future. While considering all this, the facilitator must also be thinking about whether to intervene, what interventions to make, when to make them, how deep to make them, to whom to address them, and the effects of the interventions on the group once they are made. Then the facilitator must intervene. The facilitator often must do all this in less time than it takes to read this paragraph.

Because of the high demands of the work, facilitators sometimes work together as cofacilitators to the same group. In cofacilitation, both facilitators are usually with the group at all times. This chapter considers the advantages and disadvantages of cofacilitating and describes factors to consider when selecting and working with a cofacilitator (Resource E provides a guide for deciding whether to cofacilitate and how to cofacilitate). The chapter also describes different ways that cofacilitators can divide and coordinate their labor.

Deciding Whether to Cofacilitate:
Advantages and Disadvantages

When cofacilitators work well together, the group and each cofacilitator can reap benefits that are less likely to accrue if there were only one facilitator. However, when cofacilitators work poorly together, both the group and each facilitator can suffer to the point that the group would have been better served by a single facilitator. Deciding whether to cofacilitate requires weighing the potential benefits against the potential disadvantages for the group. This section, based on the work of J. William Pfeiffer and John Jones (1975), describes the advantages and disadvantages of the choices. The underlying principle in choosing to have two facilitators is that **together, the cofacilitators should be able to diagnose and intervene in a greater range of situations and with greater skill than one facilitator could.**

Complementing Versus Competing Orientations or Styles

Different facilitators have different orientations that guide their work. For example, some facilitators focus more on helping individual members improve their communication skills; others focus more on improving group structures. The individual-level facilitator believes that groups are effective when individual members act effectively; the group-level facilitator believes that effective groups are more the result of group structures, such as group norms or a motivating task.

Cofacilitation can be effective to the extent that the facilitators' orientations are either congruent or complementary. Facilitators with different orientations usually hold different assumptions about what makes groups effective and how to effectively intervene. Consistent with the law of the instrument described in Chapter Four, the problems that facilitators identify and the actions they take are shaped largely by the knowledge and skills they have. Similarly, facilitators also have favorite interventions and, as a result, may use them when other interventions might be more appropriate. However, when individual-level and group-level facilitators work as cofacilitators, for example, they can compensate for each other's blind spots and misplaced interventions rather than reinforce them, which occurs when cofacilitators have the same orientation. Complementary cofacilitators can work well together as long as they consider each other's orientation appropriate.

Cofacilitation becomes less effective as the facilitators' orientations are more incompatible. For example, facilitators differ over the extent to which they believe groups should jointly control the process. As a simple illustration, some facilitators unilaterally enforce predetermined time frames for discussing agenda items, while others ask group members if they want to alter the schedule as they proceed. It is not possible to give the group both more and less control of the same decision. Therefore, such a difference in orientation would make it difficult to cofacilitate.

Another relatively incompatible difference involves the levels of inference that facilitators use to diagnose and intervene. Some facilitators (including me) rely more on low-level inferences, while others tend to make high-level inferences to guide how they observe and intervene in the group. Where a low-level inference facilitator might infer that members have "withheld information from each other," a high-level inference facilitator might infer that members are "engaged in a power struggle with each other." The difference is a relatively incompatible one because higher-level inferences tend to lead to deeper interventions, which expose clients to greater risks. And interventions cannot be simultaneously superficial and deep. In a study of coleaders of therapy groups—a role relationship similar to cofacilitators—different orientations was the reason most cited for not wanting to work together again (Paulson, Burroughs, & Gelb, 1976).

Still, facilitators with seemingly incompatible inferential orientations should not assume that they cannot bridge their differences. The facilitators might agree to begin with lower-level interventions before moving to deeper interventions. The key point is that differences in orientations can be advantageous if they are complementary rather than incompatible.

In addition to different orientations, facilitators have different styles. Whereas *orientation* refers to fundamental assumptions that guide the facilitator, *style* refers more to the particular ways in which facilitators conduct themselves in applying their orientation. But the two are sometimes related; a particular orientation can affect a person's style. Facilitator styles vary along many dimensions, including the facilitator's degree of seriousness versus humor, support versus confrontation, questions asked versus statements made, and the pace of intervention.

Here too, different styles can help the group if they are not incompatible. For example, cofacilitating makes possible a faster pace that lets issues emerge that otherwise would not. Each facilitator has time to move "off line" (that is, time to observe the group without having to actively facilitate) and can observe things that might otherwise go unnoticed. However, if the facilitators intervene at very different paces, their differences can become a hindrance; each may find it difficult to conduct off-line diagnosis at the other's pace. And the client group is likely to be distracted by having to adjust to two facilitator's speeds. Irene Paulson, Jane Burroughs, and Charlotte Gelb (1976) found that coleaders were less satisfied with each other when they had different styles and skills.

Being Overwhelmed Versus Overintervening

A facilitator working alone sometimes leaves a session overwhelmed, feeling that much more was occurring in the group than he or she could even perceive, let alone intervene on. In addition, the facilitator wonders whether his or her perception of the situation was realistic or distorted. This often happens when there is a high level of overt activity or energy in the group; many things are occurring at different levels simultaneously and at a fast pace. High-conflict situations are one example. But an individual facilitator can also get overwhelmed when the level of activity is not observably high, but every interaction is laden with interpersonal issues in the group. Cofacilitating reduces the chance that both facilitators will be overwhelmed and gives each an opportunity to use the other for a reality test. Cofacilitating is also useful when a group is large or when a group plans to work part of the time in subgroups.

The extra capacity to intervene that cofacilitators can bring to the group can become a liability if it leads to excessive intervention. Facilitators have a need to feel useful and that need is usually met in the course of intervening. However, at times one cofacilitator has little opportunity for intervening because the partner is already making the necessary interventions. If facilitators attempt to meet their own needs rather than their clients', they may intervene unnecessarily and slow the group's progress. The problem can be reduced or prevented so long as each cofacilitator places the group's needs first and if they divide the labor so that each cofacilitator has ample opportunity to intervene. Finally, each facilitator can reframe the meaning of *being useful* to include refraining from unnecessary interventions.

Development and Support Versus Competition

Cofacilitation enables facilitators to expand their professional skills and get emotional support. Assuming that no single approach is most effective in all situations, cofacilitators can expand the range of their effectiveness by learning from partners who have different orientations or styles. Cofacilitators can also support each other in the process. This is true for facilitators in training and experienced facilitators.

In facilitation, the relationship between personal development and professional development is strong. This is captured by a Talmudic saying, "We do not see things as *they* are; we see things as *we* are." To diagnose and intervene accurately and to cofacilitate, the facilitator's personal issues must not influence the facilitator's observations and actions. Personal issues include problems dealing with authority, ambiguity, control, commitment, status, and intimacy. A facilitator who has problems with authority, for example, may inappropriately confront or avoid the formal leader of a group. A facilitator who has problems with ambiguity may frequently interrupt while the cofacilitator is making a series of complicated interventions. When cofacilitators trust enough to share their personal issues with each other, they can help each other monitor and reduce the negative effects. Ideally, however, the long-term solution lies in eliminating or reducing negative effects.

Depending on their personal issues, the cofacilitators' relationship may be more competitive than developmental and supportive. For example, if both cofacilitators have a high need for approval, they may compete with each other for active facilitation time, at the expense of the group.

Effective Versus Ineffective Behavior

Good cofacilitators are models of effective interpersonal behavior for the group. In developmental facilitation, model behavior becomes more useful because the group can observe more of the cofacilitation relationship. The more cofacilitators are willing to divide and coordinate their labor, establish their expectations, and manage their conflicts in front of the group, the more the group can learn. If cofacilitators save their disagreements for private sessions, members may infer that the cofacilitators share the members' belief that team members, to avoid being seen as incompetent or vulnerable, should not disagree in front of nonteam members. Consequently, the cofacilitators make their work more difficult, because members refrain from discussing their disagreements.

Obviously, when cofacilitators do not work well together, they do not provide a useful example for members. They also reduce their credibility. Members legitimately question the ability of cofacilitators to help them improve their process if the cofacilitators cannot manage their own relationship.

When group members have different demographic characteristics, the cofacilitators' demographic characteristics are important, especially when the different characteristics are part of the group's problem. For the facilitator to serve as a credible example, members must identify with a facilitator. With a racially mixed group of employees torn by racial tensions, a cofacilitator pair that parallels the group members' races can have greater credibility than two cofacilitators of the same race. Each member can identify with one cofacilitator and expect that that facilitator will help interpret to the full group the perspective of the group members of that race. Whether members' differences stem from differences in language, sex, race, age, class, or ethnicity, all can be viewed as differences in cultures.

Matching cofacilitators' demographic characteristics to the group heightens the issue of cultural differences within the group. For example, if men discount women in the group, they will—through transference—also tend to discount a woman cofacilitator. When the discounting is sophisticated and subtle, the cofacilitator has a better chance of recognizing it if it is directed at her in addition to women group members. This also lets the cofacilitator identify the larger pattern of men members discounting women's contributions, which makes the observation stronger.

It is not always possible—or necessary—for two cofacilitators to match all the demographic backgrounds of group members. The principle is that **cofacilitators become more credible as they more closely match the group's relevant demographic characteristics.** The characteristics become relevant when they significantly affect how members act toward each other. In a city council that has its first elected African-American members because of redistricting prompted by a civil rights lawsuit, for example, differences in race are likely to have more of an effect on the members' behavior than differences in, say, religion or sex. Identifying the relevant demographic differences should occur early in the contracting phase.

Raising problems associated with cultural differences is essential for developmental facilitation. For basic facilitation, the issues are relevant only when the group has made them the subject of discussion or when the group cannot accomplish its content task without discussing them.

Internal-External Versus Same-role Cofacilitation

Internal facilitators are employed in the same organization as the groups they facilitate. External facilitators work for themselves or another organization. Sometimes, internal and external facilitators have a chance to work together. An internal facilitator may seek an external cofacilitator to help in a large or difficult assignment. Internal and external facilitators have different advantages that stem from their positions vis-á-vis the client organization.

Internal facilitators are in a position to know the organization's culture and the unwritten rules about how things should be done. They should know how people are supposed to talk, act, and dress. This gives them greater ability to facilitate without violating cultural norms, which would be considered offensive or would lead to misunderstanding. It also gives them a head start in understanding the client group's situation. Internal facilitators may even know some members of the client group and the problems they face. The group also has more access to the internal facilitator. This is particularly important in developmental facilitation, in which the group sometimes needs help on short notice.

External facilitators have the power of independence. They have greater freedom to take risks in raising important issues, even if they will make the group uncomfortable. They can challenge members' assumptions and logic without seeming insubordinate or disloyal. They can decline to evaluate clients, collude with clients, play messenger, or act in any other way that weakens their ability to facilitate. At the worst, external facilitators may lose a client—but internal facilitators may lose their job.

External facilitators may wish they had the internal facilitator's local knowledge, while internal facilitators may wish they had the external facilitator's independence. As cofacilitators, they can have both.

But the reasons for collaborating are also sources of tension. When they disagree, the external facilitator may think the internal facilitator does not focus enough on process issues, is too deferential to authority, or is inhibited by the culture of the organization. The internal facilitator may think the external facilitator is too idealistic and challenging and does not appreciate the culture of the organization and the need for the group to get its work done. Because the tensions stem from the different roles that each facilitator has with the organization, they are likely to exist even between facilitators who have the same orientation, style, and cultural background.

Synergy Versus Expending Extra Energy

People work together because they can accomplish together what one person cannot accomplish alone. When cofacilitators work well together, their efforts have synergy—their joint effort is greater than the sum of either of their individual efforts. But the potential of increased benefits carries a cost.

In addition to the energy that every facilitator must expend working with the groups, cofacilitators must expend energy coordinating their work with each other. First, cofacilitators must spend time talking with each other to determine whether they are compatible enough to cofacilitate. Second, if they decide to cofacilitate, they must plan how to manage differences in their orientations and styles. Third, they must divide the facilitation labor between them and develop ways to coordinate their division of labor. Some of this can be done off line. For example, before a session, cofacilitators can plan how they will divide up the opening remarks and how they will hand off control to each other at the session. Less predictable aspects of coordination can be partially planned but must also be partially coordinated on line (at the time of the interventions and in front of the group). As a simple illustration, if one facilitator agrees to write at the flip chart while the other intervenes (division of labor), both need a way to ensure that what one facilitator writes on the flip chart—and when—is congruent with the other facilitator's interventions (coordination). A much more difficult and frequent problem is coordinating the different interventions that each cofacilitator makes so that together they help the group make progress rather than take the group in different directions. Coordination is difficult because it can only be done on line and must be done continually.

Aside from expending energy dividing and coordinating their labor, cofacilitators expend psychological energy. Cofacilitators commonly worry that their partners will make significant mistakes, that they themselves will make mistakes, or both. Finally, cofacilitators spend psychological energy struggling with a tension inherent in collaboration: each person must temporarily yield some identity to the collaboration so that, together, they can become something neither alone can be (Smith & Berg, 1987).

The best way for cofacilitators to find out about each other's orientation, style, and so on, is to discuss the issues directly. Facilitators can use the questions and statements in Resource E to guide their discussion. The questions and statements can be used by two individuals to determine whether they can cofacilitate effectively and to reach agreements about how to work together.

At the end of the discussion, the facilitators can jointly decide whether to work together. But each facilitator must also decide whether the increased benefits from cofacilitation will be worth the extra energy needed to coordinate the work. Ultimately, the question can be answered only by each facilitator alone.

Dividing and Coordinating the Labor

To benefit from cofacilitation, cofacilitators must decide how they will divide their work during the facilitation sessions. Exhibit 11.1 lists six options, and the coordination issues that arise from them are discussed next. Although the divisions of labor are discussed as if they were completely separate, they are not. By keeping an eye on the partner's domain, each cofacilitator facilitates coordination.

Exhibit 11.1. Six Ways to Divide the Cofacilitation Labor.

1. Intervener-recorder
2. Primary-secondary
3. On-line–Off-line
4. Task-relationship
5. Intervention-reaction
6. No explicit division of labor

Intervener-Recorder

In this arrangement, one facilitator intervenes while the other writes on the flip chart. The technique is useful when the group is generating many ideas—as in brainstorming—and does not want to be slowed down by the facilitator's writing each idea before asking for the next one. Still, either the intervener or recorder should check that the written statements represent what the members have said.

Coordinating the two roles also requires that the cofacilitators and members agree on when a member's idea will be written on the flip chart. This can be as direct as saying, "Let's write down all the potential causes of the delays." The issue is simple, but it can create problems if not addressed. Writing a member's idea on the flip chart symbolizes that the idea—and therefore the member—is worthwhile. A member whose contributions are not written down and does not know why may feel discounted and begin to distrust the facilitator and recorder. Therefore, when the recorder decides not to write down an idea, a brief explanation is appropriate. For example, the recorder might say, "Dan, I was asking for causes and you gave a solution. Do you agree? Can you think of any causes?" In this way, the recorder temporarily becomes the intervener.

Primary-Secondary

In this arrangement, one facilitator is the primary facilitator for all interventions, while the other plays backup, intervening only when necessary, like a left fielder who scoops up ground balls that get past the shortstop. This works well when the group process is easy enough for one facilitator to manage or when the facilitators are concerned about intervening too much. It also gives the secondary facilitator a chance to rest.

The coordination problem here is that the secondary facilitator may intervene on some behavior that the primary facilitator intentionally avoided. For example, the primary facilitator may avoid clarifying an off-track disagreement among members and instead try to get the group on track. If the secondary facilitator jumps in and clarifies the disagreement, the clarification would continue to take the group off track. While coordination problems can occur with any division of labor, here the problem may be greater because the secondary

facilitator is actively looking for opportunities that the primary facilitator
missed. To avoid the problem, cofacilitators must understand each other's
intervention orientation well enough that the secondary facilitator can distinguish between a missed opportunity and one intentionally avoided.

On-line–Off-line

In the on-line–off-line division of labor, one facilitator intervenes (on line), while
the other pays no attention to what is happening in the group but instead silently
works on some problem associated with the facilitation. The problem could be
how to get members to see each other's perspectives, how to describe a complex
group pattern, or how to spend the remaining facilitation time when a group has
fallen behind schedule. The arrangement is useful when the cofacilitators need
to solve a problem that is too difficult to solve while observing and intervening
and that is either not appropriate to raise with the group or not a good use of
the group's time.

Of course, the cofacilitator needs to cue for going off line. This is easy to
do when the decision to go off line results from a brief meeting during a break.
But, a cofacilitator who wants to go off line in the middle of a session needs
another way to cue the partner and determine whether the partner consents.
Going off line is relevant information to share with the group, because group
members may expect that both facilitators will be continually on line.

Task-Relationship

In this arrangement, both facilitators actively observe and intervene, but one
focuses on what is referred to as *task process*, while the other focuses on what is
referred to as *relationship* (or *interpersonal*) *process* (Schein, 1987). If, for example, a group is setting performance goals, the task-process facilitator focuses on
the content by helping the group keep on track, think logically about what goals
are needed, and establish clear goals. In contrast, the relationship-process facilitator pays attention more to the group's social and emotional interactions, by
silently asking, What do the members' words, style, and nature of discussion say
about how they are feeling about the task, each other, and the cofacilitators?
(Yalom, 1985,).

Task-relationship is often a natural way for cofacilitators to divide the
labor. Research shows that some people are more task oriented and others are
more relationship oriented (Bales, cited in Yalom, 1985; Blake, 1964). Task and
relationship orientations are relative. Whether a cofacilitator is more task or
relationship oriented depends on how task or relationship oriented the other
cofacilitator is. For example, I have two colleagues with whom I cofacilitate. One
is very task oriented and the other, while capable of being very task oriented, also
has a keen eye for relationship issues. My ability to diagnose relationship issues
falls between that of my two colleagues. Consequently, when we divide our roles

along this dimension, I assume the relationship role with one colleague and the task role with the other. This approach lets cofacilitators take advantage of their strengths. It works well when the group generates many task and relationship issues simultaneously.

Because groups—especially basic facilitation groups—view task interventions as more appropriate than relationship interventions, the relationship cofacilitator often needs to clearly show how the relationship issue affects the group's ability to complete its task.

Intervention-Reaction

In this arrangement, one facilitator concentrates on intervening with one or a few members, while the other pays attention to the rest of the group. The division is useful when a member is the subject of much intervention and other members of the group react strongly to the member's comments or to the interventions. For example, a facilitator may need to spend several minutes questioning and supporting one member who hesitates to express strong dissatisfaction with the group, the organization, and the facilitation. Knowing the other members' reactions provides important diagnostic data.

The coordination problem here involves knowing whether or when to shift the focus of the intervention from one member to the others' reactions. Should the second facilitator immediately point out the reactions or wait until the first facilitator completes the interventions?

No Explicit Division of Labor

No explicit division of labor does not mean there is no division of labor. It means that each cofacilitator pays attention to what appears to need attention, without first talking with the other. Using this approach, cofacilitators can instantly switch their roles to adjust to the group's needs and the needs of their partners. The approach can potentially make the best and quickest use of the cofacilitators' skills.

As the least structured way to divide the labor, it is also the most difficult to coordinate. Cofacilitators risk intervening on the same issues while ignoring others, failing to capture members' ideas on the flip chart, and both going off line at the same time, temporarily abandoning the group. The approach works only when cofacilitators have worked together long enough and in enough situations that they can anticipate each other's moves and adjust automatically. Hockey player Wayne Gretzky attributed his success to a similar intuitive ability when he said, "I skate to where I think the puck will be." The less skilled and experienced the cofacilitators, the less likely they will be able to predict when and how their partners will intervene, and the less successful they will be in dividing their labor this way.

It is not necessarily desirable for cofacilitators to use only one division of labor throughout an entire session. Skilled cofacilitators can shift among divisions of labor to meet the changing needs of the group.

Allocating Roles Within a Division of Labor

After selecting a division of labor (for example, intervener-recorder or task-relationship), cofacilitators must decide who will play which role. **Cofacilitators should allocate roles in a way that makes the best use of their skills and characteristics.** Because all but two of the divisions of labor designate a primary intervener in some respect (the exceptions are task-relationship and no explicit division of labor), applying the principle usually means ensuring that the primary intervener (or active facilitator) is the one with the skills or characteristics needed most by the group. When making this decision, cofacilitators can consider a number of factors.

Skill with Potential Interventions. To a certain extent, facilitators can predict the kinds of interventions they will have to emphasize, given the group's situation and the task it seeks to accomplish. When a group is in an openly hostile conflict, the facilitator will spend a lot of time ensuring that members let each other finish their comments, testing their highly inferential negative attributions about each other, showing members how their statements are more similar (or different) than they thought, and identifying cheap shots. When a group is developing a strategic plan, the facilitator will spend a lot of time helping members clarify their visions of the organization, establishing criteria for evaluation, and setting priorities. Discussions about role expectations and team building usually require deeper interventions than discussions about creating a new organizational structure.

Cofacilitators can divide their roles so that the facilitator who has primary responsibility for intervening is the more skilled at the predicted interventions. In addition, they can switch roles if the necessary interventions become those at which the less active facilitator is more skilled. If the facilitators do not need to switch roles frequently, the intervener-recorder division of labor works well. Otherwise, the primary-secondary, task-relationship, or intervention-reaction roles allow more frequent role switches without disruption.

Knowledge of Substantive Problems. Cofacilitators vary in their knowledge about substantive problems their clients face. For example, one of my cofacilitators knows a lot about finance. When we cofacilitate a group that is discussing financial issues, he usually takes the first role in either the intervener-recorder, task-relationship, intervention-reaction, or primary-secondary divisions of labor. He can keep up when the discussion becomes so technical that I would have to slow the group's pace by frequently asking for definitions of terms. (Here I am assuming that members agree on the definitions of the terms and would be clarifying them only for me.) Still, when a cofacilitator's knowledge about and interest in a substantive issue tempts the facilitator to stray into the substantive discussion, the less knowledgeable partner should actively intervene.

Internal-External Differences. Similarly, the internal facilitator can often more easily intervene in highly technical discussions. In contrast, if the cofacilitators want to confront the group—especially about members' core values and beliefs— without risking loss of credibility or seeming disloyal, the external facilitator should actively intervene. But in developmental groups, having the internal facilitator confront the group about its assumptions is powerful, because it highlights the issue of credibility and disloyalty. Done well, the cofacilitators can use members' reactions to the internal facilitator to discuss why members who challenge the assumption of the organization are seen as disloyal.

Reactions to Cofacilitators. Members react differently to each cofacilitator. How they react depends partly on how each cofacilitator acts. But members' reactions are sometimes based on their experiences with similar others. The reaction is called *transference.* Transference is the attitude of a group member toward a facilitator and is produced by displacing onto the facilitator positive or negative feelings or desires that come from the member's previous experiences with other figures in the member's life (Yalom, 1985). Transference is an irrational reaction because the person's reaction to the facilitator is based not on the facilitator but on a reaction to some other figure whom the member associates with the facilitator. Other figures include supervisors, coworkers, parents, siblings, spouses, or people who may have the same physical, behavioral, or demographic characteristic as the facilitator.

Cofacilitators can use transference to intervene when members' reactions to them parallel the members' reactions to each other (or to members of the larger organization). Because members react differently to each cofacilitator, cofacilitators can decide who should actively intervene to evoke positive or negative transference from the group.

Why would facilitators divide their roles in a way they know will evoke negative transference? As previously discussed, cofacilitators can use group members' negative reactions to the internal facilitator's challenging assumptions to help group members examine their feelings toward group members who do the same thing. But another reason to evoke negative transference arises when members have mostly positive transference toward one cofacilitator and mostly negative toward the other; assigning roles to avoid negative transference would lead to always making the latter facilitator the passive partner. This reduces the cofacilitators' effectiveness and legitimates the group members' irrational reaction.

To varying degrees, transference affects every facilitation. But facilitators should use transference to intervene in developmental facilitation only, and then only with extreme caution. The interventions involve the two deepest levels (interpersonal and intrapersonal), which can be inappropriate, given the group's task. Also, facilitators must reach far beyond the directly observable data and make high-level inferences or attributions to identify the transference, which means that the inferences are difficult to confirm or eliminate. In short, by intervening on transference, facilitators can easily act inconsistently with the core values of facilitation.

Energy and Pace. Cofacilitators can switch roles so each can assume the less active role when one gets tired. Cofacilitators can also take advantage of their different paces by matching them to the needs of the group. For example, the faster-paced partner can actively intervene when the group is behind schedule and nearing the end of the session. The slower-paced partner can actively intervene when members are struggling to understand each other.

Training and Development. At times, cofacilitators should choose to play weaker roles to develop particular skills. This is true for experienced facilitators as well as those in training. This is a legitimate way to temporarily select roles, so long as cofacilitators seek feedback about their performance from their partners and do not attempt interventions so far beyond their ability that they harm the client.

When cofacilitators use their strengths and weaknesses to decide who should play which role, not all the relevant factors will indicate the same choice. For example, if the situation requires handling openly hostile conflict, the cofacilitator most skilled in this intervention may be much more emotionally exhausted than the other cofacilitator. Cofacilitators need to decide quickly which factors are more important at any given time.

Maintaining Boundaries Between Cofacilitators

Cofacilitators must avoid intervening too much or too little with each other. In a good cofacilitator relationship, the partners agree on when and how to modify each other's interventions, "correct" each other, reinforce each other's interventions, and help each other when one gets tangled in a conflict with the group. They must do this in a way that integrates their skills while preserving their individual identities, which made the collaboration appealing in the first place. It is a matter of setting boundaries (Alderfer, 1976). If cofacilitators allow each other to constantly interrupt and modify the other's interventions, they lose their individual identities. However, if they never do so, they lose the collaboration. Cofacilitators should discuss and agree on several issues before working with a group.

The Zone of Deference. An important part of intervening is knowing when not to. Organizational theorist Chester Barnard (1938) used the phrase "zone of indifference" to refer to the range within which employees obey orders without considering their merits. I use the phrase "zone of deference" to describe the area in which one cofacilitator lets the other cofacilitator's interventions stand, although the facilitator would have intervened differently. Without an agreed-on zone of deference, cofacilitators may constantly correct each other's interventions, confusing the group in their attempts to make things clearer. Or, to avoid seeming nit-picking or overbearing, cofacilitators may fail to modify any of each other's interventions, depriving the group of the benefits of cofacilation.

What types of interventions fall in the zone of deference? It is easier to describe which interventions fall outside the zone of deference. Ultimately, the answer lies with each cofacilitator team. However, cofacilitators can consider several overlapping questions. When the answer to at least one of the questions is yes, the cofacilitator should intervene on the partner's intervention.

1. *Will the client suffer harm?* The most elementary responsibility of facilitators to their groups is to do nothing that harms them. Interventions that cause harm include deceiving or demeaning members, cheating, breaking promises, and disobeying the law (Gellermann, Frankel, & Ladenson, 1990). Making interventions that are beyond the cofacilitators' skills can also harm the group.
2. *Is the intervention inconsistent with the core values of facilitation or the ground rules?* Any intervention that is not based on valid information or that does not enable the group to make free and informed choices that lead to internal commitment reduces the cofacilitators' effectiveness and integrity. Acting inconsistently with the ground rules has the same effect, because the rules are based on the core values.
3. *Does the intervention change the facilitator's role?* Leaving the role of facilitator violates the client-facilitator contract, unless the group and cofacilitators explicitly agree that a cofacilitator will temporarily leave the role of facilitator. Examples include acting as a group member, a group decision maker, a content expert, or intermediary between the group and others.
4. *Will the intervention prevent or hinder the client group from accomplishing its goals?* Interventions that prevent or hinder the client group from accomplishing its goals include taking the group off track, establishing agenda items in an order that requires the group to return to items members have already discussed, and providing interesting exercises that neither contribute to the task nor meet the group's maintenance needs.

Beyond excluding these areas, whether an intervention falls in the zone of deference depends on the groups' needs and the cofacilitators' preferences. Some cofacilitators work well by frequently interrupting each other, while others (and their groups) find the practice more distracting than helpful.

Given that cofacilitators have different needs and preferences, the zone of deference can be different for each cofacilitator. However, both cofacilitators must agree to each zone of deference. Still, one potential problem is that when members observe that the cofacilitators do not show equal deference toward each other, members may inaccurately attribute the difference to some conflict or status difference between cofacilitators. Cofacilitators can mitigate the problem by telling members why their zones are different.

Finally, the group's needs take priority over honoring a cofacilitator's zone of deference. At times, while on line, one cofacilitator realizes that the other's intervention should be corrected and that their agreement does not allow it. The cofacilitator should make the correction and deal with the inadequate agreement later or simultaneously, if possible.

Supporting an Intervention. While the zone of deference applies to situations in which one cofacilitator disagrees with the other's intervention, supporting an intervention occurs when one cofacilitator emphasizes the other's intervention. Here conflicts can occur when the cofacilitator who made the initial intervention expects support, while the other cofacilitator, believing the first cofacilitator does not need it, does not provide it. In the reverse situation, a cofacilitator offers support when the initial cofacilitator thinks it is unnecessary. Again, to avoid discrepant expectations, cofacilitators should discuss when and how they will support each other's interventions and how each cofacilitator can ask for support.

Rescuing a Cofacilitator. Sometimes, a cofacilitator gets in a conflict with the client group. This can happen in several ways. First, the cofacilitator can start the conflict by behaving ineffectively. For example, if the cofacilitator offers an opinion on an issue that divides the group, that part of the group that disagrees may attack the cofacilitator's opinion and competence for leaving the facilitator role.

Second, if the group considers one cofacilitator a safe target (Krantz, 1990), it may make the cofacilitator a scapegoat; that is, group members project their anger, frustration, or other feelings onto the cofacilitator, deny that they have the feelings, and try to exorcise the cofacilitator from the group, without acknowledging what is happening (Wells, 1990). The cofacilitator's response may escalate the conflict.

Third, the group may actively draw a cofacilitator into its conflict. When two parties (A and B) are in conflict, one party (for example, A) tends to draw a third party (X) into the conflict, in order to have an ally (X) and isolate party B (Bowen, 1978, cited in Smith, 1989). In cofacilitation, when a conflict divides the client group, one faction may try to draw a cofacilitator into the conflict. If successful, that cofacilitator finds herself in conflict with the other group members.

In a variation, the group splits the cofacilitators; that is, they assign their negative feelings to one cofacilitator and their positive feelings to the other cofacilitator. This is an irrational action, because whom the group designates as positive or negative has more to do with the group's issues than with the cofacilitators' actions. Again, depending on how the "negative" cofacilitator responds, the conflict can escalate.

What should one cofacilitator do when the other is in a conflict with the group? A natural reaction is to intervene and protect or rescue the partner from the conflict with the group. The reaction saves the partner and relieves the helping cofacilitator's concern about becoming a victim of the partner's conflict with the group (Steiner, 1974). Unfortunately, this discounts the partner and reinforces the group's belief that the rescued cofacilitator is bad or incompetent. Group members may reason that if the cofacilitator cannot extricate from the conflict without the help of the other cofacilitator, the group's negative assessment of the cofacilitator in conflict (and positive assessment of the helping cofacilitator) must be accurate.

A more effective response—one that avoids reinforcing the group's negative views—is to wait for the cofacilitator in conflict to ask for help. Waiting increases the chance that the cofacilitator will manage the conflict with the group and may simultaneously enhance the group's image of her. Allowing the cofacilitator to choose when to receive help increases the facilitator's free choice and reduces the image of the cofacilitator as helpless. If, however, the cofacilitator is acting inconsistently with the core values, principles, or ground rules, the other cofacilitator has a responsibility to intervene.

In some cases, a conflict between one cofacilitator and the group becomes known to the other cofacilitator first. For example, a manager in a top management retreat approaches cofacilitator A during a break and says, "Listen, A, [cofacilitator] B is a nice guy, but he's stirring up issues the group doesn't need to deal with, and people are getting upset with him. Don't tell him I said anything, but just steer the conversation back when he starts challenging the group." To avoid rescuing B, colluding with the client, or acting as an intermediary, cofacilitator A should explain that unless cofacilitator B can talk directly with those who are concerned, B will not have valid information to make a free and informed choice about whether or how to change his behavior. This is true whether or not cofacilitator A believes cofacilitator B is acting ineffectively. The conversation with cofacilitator B should occur with the entire group because it involves all members. Once the conversation is raised with the entire group, cofacilitator B can ask cofacilitator A for help.

Coordination and Openness with Clients

Because interventions are based on diagnosis, to coordinate their work, cofacilitators must discuss with each other what is happening in the group. Aside from telepathy, there are only two ways for cofacilitators to coordinate their work in front of the group: they can either talk openly or try to hide their discussions, using some secret language.

The genesis of the Training Group (T-Group) (Benne, 1964; Marrow, 1969), which is a source of many of the group facilitation techniques discussed in this book, reveals the advantages and risks in the open approach. The principles of the T-Group were determined in the summer of 1946 by social psychologist Kurt Lewin and his colleagues. Lewin, then a professor at the Massachusetts

Institute of Technology (MIT), was responding to a call from the director of the Connecticut State Commission, who was troubled by his staff's inability to help communities overcome bias and discrimination. Lewin—following his motto of "no action without research; no research without action" (Marrow, 1969, p. 193)—proposed a workshop that would simultaneously train commission staff members and provide research data on what produced the changes. The two-week workshop trained three groups of ten staff members, each of whom hoped to develop skills in working with people, changing others' attitudes, and learning about personal values and attitudes. Each group was led by one of Lewin's psychologist colleagues.

The training leaders used group discussion, supplemented by role playing. No here-and-now analysis of the groups' behavior was planned. Lewin and some of his graduate students served as researchers, observing each of the three groups and noting members' interactions. The researchers did not plan to share their observations with group participants.

However, each evening, the researchers met with the group leaders to discuss and record on tape their process observations of the groups and the leaders. The evening meetings were planned to include only the researchers and group leaders. One day, a few participants asked to attend the evening meetings. Most researchers and group leaders feared that it would be harmful for the participants to hear discussions of their behavior. They also had no plans for handling participants' (or their own) reactions to the experience. But Lewin, an advocate of feedback, saw no reason why the researchers and leaders should withhold data from the participants and believed the feedback could be helpful.

The evening sessions had an electrifying effect on everyone involved. When leaders and researchers analyzed an event in a group, the group participants interrupted with their interpretations. Energetic discussions followed—some lasting three hours—as researchers, leaders, and participants tried to make sense of the different perspectives. Members found that when they participated nondefensively, they learned important things about their behavior, how others reacted to them, and how groups in general behave. Together, the researchers, leaders, and participants had found a powerful method of learning.

By watching leaders discuss their work, group members learned how groups act and how leaders can create change. By participating in the discussions, members clarified leaders' diagnoses and helped the leaders select more appropriate interventions. Finally, by participating in the sessions with leaders and researchers, they learned effective group behaviors and methods of change.

Lewin's findings suggest that developmental cofacilitators should openly coordinate their work in front of the group and encourage members to participate. In developmental facilitation, the division of labor between cofacilitators and members must shift so that ultimately, members facilitate their process. Cofacilitators take the first step in the shift when they allow members to observe and question the "backstage" part of their cofacilitation.

There are many risks in open coordination. When the group is angry with the cofacilitators, members may use the cofacilitators' openness to suggest that the facilitators are not competent. In some situations, cofacilitator openness does not help the members achieve their goals. When cofacilitators intervene with each other at a depth much greater than their intervention with the group, the group may consider it a waste of time or become uncomfortable. Another problematic situation is when cofacilitators disagree with each other without using effective behavior (Dies, Mallet, & Johnson, 1979). In the first few meetings, the lack of group cohesiveness can lead to divisiveness when cofacilitators disagree with each other, even if they do so appropriately (Yalom, 1985). But cofacilitators must be careful not to discount members' abilities. It is easy to justify not being open with members by claiming they are not ready to handle it or would consider it a waste of time.

In basic facilitation, even when cofacilitator openness does not help the group directly achieve its primary goal, it normally enhances trust. Members are less likely to become suspicious when cofacilitators coordinate openly than when they allow members to interpret ambiguous gestures such as nods, frowns, and hand motions. Like whispering or note passing, secret signals raise suspicion among members by destroying the impression that a cofacilitator is "only what he appears to be and that things are as he claims them to be" (Goffman, 1959, p. 176).

To illustrate how secret signals affect clients, consider my nonfacilitation experience with my university's gym service counter; I was trying to get a locker assignment. My old locker had been cleaned out and the combination changed when I had missed the deadline for paying the locker renewal fee. When I asked for my old locker because I liked its location, the employee said it was not available and that only a few were left, none near my original locker. Overhearing the conversation, the employee's supervisor said to me, "Let me look in my office and see what I can do." She winked at the employee. I wondered what the wink meant. What was the supervisor secretly telling her employee that she could not say in front of me? Was she telling the employee she would return without a better locker but would go through the motions of looking so that I would feel she had tried to help me? Was she telling the employee that she knew my locker was available, that she would give it to me, and that the employee should not be concerned, because the employee had acted correctly by initially refusing my request? In a minute, the supervisor returned smiling and said, "Look what I've got here. Your old locker is available." I was pleased with the result, but I distrusted them. I felt that they had colluded to manipulate me in some way, perhaps to make me feel grateful that they had gone out of their way to accommodate me.

Unlike locker supervisors, cofacilitators cannot provide their service unless the group trusts them. Cofacilitators cannot risk coordinating their work in a way that raises questions about their credibility. And yet there are times when a secret language is useful, not because the cofacilitators want to hide what they are saying or even that they are saying something but because openly coordinating would simply be distracting. How do cofacilitators solve the problem?

One approach—based on the ground rule "share all relevant information"—is to tell members about the coordinating actions they might observe (for example, nodding or hand signals) and to point out that their purpose is to avoid distracting the group, not to keep secrets from them. As assurance, the cofacilitators can promise to share their private discussions whenever a member asks. Finally, members can agree to tell the cofacilitators if the secret coordination becomes distracting. The approach maintains or enhances trust in the cofacilitators. The underlying principle is that **cofacilitators should coordinate their work in a manner consistent with the core values and the client's goals.**

Cofacilitator Self-critiques

After each facilitation session, cofacilitators should conduct a self-critique. The critique is in addition to the self-critique at the end of each session conducted with the group. Although the group's self-critique also focuses on the cofacilitators' behavior, it is not nearly as extensive as the cofacilitators' self-critique. Cofacilitators will remember many more details of the session if they conduct their self-critique immediately after the session. In developmental facilitation, group members can learn by having the cofacilitators share relevant parts of their self-critique with them.

In addition to discussing what has happened in the group, the cofacilitators should discuss ways in which they worked together well and ways in which they need to improve. One approach is to analyze the critical incidents during that session, comparing how they handled them with their cofacilitation agreement. For example, after a recent facilitation session, I asked my cofacilitator whether I was adding to his interventions too frequently. I said I was concerned that he might see my additions as intrusive. He saw my additions as appropriate, consistent with our agreement, and wanted me to continue them.

Cofacilitators should also discuss their behaviors, feelings, and thoughts toward each other and deal with them so that they do not contribute negatively to the group's dynamics. Sometimes, the behaviors, feelings, and thoughts stem from the cofacilitators' actions, such as when one cofacilitator frequently interrupts the other. But other times, the feelings between cofacilitators stem from and parallel a situation within the client group (Alderfer, 1990). For example, if the group has split the cofacilitators, assigning negative feelings to one cofacilitator and positive feelings to the other, the cofacilitators can end up in conflict with each other because the group is treating them differently. If cofacilitators do not discuss and trace the source of the feelings, they become victims of the group's dynamics. Whatever the source, cofacilitators' feelings, thoughts, and behaviors toward each other about status, control, intimacy, and attraction are all important to discuss. The principle is that **the cofacilitators' effectiveness depends on their openness with each other about issues that may affect their working rela-**

tionship. If cofacilitators withhold relevant information from each other, their relationship is doomed.

Summary

This chapter explored how cofacilitators can work together to better serve their groups and improve their own skills. The chapter began by discussing the potential advantages and disadvantages of cofacilitating. In deciding whether to cofacilitate, the underlying principle is that together, cofacilitators should be able to diagnose and intervene in a greater range of situations and with greater skill than one facilitator could alone. Cofacilitators can work together effectively to the extent that the facilitators' orientations and styles are either congruent or complementary.

The chapter also described different ways that cofacilitators can divide and coordinate their labor and, after selecting a division of labor, factors that facilitators can consider when deciding who will fill which role. In making the role decision, cofacilitators should usually allocate roles in a way that makes the best use of their skills and characteristics. This section also considered how cofacilitators maintain boundaries and how they coordinate their work in front of groups. Finally, the chapter discussed how cofacilitators can use self-critiques to improve their effectiveness.

Part Four Using

Facilitation Skills in

Your Own Organization

Chapter Twelve Serving as Facilitator in Your Own Organization

Many facilitators facilitate groups in their own organizations. Such facilitators are known as *internal facilitators*. Some examples include a manager who facilitates quality teams throughout the organization, a human resources director who facilitates an employee-management group from the marketing division, or an employee who facilitates a meeting of the top management group. Internal facilitators face special problems. They may be pressured by their bosses to facilitate inconsistently with the core values, or their behavior in their nonfacilitator roles in the organization may reduce their credibility when serving as facilitators.

This chapter describes how the effectiveness of internal facilitators depends in part on how their facilitator role develops in their organizations. It discusses strategies that internal facilitators can use to improve their role and increase their effectiveness.

Throughout the chapter, except where noted, the term *facilitator* refers to internal facilitator.

How the Facilitator's Role Develops

The special issues that an internal facilitator faces stem from his role in the organization. To understand the nature of their role and how they can shape it, it is necessary to understand how the facilitator's role develops.

Like any organizational role, the internal facilitator's role develops through a cyclical process involving people who are directly associated with the facilitator. The people—collectively called the facilitator's *role-set* (Katz & Kahn, 1978)— include the facilitator's immediate supervisor and immediate subordinates, the facilitator's primary client groups, and the supervisors of the primary client groups. Because each person in the facilitator's role-set depends on the facilitator in some way, each has some stake in how the facilitator performs. As a result, each develops some beliefs and attitudes about what the facilitator should and should not do in the facilitator role.

The constituents of the role-set may communicate their expectations to the facilitator, either directly or indirectly. For example, the facilitator's supervisor may state explicitly that the facilitator should not work with certain groups in the organization. Or, the supervisor may simply imply through actions that the facilitator should evaluate client-group members for purposes of merit increases. Similarly, the expectations that role-set constituents send may be specific, such as "Do not turn down any assignment from a client group high in the organizational hierarchy." Or, the expectations can be vague, such as a client group that says, "We want you to be available when we need you."

Facilitators also have expectations about how they should fulfill their facilitator role. Just as the people in the role-set communicate their expectations to facilitators, facilitators communicate their expectations to their role-set. For example, facilitators may tell client groups that they cannot mediate between the group and its supervisor but they can help the client group figure out how to raise difficult issues with its supervisor. Or, they may tell their own supervisor that the rules of confidentiality in the group prevent them from sharing specific comments that members make in their meetings.

The facilitator's role develops as constituents of the role-set communicate their expectations to the facilitator and vice versa. The more similar the expectations, the less conflict the facilitator will experience with these people.

One reason it is difficult for facilitators to fulfill their role is that they have a potentially large number of people in their role-set. If the facilitators' potential clients include all employees of their organizations, over time every employee could be sending expectations of how facilitators do their job. As the number of people in the role-set increases, so does the likelihood that some of their expectations for the facilitator will be incompatible. Therefore, the larger the number of people in the facilitator's role-set, the greater is the potential for conflict with those people.

To make matters more complex, **the facilitator and the people in the role-set do not send and receive their expectations in isolation. Organizational, interpersonal, and individual factors also influence what each person believes the facilitator's role should be.** Consider some examples. In organizations in which hierarchical status is considered important, role-set constituents may expect that the facilitator will not openly confront client-group members who have greater hierarchical status than the facilitator. If the interpersonal relationship between facilitator and supervisor has been characterized by competition, the supervisor may expect the facilitator to function with relatively little autonomy. Finally, if clients see the facilitator as a humorous person, they may expect the facilitator to use humor to diffuse tense situations.

This chapter also discusses how facilitators can influence organizational, interpersonal, and individual factors in order to influence how their role develops. Not coincidentally, the factors are sometimes the same ones that contribute to the problems that led a group to ask the facilitator for help.

Finally, **the internal facilitator's role is complicated by the fact that he or she typically fills another role in the organization.** The organization may consider the facilitator role to be a part of the larger organizational role the person fills. Internal facilitators are often also *human resources managers, organization development managers,* or *trainers,* because all these roles require skills that are useful in facilitation. **But any organizational member can also serve as an internal facilitator, regardless of his or her other organizational role.**

Complications arise when the people in the role-set expect the facilitator, when serving as facilitator, to act in a way that is consistent with his or her nonfacilitator role but inconsistent with the facilitator role. For example, if the facilitator's nonfacilitator position is higher in the organizational hierarchy than the clients' positions, members may expect the facilitator to convey messages to their superiors. The facilitator's superior may expect the facilitator to evaluate the group members' performance as part of the performance appraisal process. If the facilitator is also the human resources director, the client group may expect the facilitator to make decisions on personnel matters. If the facilitator is also the budget director, the client group may expect the facilitator to pass judgment on budget matters.

The problem arises partly because role-set constituents often do not think of the person's work in terms of roles. Rather, they think of the person as someone who does different tasks and who can perform any task or behavior in any context. **The challenge for the facilitator is to help role-set constituents think in terms of roles and to explain that while serving as facilitator, he or she cannot engage in nonfacilitator role behaviors that conflict with the facilitator role.**

Advantages and Disadvantages of the Internal Facilitator Role

As the internal facilitator's role develops, the role can create problems for effective facilitation. But, like the role of external facilitator, the role of internal facilitator also has a number of advantages. Drawing heavily on the work of Fritz Steele (1982), this chapter considers the advantages and disadvantages in the context of the same overlapping factors that generate both of them.

Accessibility

Accessibility works in two directions in the facilitator-client group relationship.

Access and Information About the Organization. An internal facilitator knows a lot about the organization's history, structure, dynamics, and its people. Sometimes, the facilitator also knows a lot about the potential client group. In role terms, many of the facilitator's clients may be members of his or her nonfacilitator role-set. All this information helps the facilitator quickly understand the client group's situation. It can also help the facilitator to quickly diagnose problems in a group's behavior and help the group analyze its decisions in the context of the culture of the organization. However, the internal facilitator's familiarity with the client's situation can lead him or her to presume that information, assumptions, and inferences are valid, even if they have not been tested.

Access and Continuity of Work. Internal facilitators are typically more accessible to groups. They are relatively easy to contact and, depending on the nature of their nonfacilitator role, may be able to spend more time with the group than an external facilitator. Internal facilitators can more easily be involved in a project from its beginning to its end, and they can see the long-term results of the project. Groups view internal facilitators as more available for ongoing support, and internal facilitators may have more opportunities to build on earlier efforts. An internal facilitator's continuous visibility in the organization reminds others of the facilitator's work, so that word of an internal facilitator's successful facilitations spreads more broadly in the organization.

However, groups' increased accessibility has disadvantages. Groups may expect the facilitator to devote more time than the facilitator can allot to any particular group. This can be especially difficult if a facilitator's supervisor expects him or her to devote less time to facilitation. Because facilitators are more available for ongoing support and the design of follow-up projects, it is more difficult to determine when a project has ended and the terms of the project agreement have been fulfilled. Facilitators are also more available to be a scapegoat of an unsuccessful project. Finally, just as word of facilitators' successes is more likely to spread throughout their organizations, so is the word of failures. However, if facilitators value valid information, word of failure is only a disadvantage when a facilitator is made a scapegoat.

The Insider Image

There are several advantages to being considered an insider. Groups may consider an internal facilitator "one of us." They are likely to value the facilitator's insider knowledge of the organization and of them. As members of the same organization, they have mutual interests. For these reasons, groups may be more comfortable with an internal facilitator at the beginning of a project. If a facilitator is part of an internal staff group that provides facilitation services, the group's reputation may allow client groups to feel some confidence in the facilitator, even if they have not worked with him or her personally.

However, being "one of us" is a liability if clients see facilitators as either too close to the problem to be neutral or too blind to their assumptions to challenge their thinking. If the reputation of the facilitator or the facilitator's department is negative, the group may consider the internal facilitator an organizational adversary—"one of them" rather than "one of us." This is worse than the typical reputation of the external facilitator, which is "not one of us but not one of them."

Finally, an internal facilitator has a more difficult time establishing credibility as a facilitation expert, in contrast to an external facilitator, who is brought in to help with a specific situation. This is especially true when the facilitator raises issues that challenge the culture of the organization. One of the most subtle but powerful expectations of members—including of an internal facilitator—is that all employees perform their work in a manner consistent with the culture of the organization. Although members may not agree with aspects of the culture, at some level they value it because it is predictable and it meets some of their needs. Consequently, when interventions identify how group members contribute to the dysfunctional aspects of the culture, group members or the facilitator's supervisor may see the facilitator as disloyal or heretical.

Job Security

An internal facilitator has the security of a regular paycheck, and many potential clients are available without much marketing effort. However, the increased security that comes from working for a single organization also creates increased risk when that security is threatened. If a single project fails, the external facilitator may lose a client, but the internal facilitator may lose a job. Consequently, the internal facilitator has more financial security to lose when confronting a group or supervisor.

Strategies for Improving the Internal Facilitator's Role

The role of internal facilitators is not fixed. Because they are part of the cyclical process through which the role develops, they can influence how the role is defined. This section describes general strategies that internal facilitators can use to increase the effectiveness of their role. Some of the strategies are from the work of Fritz Steele (1982). Many involve actively shaping the role (Steele, 1982) before finding that others have established firm expectations that reduce the facilitator's effectiveness. In doing so, facilitators attempt to reduce ambiguities and conflicts that role-set constituents and facilitators have about the role.

When considering the strategies, it is important to realize that **there is essentially no difference between what constitutes effective behavior for internal facilitators and external facilitators. The core values of valid information, free and informed choice, and internal commitment guide the behaviors of internal and external facilitators alike. These are the same core values that generate effective behavior for all members of an organization. Therefore, the core values must logically define effective behavior for the internal facilitator, who is both a facilitator and a member of the organization.**

The strategies (shown in Exhibit 12.1) deal with increasing the effectiveness of facilitators, not their political acceptance in the organization. This means

Exhibit 12.1. Strategies for Improving the Internal Facilitator's Role.

1. Clarify personal interests regarding the role of facilitator.

2. Anticipate and discuss role conflicts before the conflicts arise.

3. Create opportunities to educate others about the facilitator's role.

4. Become identified with different groups in the organization rather than one particular group.

5. Clarify when one is switching roles.

6. Use the core values in one's nonfacilitator role.

7. Discuss problems in past working relationships with potential client groups.

8. Turn down facilitator assignments when it is impossible to be substantively neutral.

9. Be willing to give up the facilitator role.

10. Become an informal internal organizational change agent.

that the facilitator's primary concern is to define his role consistently with the core values. This creates a paradox. In the short-term, facilitators may have more opportunities to help groups if they violate the core values. Yet by violating the core values, facilitators become less able to help groups. The strategies deal with this paradox by helping the facilitators create conditions that do not require them to violate the core values. Most of the strategies (they are also principles) can be used continually, not only when facilitators are actively facilitating a client.

1. *Clarify personal interests regarding the role of facilitator.* Specific expectations that role-set constituents and the facilitator have for the facilitator role (for example, the facilitator should not facilitate groups in her department) are simply positions, not interests. To effectively shape the facilitator role, internal facilitators must clarify the interests underlying their expectations for the role. In many cases, the interests will lie in acting consistently with the core values. But they may have other interests. For example, facilitators may expect that they can decide whether to work with a group because they are interested in avoiding overcommitments that would make them insufficiently accessible.

Sometimes, role conflicts occur between the role-set and the facilitator simply because the facilitator's expectations for the role are in conflict. For example, the facilitator expects that he will be available to facilitate throughout the organization while expecting to provide intensive developmental facilitation for one department. Alone, each expectation is appropriate; together, they are incompatible. After identifying the conflicting expectations, the facilitator should determine whether the underlying interests are also incompatible or whether the interests can be met through different but compatible expectations.

Similarly, facilitators need to understand the interests behind others' expectations for the facilitator role. Following the ground rules, when facilitators discuss expectations with members, they should focus on the interests behind the expectations before deciding on the expectations.

2. *Anticipate and discuss role conflicts before the conflicts arise.* It is easier for people to discuss their conflicts about their expectations for the facilitator's role before the conflicts actually arise than after they are engaged in conflict. For example, it is easier to discuss whether the facilitator should serve as a mediator between a client group and its supervisor before the supervisor asks the facilitator to do so. This requires that facilitators anticipate the kinds of role conflicts that are likely to arise with different members of their role-set.

In simple cases, facilitators will have an expectation different from one or more of their role-set constituents'. In complicated cases, different role-set constituents will have expectations that conflict with each other as well as with the facilitator. The challenge for the facilitator is to reach agreement with different role-set constituents so that everyone's expectations are compatible. Discussing the role conflicts and reaching agreement is similar to—and, in some cases, part of—contracting with clients.

3. *Create opportunities to educate others about the facilitator's role.* Role conflicts often arise simply because the role-set does not know what a facilitator is or does. In fact, many people equate facilitators with mediators or arbitrators (see Chapter One for a discussion of the mediator role). Consequently, the expectations for a facilitator are borrowed from another role. The conflicts can be avoided or reduced by creating opportunities to educate others about the facilitator's role. This also helps constituents reframe the meaning of the facilitator's actions. For example, once a role-set constituent understands the facilitator's role, the constituent may no longer necessarily consider the facilitator remiss upon hearing that the facilitator allowed a client group to make a poor decision. Educating others also generates future clients as employees understand how the facilitator can help them. But education is a process, not an event. To get results, the facilitator must continually find ways to help other employees understand the role and its benefits.

4. *Become identified with different groups in the organization rather than with one particular group.* Clients consider external facilitators objective because they are not aligned with any particular part of the organization. But every internal facilitator has a role somewhere in the organizational chart. **The more groups with which the facilitator becomes identified, the less likely it is that any one group will consider the facilitator an organizational adversary.** Consider a potential client group that is thinking about working with the facilitator, and assume that the potential client group is likely to consider some other organizational groups as supporters and others as adversaries. If the facilitator were identified only with the potential client group's adversary group, by extension the facilitator would also be considered an adversary. Similarly, if the facilitator were identified only with the potential client group's supporter group, by extension the facilitator would also be considered a supporter. However, if the facilitator were identified with both adversary and supporter groups, members of the potential client group would conclude that the facilitator is neither purely a supporter nor an adversary. And, in somewhat different terms, this describes

the facilitator's role—to support the client group while challenging and confronting it.

However, the purpose of being identified with different groups is not merely to avoid being labeled a supporter or adversary. Spending time with different groups increases the facilitator's knowledge about different groups, which helps the facilitator help groups look at problems from multiple perspectives. It also provides opportunities to educate others about the facilitator's role and makes the facilitator more accessible to potential clients. *Different groups* refers to formal groups such as different departments or units and informal groups such as employees and managers, men and women, or older and younger employees.

Spending time with different groups may be difficult, given the facilitator's other organizational role. But for the facilitator who also holds a staff position (for example, budget, personnel, training, organization development) that serves the entire organization, the strategy can also improve the facilitator's effectiveness in her or his nonfacilitator role.

A similar problem occurs with the facilitator's position in the organizational hierarchy, which is associated with her role. External facilitators do not have any fixed hierarchical status in the client organization. Rather, their hierarchical status as external facilitators is tied to the level of the primary client group. If they are working with the board or top management of the organization, their status will be higher in the organization than if they are working with a group of first-line supervisors. In contrast, the internal facilitator's position in the hierarchy is fixed. Even if the internal facilitator's position does not affect his actions as a facilitator, it is likely to affect the group's perception of him, just as his departmental location influences members' perceptions. Similarly, facilitators are more likely to reduce any negative perceptions regarding their position in the hierarchy if they identify with employees at all levels of the hierarchy. Given the culture of organization, this is more difficult for facilitators located at lower levels of the hierarchy.

5. *Clarify when one is switching roles.* When facilitating, sometimes it is appropriate for facilitators to switch to their nonfacilitator role. The next section discusses when it is appropriate to switch roles. Here, it is enough to note that facilitators should clearly identify when they are switching to their nonfacilitator role. For example, the facilitator may say, "I'm answering this question in my role as human resources director." When the group asks the facilitator a question that could be answered in either the role of facilitator or human resources director, the facilitator can ask, "Are you asking me this in my role as facilitator or as human resources director?" Similarly, facilitators should also clearly identify when they have returned to the facilitator role. They can do this simply by saying, "I'm back in the facilitator role."

6. *Use the core values in one's nonfacilitator role.* As noted previously, the core values of effective facilitation are also the core values that generate effective behavior for all employees in an organization. This implies that facilitators

should perform their nonfacilitator role in a manner consistent with the core values. Doing so has several consequences.

First, employees make inferences about the facilitators's ability from observing how the facilitators behave in their nonfacilitator role. Internal facilitators cannot use the core values in their facilitator role and a different set of values in their nonfacilitator role and expect that organizational members will completely trust them as a facilitator. If facilitators do not perform their nonfacilitator role in a manner consistent with the core values, employees will question their ability to facilitate effectively.

Second, using the core values positively affects how the facilitator role develops, by influencing the interpersonal relationships between the facilitators and their role-set. Just as the core values generate effective group behavior, they also generate effective interpersonal behavior. For example, ineffective interpersonal relationships often result from untested inferences. Using the core values will lead the facilitator to test inferences that she makes about role-set constituents and to inquire about inferences they make about her. Finally, consistently using the core values over time changes certain individual attributes of the facilitator. For example, if facilitators genuinely seek valid information and encourage free and informed choices, they are less likely to be seen as defensive, controlling, or manipulative.

Part of using the core values means facilitators explain to their role-set how the core values guide facilitators' behavior. This helps the role-set understand why the facilitators act as they do.

In short, the core values represent a way of managing, not only a way to facilitate. Consequently, facilitators should consider every interaction with employees of the organization as an opportunity to establish their credibility for generating valid information, free and informed choice, and internal commitment.

7. *Discuss problems in past working relationships with potential client groups.* Even if facilitators begin using the core values in their nonfacilitator role, they still have a history with potential client groups who knew them before they used the core values. If that history includes problems in working together, the potential client may not trust facilitators enough to use them. *Redeveloping trust with potential clients is a critical process for internal facilitators.* A facilitator begins to redevelop this trust by asking potential clients directly whether anything has occurred in their past working relationship that would lead the client to have reduced trust in the facilitator.

Also, if, in their previous experiences with a potential client, facilitators are aware of times when they acted inconsistently with the core values, they should share the relevant information, explain why they considered their behavior ineffective, and explain how they would act differently now. (Following the ground rules, facilitators should also ask whether the potential client considered their [the facilitator's] behavior ineffective.) Volunteering the information shows the potential client that facilitators are aware of their own previously ineffective behavior and that the facilitators are capable of making significant changes in their own behavior. Sharing the information also demonstrates that facilitators can discuss their own behavior without getting defensive. This makes it easier for potential clients to raise concerns that they had considered undiscussable with the facilitator. Through such discussions, potential clients begin to increase their trust in the facilitator. In essence, **facilitators redevelop trust with potential clients not only by using the core values but also by using the core values to talk with potential clients about how they (the facilitators) have acted ineffectively in the past.**

8. *Turn down facilitator assignments when it is impossible to be substantively neutral.* Sometimes, the facilitator cannot facilitate a potential client group and remain substantively neutral. This occurs when the facilitator has strong feelings about the subject of facilitation. In the extreme case, the facilitator's own work group may ask her to serve as a formal facilitator on issues that involve her directly. *Substantively neutral* is a relative term; one could argue that an internal facilitator can never be totally substantively neutral about issues within the organization. However, there are two working criteria for judging neutrality: facilitators must believe that their personal views about the substance of the facilitation will not significantly affect the facilitation, and the client group must believe that facilitator's personal views about the substance of the facilitation will not significantly affect her facilitation.

When facilitators cannot meet both criteria, they must turn down requests in order to maintain the credibility of the facilitator's role. But even if the facilitator could facilitate and remain substantively neutral, there is another reason for turning down the request when the facilitator is a member of the client group. Facilitating is mentally demanding work that requires complete concentration. It is almost impossible to simultaneously facilitate and participate as a member of the group. By serving as formal facilitators, people give up the opportunity to participate in the substance of discussions that directly affect them.

The conflict occurs only when the person is simultaneously serving as a *formal* facilitator and participating as a group member. In contrast, no conflict occurs when the person *informally* uses facilitation skills to help improve the group's process while simultaneously participating as a group member. The difference between the two situations stems from role expectations. Members who understand the facilitator role will expect anyone who formally fills that role to remain substantively neutral. However, if any member informally uses facilitation skills as part of the role of member, other members do not expect that individual to remain substantively neutral. The difference is not one of semantics. The work that each employee does, the amount of formal authority he or she has, and the expectations others have stem from the formal role he or she fills. The role of facilitator prohibits engaging in the substantive discussions of group members. In contrast, the role of group member does not prohibit using facilitation skills to improve the group's process.

9. *Be willing to give up the facilitator role.* Facilitators should be willing to give up the facilitator role if they cannot fill that role in a manner consistent

with the core values. Such willingness makes it more likely that facilitators will take the risks necessary to openly confront role conflicts, including those with their superiors. Ironically, willingness to step aside may lead to a set of role expectations that cancel the need to give up the role.

Still, in some cases, facilitators will find that despite their efforts to shape their role, it is not possible to fill the facilitator role without repeatedly violating the core values. For some people, giving up the internal facilitator role may also mean having to leave their jobs and their organizations. Financially, this is the most serious consequence an internal facilitator faces. Yet continuing to facilitate while violating the core values leads back to the problem that opened this section. By violating the core values, the facilitator becomes less able to help clients.

10. *Become an informal internal organizational change agent.* Material earlier in the chapter described how the role-set's expectations of the facilitator are influenced by organizational factors. Some factors may hinder the facilitator's ability to fulfill that role effectively. For example, in an organization with a strong hierarchy, potential client groups may not be permitted to contact the facilitator directly. In some cases, the organizational factors that hinder the facilitator from fulfilling the role of facilitator are the same factors that contribute to the client group's problems and lead them to ask a facilitator for help.

One choice facilitators face is whether to attempt to change the group or organizational culture that hinder them from fulfilling the role. Culture has a pervasive and strong influence on the behaviors of members, and culture is very difficult to change. However, changing a group or organizational culture can lead to significant change in the facilitator's role. Of course, using the core values in the role of informal internal change agent is essential.

Managing Role Issues Throughout Facilitation

With some variation, internal facilitators and external facilitators must deal with the issues that we have discussed in earlier chapters: establishing the role of the facilitator, contracting with clients, diagnosing behavior in groups, intervening in groups, and working with a cofacilitator. Internal facilitators are always managing expectations about their role, whether they are formally discussing their role or contracting, diagnosing, intervening, or cofacilitating. This section revisits previous chapters and highlights the issues and situations that arise throughout facilitation and that require internal facilitators to manage expectations about their role. Many situations represent potential pitfalls for facilitators. Facilitators manage the situations and avoid the pitfalls by using the ten strategies described in the previous section.

The Role of the Facilitator

The limits of the facilitator's responsibility. Compared with external facilitators, internal facilitators experience more pressure to take responsibility for the group.

Consider, for example, a facilitator who is also the personnel director and reports to the city manager and whose client group is a citywide task force that also reports to the city manager. The city manager tells the facilitator that she is concerned the task force is not making progress quickly enough. The facilitator, in an effort to address the city manager's concern, acts as a mediator and conveys the message directly to the group. Or, the facilitator attempts to speed the group's progress by making content suggestions. While the responses to the city manager might be appropriate for a personnel director, they are inconsistent with the facilitator's role.

To remain consistent with the role, the facilitator needs to explain his interests behind having the city manager convey her message directly to the client group. If the facilitator is concerned that the city manager thinks the facilitator is not doing his job effectively, he tests the inference with the city manager. In doing so, the facilitator may learn that the city manager either has unrealistic expectations for the facilitation process or is unclear about the facilitator's role.

Switching from the facilitator to the expert or resource role. Chapter One discussed conditions under which it is appropriate for facilitators to leave their role. Unlike external facilitators, the internal facilitators must also decide when it is appropriate to switch to their nonfacilitator organizational role. The nonfacilitator is the role of expert or resource person discussed in Chapter One.

Consider, for example, a client group that is discussing how to establish self-managing work teams in its department, in which team members decide how to plan, divide, and coordinate the work among themselves. To foster the change, the group may see the need to change the job descriptions of all team members involved. The facilitator who also serves as a personnel manager will know how the client group gets job descriptions changed. It is appropriate for the facilitator to temporarily leave that role and, in the role of personnel manager, describe the process by which the client group can request changes in job descriptions.

It is appropriate to switch to the nonfacilitator role when the group requests it. In this situation, the facilitator becomes like any other organizational member from whom the group seeks information. The only difference is that in this case, the organizational member is already in the room.

The facilitator faces a dilemma when deciding whether to share relevant information in the nonfacilitator role when the group has not asked for it. If the facilitator waits to be asked by the group, the facilitator increases the likelihood that the group may make a poor decision without the information. However, if the facilitator volunteers the information, the facilitator may inappropriately increase the group's dependence on her. In resolving the dilemma, the facilitator must weigh the negative consequences of withholding the information against the risk of increasing the group's dependence.

Contracting

Shortcutting the contracting process. When facilitators are familiar with the members of a client group, it is tempting to shortcut the contracting process. If they assume that they know the client's situation or the client's commitment, they may not obtain certain diagnostic information or may not obtain agreements at a given stage. Avoid that temptation. If the facilitator's assumptions about the client are accurate, the contracting will take relatively little time. But if the facilitator shortcuts the process and the assumptions are wrong, the facilitator will develop a poor contract with the client. The poor contract will also create problems throughout the facilitation.

Establishing ground rules for confidentiality. As members of the organization, facilitators have more opportunities to share information they obtain in the sessions with nongroup members. Various organizational members, including the facilitator's supervisor, will frequently ask the facilitator how the group is doing. If the facilitation addresses a major conflict in the organization, people will want to know not only what the group has decided but what individual group members have said. Clients want assurance that the facilitator will not violate the group's ground rules for confidentiality.

Apart from expressing their commitment to maintain the group's confidentiality, facilitators can encourage members to discuss with them any reason members have to question whether they have violated the group's confidentiality.

There may also be times when groups ask facilitators a question in their nonfacilitator role and facilitators cannot answer the question without violating the confidentiality of their nonfacilitator role. For example, the facilitator who is also the personnel director may know why an employee in the department was fired but cannot legally share the information. To maintain credibility while simultaneously maintaining confidentiality, the facilitator explains that the information is confidential and the reason it is confidential.

What should facilitators do when they obtain information in the facilitator role that they would act on if they had obtained it in their nonfacilitator role? Consider the example of my colleague who is an internal facilitator and human resources director for his organization. While facilitating a quality improvement group, the group began discussing a departmental policy about overtime. The facilitator quickly realized that if the members' comments were accurate, the departmental policy was in violation of the organizational policy. Had he heard the discussion when he was acting in his human resources director's role, he would have contacted the department head to discuss the apparent violation. The question is, should the human resources director take different action because he obtained the information in his role as facilitator and in the context of a confidentiality agreement?

The situation poses a dilemma because part of the clients' trust in the facilitator stems from the fact that, theoretically, the facilitator has no influence over what happens to the members outside the facilitated group. But if the facilitator acts on the information in his human resources director role, he does have influence. While in this situation the influence would have benefited the group members, in other situations it may disadvantage them personally. If the facilitator does not act on the information and neither does the group, the facilitator is in the untenable position of knowing that some personnel procedures are being violated but not being able to act on that knowledge. On the other hand, if the facilitator acts on the information in his human resources director role, group members may in the future withhold relevant information, concerned that the facilitator will act on it in his other role.

One approach to the dilemma lies in the core value of generating valid information. In an organization that acts consistently with this value, members would consider it appropriate for the facilitator to act on the information in his human resources director role. This would suggest that a client group that espouses the core values would act accordingly.

However facilitators decide to deal with the dilemma, clearly contracting with members about how they will treat such information provides them with valid information with which they can then decide whether to share or withhold certain information in their discussions. Anticipating a conflicting issue means contracting about it before it arises.

Length of contract. Because internal facilitators are relatively available to provide ongoing support to clients, it is easy for the facilitator's work with the group to extend beyond their agreement. The problem is not in providing ongoing support or extending the length of a project. It is in doing so without an agreement to guide the work. The facilitator addresses the problem by clearly identifying when a group's request surpasses the initial agreement and then reaching a new agreement with the group about the new request.

In addition to contracting with their clients, internal facilitators often need to contract with their supervisors about such issues as how they will receive facilitation requests and how they will balance their facilitation work with other work. These issues are discussed in Resource F, which includes a contracting questionnaire for internal facilitators and their supervisors to use.

Diagnosis

Testing inferences. Internal facilitators face the same problem in diagnosing as they do when contracting. Their familiarity with the organization, the group, or its members can lead them to misinterpret members' behavior. For example, if they believe that one member of the group is a so-called difficult person, they are likely to find that person violating ground rules even when the person is not. The challenge for facilitators is to use their information about the client group and the organization as hypotheses to be openly tested with the client group rather than as predetermined truths. If facilitators seek valid information in their non-facilitator roles, they mitigate the problem.

Things to Consider Before Stepping In

Developmental facilitation. Because developmental facilitation relies more on deeper interventions, it creates more risks for clients but also creates the potential for more fundamental and permanent changes. As facilitators make deeper interventions, they raise issues about the culture of the organization and about group members' deeply held values and beliefs. As discussed previously, when facilitators' interventions identify how group members contribute to the dysfunctional aspects of the culture, group members or the facilitators' supervisors may see them as disloyal or heretical.

Facilitators reduce the chance of this happening by educating the group and their supervisors about the kinds of cultural issues that might arise in the facilitation. By giving some examples, facilitators can determine whether the client or supervisor is willing to have the issues raised. If not, facilitators decide whether there is enough support to proceed with the facilitation.

How to Intervene

Choosing your words carefully. Just as the terms people use can identify which region of the country they are from, so the terms employees use can identify which part of the organization they are from. The different terms describe the same object, situation, person, entity, or event but sometimes convey different meanings. For example, in universities that have more than one campus, employees of the campus at which the university was founded often refer to their campus as the *main campus.* However, employees at other campuses refer to the founding campus simply by its name (such as the Ann Arbor campus or Chapel Hill campus) rather than bestow on it any greater importance. In one organization, what managers called an *efficiency expert,* line workers called *the snooper* (Roy, 1960).

Choosing words carefully requires that the facilitator avoid using terms that have a different meaning in another part of the organization and that would create a barrier in communicating with the group. This is one part of identifying with different parts of the organization.

Working with Another Facilitator

As Chapter Eleven discussed, cofacilitating has advantages and disadvantages. If the cofacilitators are both internal facilitators, it is an advantage if their nonfacilitator roles are in different parts of the organization (for example, production and training). As a team, the differences increase their perspectives and reduce the disadvantages that stem from being associated with one part of the organization.

An internal facilitator may want to cofacilitate with an external facilitator when the facilitation is likely to raise challenging issues about the culture of the organization or about how group members contribute dysfunctionally to that culture. In such situations, an external facilitator can lend objectivity to the internal facilitator's efforts.

Summary

This chapter examined the issues that facilitators face when they facilitate groups in their own organizations. Considered were the advantages and disadvantages of the role of internal facilitator, strategies for improving the internal facilitator's effectiveness, and issues that arise for internal facilitators throughout the facilitation process.

Although the expectations that employees have for internal facilitators often are different from the expectations they have for external facilitators, a basic principle underlies this chapter: there is essentially no difference between what constitutes effective behavior for internal facilitators and external facilitators. The core values of valid information, free and informed choice, and internal commitment guide the behaviors of internal and external facilitators alike. These are the same core values that also generate effective behavior for all employees of an organization. Therefore, the core values must logically define effective behavior for the internal facilitator, who is both a facilitator and an employee of the organization.

Chapter Thirteen The Facilitative
Leader

This book focuses on the facilitator as a separate role. But **the core values and
principles can be used by employees throughout an organization, regardless of
their specific roles. Everyone is capable of becoming a facilitative leader.** This
chapter explores how **employees of organizations can become facilitative leaders
by applying the core values and principles of facilitation in their everyday roles.**
A facilitative leader helps groups and individuals become more effective by helping them reflect on and improve the process they use to solve problems and make
decisions. Ultimately, like developmental facilitators, facilitative leaders help
others learn how to learn.

　　　This chapter is as much an exploration of facilitative leadership as it is
an extension of the core values and principles of facilitation, because my thoughts
about facilitative leadership are not as well formed as my thoughts about facilitation. With this in mind, I invite readers to reflect on the ideas, evaluate them,
and build on them, using their own experiences.

Creating Empowered Employees, Self-managing Groups, Learning Organizations, and Partnerships

In recent years, organizations have begun to shift from a management philosophy
based on the values of unilateral control and compliance to a philosophy based
on the values of joint control, empowerment, and commitment. Whereas in the
1960s and 1970s managers began using participative management approaches,
more recently managers have sought ways for employees to become more highly
involved in and committed to their organizations. To this end, organizations have

engaged in total quality management and established continuous improvement teams. They have empowered employees by providing them with more decision-making authority and by developing self-managing work teams. Even more fundamental, organizations are seeking to become learning organizations capable of identifying, challenging, and changing the very assumptions that undermine their effectiveness.

At the same time, organizations are increasingly finding that they face problems that cannot be resolved through unilateral control and compliance-based leadership. Instead, organizations are learning that by developing partnerships with their suppliers, distributers, customers, and the communities in which they do business, they can synergistically increase their effectiveness and that of their partners. Similarly, in the public arena, government, private sector, and nonprofit organizations are increasingly working together to solve difficult social and economic problems, and no single organization has control over the process.

The reasons for all the innovations are several. When employees are empowered, they can be more responsive to customers, and the organization can adapt more quickly to changing conditions. At the same time, as employees have more choice about how to do their work, their work becomes more motivating, and commitment to their work is likely to increase. Similarly, by becoming a learning organization and engaging in partnerships, organizations can better identify the root causes of their problems and increase their effectiveness.

The Need for a New Kind of Leader

Underlying all the innovations lies a question, What kind of leaders are needed in the new kinds of organizations? While some authors have suggested that there is relatively little need for leadership where self-management exists, others have argued that leadership is both more demanding and more important in such situations (Hackman, 1986). I share the latter view.

It seems logical that the role and philosophy of managers must change as employees become more empowered and take on more responsibility for managing their work and improving the organization. As Charles Manz and Henry Sims have put the question (1984, p. 410), "How does one lead employees who are supposed to lead themselves?"

Clearly, leaders whose core values include unilateral control and compliance cannot fill the role. Their values are inconsistent with the directions in which these organizations seek change.

Even visionary heroic leaders (Manz & Sims, 1993) may not be completely up to the task. A visionary heroic leader has the ability to paint a vivid and compelling picture of the mission and vision of the organization, that is, how the organization should look and act as it seeks to accomplish the mission. The vivid and compelling picture and the leader's inspirational and persuasive manner enroll employees in helping to create the leader's vision. To be sure, such leadership is energizing, and organizations have achieved much through it.

Yet the strengths of heroic leadership are also its limitations. The source of wisdom, direction, and inspiration is the leader, and employees act according to the leader's vision (Manz & Sims, 1993). However, as Peter Senge has noted, the only visions to which an individual can truly become committed are those that are "rooted in an individual's own set of values, concerns, and aspirations" (1990, p. 211). This does not mean that leaders cannot shape visions; they must. It does mean, however, that for the vision to motivate and provide purpose for employees' work, employees must genuinely share the vision, not just adopt it. Finally, the power of visionary, heroic leadership, though inspirational, lies with the leader (Manz & Sims, 1993). In short, the focus of visionary heroic leadership is on the leader. As Peter Block has written, "To put it bluntly, strong leadership does not have within itself the capability to create the fundamental changes our organizations require. It is not the fault of the people in these positions, it is the fault of the way we have all framed the role" (1993, p. 13).

The Facilitative Leader

The type of leader innovative organizations need is one who works from a set of core values consistent with the concepts of empowerment, commitment, collaboration, learning, and partnership. The core values and principles underlying the facilitation approach in this book provide a foundation for becoming such a leader—what I call the *facilitative leader.*

Most of this book has considered how a facilitator uses the core values and principles. This chapter explores how a facilitative leader applies the core values and some of the key principles of facilitation to help increase group effectiveness. To do so, I have integrated the key principles under several headings: Serving Everyone's Interests and Thinking Systemically, Increasing Responsibility and Ownership and Reducing Dependence, and Creating Conditions for Learning.

The roles of a facilitator and a facilitative leader are different in several ways (Table 13.1). A facilitator is a third party; a facilitative leader is part of the group. A facilitator remains substantively neutral; a facilitative leader becomes deeply involved in the substance of the group's work. A facilitator is a process expert but not an information resource or content expert; a facilitative leader is an expert in both content and process. A facilitator has no decision-making authority; a facilitative leader does. The differences mean that **a facilitator and a facilitative leader use the same core values and principles, but apply them in different ways consistent with their roles.**

Valid Information

Facilitative leaders understand that valid information (Chapter One) helps form the foundation of effective relationships. Working consistently with this value means that facilitative leaders share all relevant information with group members. At a simple level, group members have access to information about the

Table 13.1. Differences Between Facilitators and Facilitative Leaders.

Characteristic	Facilitator	Facilitative Leader
Group membership	Third party	Leader of group
Involvement in substantive issues	Substantively neutral	Deeply involved in substantive issues
Use of expertise	Process expert	Content and process expert
Decision-making authority	No	Yes

organization's strategy, financing and budgeting, and salaries. Facilitative leaders share the reasons for their actions, statements, and questions, so others do not have to make unnecessary inferences. They test their inferences and assumptions directly with the relevant people and help others identify assumptions of which they may be unaware. Facilitative leaders recognize that not all relevant information can be quantified; they share the facts, but they also share their feelings about them.

For information to be valid, people must feel free to disagree with each other without retribution, regardless of their differences in rank or seniority. Facilitative leaders model this behavior by encouraging others to disagree with them and when they do, by responding without getting defensive. Ultimately, no issues can be undiscussable. Too many of the critical but uncomfortable conversations that employees need to have with each other take place instead either in their minds, with their families or friends, or behind closed doors with coworkers they trust to take their side but who cannot resolve their problems. Either the problems remain or employees attempt to solve them without having to deal directly and honestly with the people they consider the problem, thereby creating more problems and more undiscussable issues. Facilitative leaders interrupt the downward spiral by raising the undiscussable issues directly with those involved and by helping others learn to do the same.

Free and Informed Choice

Facilitative leaders understand that valid information becomes of consequence only when people can use it to make free and informed choices (Chapter One). With free and informed choice, facilitative leaders change the distribution of power from being held largely by the leader to being shared by the facilitative leader and group members. Shared power in turn makes possible joint control. Without shared power and joint control, empowerment, self-managing teams, and partnerships cannot be sustained.

Free and informed choice recognizes a basic truth that leaders seem to know deep down but also seem reluctant to accept: "essentially all control over employees is *ultimately* self-imposed" (Manz & Sims, 1989, p. 5). Regardless of the controls and standards that leaders set, ultimately each employee chooses whether to be influenced by them. The most powerful control comes not externally but when employees have freely choosen their course of action. Facilitative leaders understand that while external controls generate *compliance,* internal controls generate *commitment.* Consequently, they seek to increase the extent to which group members make their own choices about their work. Instead of spending their time designing ways to control other's behaviors, facilitative leaders help group members develop their own internal controls, which are necessary for managing themselves effectively.

Enabling group members to have free and informed choice does not mean that leaders give up their own. Making decisions by consensus ensures that everyone involved maintains free and informed choice. It does not, however, ensure that everyone (including the facilitative leader) will get *all* of what they want all the time. As Peter Block has noted, there are limits:

> In any community there will always be different levels of authority. The boss will have 51 percent, the subordinate 49 percent. This means that when all is said and done, others will have the right to tell us what to do. This has no effect on our right to say no, even to say it loudly. The notion that if you stand up you will get shot undermines partnership. Partnership does not mean that you always get what you want. It means you may lose your argument, but you never lose your voice. (1993, p. 30)

Internal Commitment

Although a value in itself, internal commitment (Chapter One) is also a natural result of valid information and free and informed choice. With internal commitment, employees take responsibility for their actions and initiative to do what they need to do to make their choices work. The typical over-the-shoulder monitoring by leaders becomes unnecessary to ensure that people are doing what they said they would do. With internal commitment, employees get the job done because they *want* to do it. Instead, facilitative leaders serve as resources to and partners with group members, helping them diagnose problems in implementation.

Facilitative leaders understand the paradox that to get the internal commitment they want so much from employees, they must first give up unilateral control. Similarly, by embracing the three core values, facilitative leaders come to grasp the counterintuitive notion that shared control ultimately creates greater control for all those involved.

Serving Everyone's Interests and Thinking Systemically

One thing that distinguishes facilitators from many leaders is the principle that facilitators' clients include the entire group as well as those not represented in the group (known as *ultimate clients*), not just certain members of the group or the facilitators themselves (see Chapter One). The approach engenders trust as group members realize that facilitators will not take advantage of them to serve others' interests or the facilitators' own. The facilitative leader uses the same principle, helping others to focus on the interests of all stakeholders and craft solutions that address all the interests. This does not mean that facilitative leaders give up their own interests. Rather, they think of their interests as one of many sets of interests to be considered when crafting solutions.

Underlying the principle of serving everyone's interests is the broader principle of thinking systemically. Facilitators and facilitative leaders think systemically when they understand that to remain effective, groups must maintain their ability to work together and meet members' personal needs, as well as deliver quality services or products. The three criteria for effectiveness are inseparable and mutually reinforcing; if one criterion is not met, in the long run the others will not be met. Similarly, facilitative leaders appreciate that the factors that contribute to group effectiveness and the elements that constitute them are also all interrelated (see Chapter Two). Consequently, when they help improve group process, group structure, or influence the organizational context of the group, facilitative leaders do not do it piecemeal, nor do they do it by simply borrowing innovative ideas from others who have been successful. Instead, they ask themselves and others whether the innovations are consistent with the core values of the group, recognizing that all parts of a system must be congruent if a system is to have integrity (see Chapter Two).

Finally, facilitative leaders act systemically when they shift from focusing on placing blame to focusing on understanding how problems arise and how they continue despite the sincere efforts of many talented people to solve them. People can easily convince themselves that the cause of their problems lies with "enemies" who are outside: outside their group, their department, their organization (Senge, 1990). As a result, they fail to see how their own actions interact with those of the outsiders to maintain or even escalate the problem. In the world of systems thinking, however, "there is no outside; . . . you and the cause of your problems are part of a single system. The cure lies in your relationships with your 'enemy'" (Senge, 1990, p. 67).

Increasing Responsibility and Ownership and Reducing Dependence

Like a facilitator (especially a developmental facilitator), to develop the group's long-term effectiveness, the facilitative leader seeks to decrease the group's dependence on the leader (Chapter One). In short, the facilitative leader seeks to do for the group that which it cannot yet do for itself (Chapter Four). Determining what the group can and cannot do at any point requires continual testing. Therefore, like a facilitator, the facilitative leader diagnoses and intervenes in a way that enables the group to take as much responsibility and ownership as possible for diagnosing and solving problems. To do this, the facilitative leader uses the diagnosis-intervention cycle discussed in Chapters Four and Six.

Two types of behavior are inconsistent with the core values and undermine the principle of increasing responsibility and reducing dependence. First, when probems arise, if the facilitative leader serves as intermediary either for group members or for the group and others, the parties become dependent on the facilitative leader for valid information (Chapter One). An intermediary buffers the parties from learning how their actions affect the other parties. As a result, it becomes easier to blame the other parties than to think systemically. Second, if facilitative leaders collude either with some members of the group against other members (or with the entire group against other parties), they create additional problems. Collusion requires the leader to withhold valid information and consequently prevents free and informed choice for certain group members and places the interests of some group members above the interests of the group as a whole (see Chapter One).

As for a facilitator, one of the most difficult challenges for a facilitative leader is to avoid taking responsibility for the group's ineffective behavior or its consequences so long as the leader has acted effectively (see Chapter One). To believe and act otherwise leads a facilitative leader to see group members as helpless and to rescue them, to see them as defiant and to punish them, or to see them as hopeless and to abandon them. All the responses shift the burden from the group to the facilitative leader, increase the group's dependency, and reduce its ownership and responsibility. The facilitative leader recognizes that the systemic solution lies in helping the group address the root causes of its ineffective behavior, thereby increasing the group's ability to deal with similar problems in the future (Senge, 1990).

Creating Conditions for Learning

To accomplish all these things requires that facilitative leaders and those with whom they work to have the ability to create the conditions for learning. By *learning*, I do not mean simply improving performance or learning new tasks. I mean the fundamental learning that occurs when members identify the core values and beliefs that guide their behavior (Argyris & Schön, 1974), understand how some values and beliefs undermine their effectiveness, and learn how to act consistently with a more effective set of values and beliefs.

Like facilitators, facilitative leaders create conditions for learning. They share the core values, principles, and ground rules with others and discuss what they mean, how they work, and what the barriers to using them are. In doing so, they attempt to be models of the values, principles, and ground rules and tell others that is what they are doing. They ask for specific feedback and explain that they will try not to get defensive when it is negative. They encourage others to tell them if they are responding defensively to the feedback. They promise no retribution as a result of the feedback—and they do not break that promise.

Like internal facilitators, facilitative leaders develop trust with group members not only by being models of the core values but also by using the core values to talk about how they (the facilitative leaders) have acted ineffectively in the past (Chapter Twelve). Without this conversation, members may infer that the facilitative leader has a new, sophisticated strategy for maintaining unilateral control and compliance.

Self-critiques provide a structured forum for reflecting on how people have acted consistently and inconsistently with the core values (Chapter Four).

Finally, facilitative leaders cannot lure, demand, manipulate, or coerce others to use the core values and principles discussed throughout this book. It should be obvious that to do so is inconsistent with everything for which the core values and principles stand. Yet even if others choose not to use the core values, the facilitative leader does. By being a model of the values, the facilitative leader gives people experience with them so that they may later make a more informed and free choice to embrace them.

The Facilitative Leader and the Elements of Group Effectiveness

The general discussion of the role of facilitative leader noted that to be effective, groups must have effective group process, group structure, and organizational context. The three factors and the elements that constitute them (for example, problem solving, clearly defined roles, and a supportive culture) must be effective, regardless of the type of leader the group has. Each element of the model of group effectiveness represents a foreseeable problem that a group must solve and keep solved in order to be effective. Although the elements remain the same, *who* attends to them and *how* they do so vary significantly according to the type of leadership. Table 13.2 shows the differences between traditional leadership and facilitative leadership for dealing with each element of group effectiveness. By *traditional leadership*, I mean leadership based on values of unilateral control and compliance.

Table 13.2 shows the role of facilitative leader for a group that is self-managing, self-designing, and self-governing. In practice, the specific tasks of the facilitative leader change as a group's ability to guide itself increases. For example, in a group that has just begun to manage itself, the facilitative leader would take more initiative or responsibility for those elements associated with self-designing groups, until the group is ready to learn how to deal with the elements. Similarly, the facilitative leader would continue to take initiative and responsibility for the self-governing elements, until such time as the group is in a position to deal with those elements. In this respect, facilitative leaders are like developmental facilitators, seeking to work their way out of a job with a particular group. Like the facilitator, the facilitative leader moves on to help another group. **Consequently, although the facilitative leader's tasks may change according to the group, the role remains constant and is defined by the principle that the facilitative leader does for the group that which the group cannot do for itself.**

Table 13.2. Moving from Traditional Leadership to Facilitative Leadership.

Group Element	Traditional Leader	Facilitative Leader
Group Process		
Communication	Leader controls who communicates with whom.	Leader teaches group members how to communicate effectively, using the ground rules.
		Group members initiate communication with anyone who has valid information or has an interest in the situation.
Conflict management	Leader manages conflicts among group members.	Leader teaches group members how to manage their own conflicts.
Problem solving	Leader solves problems that group members present.	Leader teaches group members the problem-solving model.
		Leader ensures that group members have access to relevant information to solve problems.
		Group members take responsibility for identifying and solving problems they encounter.
Decision making	Leader either makes decisions alone or after consultation with group members.	Group members make many decisions on their own or as a group.
		Leader and group members jointly make appropriate decisions by consensus.
Boundary management	Leader is largely responsible for communicating, coordinating, and solving problems with people outside the group.	Leader teaches members how to communicate, coordinate, and solve problems with people outside the group.
		Leader and members jointly determine the boundary-management approach.
		Leader manages boundaries largely to facilitate group problem solving rather than to solve the problem.
Group Structure		
Group norms	Leader attempts to establish norms implicitly with group.	Leader shares core values, principles, and ground rules with group members as potential bases for group norms.

Table 13.2. Moving from Traditional Leadership to Facilitative Leadership, Cont'd.

Group Element	Traditional Leader	Facilitative Leader
		Leader and group members explicitly discuss and agree on group norms.
Group culture	Leader attempts to influence culture implicitly.	Leader shares core values, principles, and ground rules as potential bases for group culture.
		Leader and group members explicitly discuss the current and desired culture and agree on steps to shape it.
Sufficient time	Leader decides how much time tasks should take and sets deadlines in consultation with group members.	Leader teaches group members how to plan and manage time.
		Group members use relevant information and support from leader to set deadlines for their tasks.
Clearly defined roles	Leader defines employees' roles with or without participation from group members.	Group members use relevant information and support from leader to define and agree on their roles.
Appropriate membership	Leader or leader's supervisor decides who will join and leave the group with or without consulting group members.	Leader ensures that group has information and skills necessary to select (and remove) group members.
		Group members use relevant information and support from leader to discuss and decide what kinds of members they need.
Motivating task	Leader or leader's supervisor designs group members' jobs, sometimes in consultation with group members.	Leader helps members understand what makes a job motivating.
		Group members use relevant information and support from leader to redesign their jobs.
Clear goals	Leader sets goals based on direction from leader's supervisor and sometimes in consultation with group members.	Leader helps group members learn how to set clear goals.
		Group members use relevant information and support from leader to discuss and set goals.

Table 13.2. Moving from Traditional Leadership to Facilitative Leadership, Cont'd.

Group Element	Traditional Leader	Facilitative Leader
Organizational Context		
Physical environment	Leader takes responsibility for trying to change the physical work environment, sometimes using information from group members.	Group members take responsibility for trying to change the physical work environment with relevant information and support from leader.
Technological and material resources	Leader takes responsibility for obtaining resources.	Group members take responsibility for obtaining resources with relevant information and support from leader.
Training and consultation	Leader takes responsibility for identifying and obtaining training and consultation needed by group.	Leader ensures that group members have knowledge and skills to assess their training and consultation needs. Group members take responsibility for identifying and obtaining training and consultation needed by group.
Information and feedback	Leader decides what information, including feedback, group members need and provides it, sometimes with participation from group members. Leader provides feedback to group members about their performance.	Group members decide what information they need and obtain it. Leader helps group members learn how to provide and seek feedback effectively. Leader and group members provide feedback to each other and critique their own performances jointly through self-critiques.
Rewards consistent with objectives	Leader (or supervisor above leader's level) designs reward system and decides who receives rewards. Leader focuses primarily on individual extrinsic rewards.	Leader ensures that group members understand the elements of effective reward systems. Group members design reward system and decide who receives rewards. Reward systems include intrinsic and extrinsic rewards and focus on group and individual rewards.

Table 13.2. Moving from Traditional Leadership to Facilitative Leadership, Cont'd.

Group Element	Traditional Leader	Facilitative Leader
Supportive culture	Leader and group members attempt to influence culture implicitly.	Leader and group members are models of the core values, principles, and ground rules and simultaneously advocate and encourage others to inquire about using them as bases for group culture. Leader and group members explicitly discuss the current and desired culture and agree on steps to shape it.

Anyone Can Be a Facilitative Leader

Anyone in an organization can become a facilitative leader, even someone who has no supervisory authority. Traditionally, the influence of a manager and traditional leader stems largely from formal authority. But a facilitative leader's influence stems largely from the ability to help others accomplish what they want to accomplish. This means practicing the core values and principles, including the principles of group effectiveness, even if others choose not to do so. In this respect, **anyone can be a facilitative leader, regardless of one's position in the organization.** Ultimately, the core values and principles represent not only a way to facilitate and lead but also a fundamental choice about the kind of life people create for themselves and others in organizations.

Resource A Guidelines
for Developing
an Effective Contract

Chapter Three discussed the need for developing a contract between the facilitator and the client group and listed a set of questions to use to develop an effective contract. This resource discusses the issues associated with each of the questions.

Who Is the Primary Client?

This question asks which group is asking for help. In practice, this usually means identifying the group that the facilitator will facilitate. The contract should specify the primary client unambiguously, so it is clear which individuals and/ or positions are included. For example, in a top management team that includes an agency director and those who report directly to her, the agreement should specify whether the assistant to the director or a student intern is part of the primary client group. In a group that includes a city council and the city manager, the contract should specify whether the assistant city manager or the clerk to the council is part of the primary client group. The contract should also specify whether individuals in the primary client group who are unable to attend may send substitutes, as is the norm in some organizations.

The contract should also specify who else will attend group meetings and what role they will play. For example, the facilitation may also include individuals who provide budget or legal information to the primary client group. The role of these individuals may be to respond to group members' requests for information but not to actively participate in discussion or decision making. Other individuals may also be invited to observe the sessions without participating.

There are two principles to consider in deciding who will attend and participate. First, **the group should not be larger than the number needed to accomplish the objectives.** Groups that are larger than the task requires take more time to accomplish their work and may end up with lower-quality decisions. This does not mean that only those who are responsible for making the decision should be present. Generating valid information and commitment may require that the primary group include individuals responsible for implementing the decision and individuals who may be affected by a decision, as well as those making the decision. Second, **when it is necessary to discuss issues that are highly conflictual or that members find difficult to discuss openly, the group should include few, if any, people from outside the primary client group.** The presence of additional people can create pressure on primary group members to withhold and distort information or to "play to the gallery" (Svara, 1990). For example, when observers include the primary group members' constituents, members who privately agree with each other may be reluctant to say so if they believe their constituents would disapprove.

Still, the facilitator must be careful that the group does not exclude potential participants solely because other group members want to avoid a conflict with them. In contracting with a group of physicians, for example, I raised the question of whether one physician, who was loosely connected with the group and about whom some members had concerns, should attend the planning-and-expectation-setting retreat. One of the physicians remarked, "Well, if he comes, we can't talk about him." I responded, "I agree. But, if he comes, you can talk *with* him." I explained that if members of the group have problems working with the doctor, the retreat would provide an appropriate forum for exploring their unmet expectations, and my cofacilitator and I could help the group discuss the issue constructively. I also mentioned that I believed the group members could not resolve the conflict with that person unless they talked directly with him about the issue. As it turned out, the planning group decided to exclude the doctor, ostensibly for other legitimate reasons. I doubt that the group members would have excluded him if they did not see themselves as in conflict with him.

Because the excluded person's presence was not necessary for the group to accomplish its retreat goals, I did not press the issue with the planning group. However, I mentioned that if, during the retreat, the individual's behavior became the subject of the group's discussion, I would raise the question of the validity of any group decisions based on untested inferences or assumptions that members made about him.

A special group of observers is the news media. The contract should state whether the facilitation is to be conducted as an open meeting (required by law for some governmental groups) and, if so, what role the media will play. In most cases, the media act only as observers. However, when the group's objectives include establishing expectations with those outside the group, the media may be willing to participate, discussing what they expect from the client group and vice versa.

What Are the Objectives and the Agenda?

The contract should state clearly the objectives of the facilitation. The objectives may include developing a mission statement or a long-range plan, establishing expectations, or resolving a particular conflict. If the facilitation is developmental, improving the group's process should be included as an objective.

If the facilitation occurs in a single session (for example, a two-day retreat), the contract should include an agenda that identifies generally how the group will spend blocks of time. The agenda must be flexible, because it is impossible to predict how a group discussion will proceed and whether an allotted block of time will be sufficient to accomplish part of the group's objectives. When the facilitation is long-term, the specific agenda for each meeting emerges from the previous meeting. Therefore, the agendas are not included in the contract.

Where and for How Long Will the Group Meet?

For matters of convenience, long-term facilitation groups usually meet at the site of the organization. For short-term basic facilitation, groups often choose to meet off site, and the contract should identify the meeting site. For long-term facilitation, this is not necessary, especially if the location is on site.

Regardless of the type of facilitation, several factors should be considered in selecting a site. The setting should enable the group to accomplish its task. It should be comfortable but not sleep inducing and should reduce such distractions as phone calls. The room setup should allow all participants to see each other and the facilitator. If observers are present, their seating should be separate from the participants'.

In basic facilitation, I prefer that the setting not be associated with the group's normal meeting location or with any particular member or subgroup. Effective facilitation often means helping participants "free up" their typical ways of thinking to find solutions that have eluded them. Because people decide how to behave in part on the setting they are in, meeting in a new location helps reduce the cues that subtly influence people to maintain their typical behavior. Meeting in a place associated with a particular group member or subgroup can also reduce the group's effectiveness, because it may inhibit members who feel they are in another member's territory. Consider, for example, a top management retreat held at the beach home of the group's leader. The "visiting" members may be reluctant to disagree with the "host" leader, because at some level they consider it impolite to argue with a host. A neutral site avoids the problem.

In developmental facilitation, however, finding a new location unassociated with previous meetings is less important. As members increase their process effectiveness, a meetingplace where ineffective meetings previously had been held takes on constructive cues for group members.

The site selected should also be consistent with the image the organization wants to project. This is an especially important consideration for groups that will receive media coverage. Boards of commissioners and city councils some-times meet in spartan, low-cost settings to encourage the media to focus on the group's accomplishments rather than on the location. Meeting at resort locations can produce such headlines as Council Retreats to Beach, even if the meeting is held at no cost to the public.

Deciding how much time the group will need depends on several factors: what objectives the group wants to accomplish, how much work will be required for the group to accomplish the objectives, the group's initial skill level, and the facilitator's skill in helping the group accomplish its objectives. It is beyond the scope of this—and probably any—book to describe how long it will take a group to accomplish such objectives as clarifying role expectations or resolving a par-ticular conflict. Groups' abilities to work effectively vary widely, and a facilitator can have only a limited understanding of a group's strengths and weaknesses before working with it.

For short-term basic facilitation, how long the group meets is often con-strained by the time the group has available. Members sometimes pressure facil-itators to help them accomplish their objectives in an unrealistically short amount of time. Facilitators may acquiesce because they want to work with the group, are pressured by their supervisors, or need the income. If the facilitator suggests that the group can accomplish its task in the allotted time when this is not likely, the facilitator has set the group up to fail.

When scheduling work, the facilitator should match the objectives with the time available and should avoid compressing work to fit the time allotted (Schwarz, 1991). A major risk in allotting less time than needed is that the group will fail to make sufficient progress and become less motivated to continue work-ing in subsequent sessions or will consider consensus decision making a waste of time. When the group is attempting to resolve a difficult conflict, for example, insufficient time may leave the group in more conflict than if members had not addressed the conflict at all.

In such situations, the facilitator can describe how much time the group will need to accomplish its objectives and let the group test whether the facili-tator's time frame is realistic. For example, a council-manager group that asked a colleague and me to facilitate its evaluation of the manager's performance wanted to complete the entire evaluation in three hours. We told the group it would take at least six hours but that we would agree to work with the group for three hours—without rushing the process. We also agreed that after three hours, the group would evaluate itself and our effectiveness, including how well we used the time, and then decide whether to continue the process. At the end of three hours, the council group realized its estimate had been unrealistic and agreed to allot more time. Again, the group allotted less time than we thought realistic, and again we reached the same agreement with the group. In this way, the group was able to make a free and informed choice about how much time to spend, and my colleague and I did not have to compress our work in a way that we considered ineffective.

This approach does not work when the initial amount of time scheduled is likely to result in unresolved issues that would harm the group. This is likely to occur when the group is faced with a difficult conflict or when personally threatening or undiscussable issues are likely to be raised. **When the group is likely to be harmed, the decision involves the facilitator; when the facilitator believes the group is not able to make an informed choice, the facilitator is ethically responsible for informing the group and declining to facilitate.** If the group cannot allot sufficient time, the facilitator should decline to work with it and explain why.

What Are the Roles of the Different Parties?

Groups often seek a facilitator without clearly understanding what the facilitator will do. Sometimes, clients equate facilitators with mediators or arbitrators. In addition, adding a facilitator to a group changes the roles that group members normally play and how they interact with each other. Therefore, the facilitator and client group need to agree on the roles that each will play.

Facilitator Role

Chapter One described the facilitator role in much more detail than is necessary to include in the contract. The contract should capture the core values, beliefs, and principles that will guide the facilitator. It should also indicate the types of behaviors that the facilitator will not engage in that the client might otherwise expect. For example, clients sometimes expect the facilitator to provide expert information or to raise issues for group members who feel uncomfortable doing so themselves. Early conversations with the group members should provide the facilitator with a clear idea of what types of facilitator behaviors require clarification.

Concerns About the Facilitator's Qualifications. Groups often have questions about the facilitator's qualifications. They may want to know whether the facilitator has worked on similar problems or with similar organizations. A potential client may want to talk with some of the facilitator's other clients or see a résumé. Underlying all the requests is the question of whether the facilitator can help the group.

Facilitators can address the concern in two ways. First, they can describe their credentials and facilitation experience, highlighting especially relevant past work. If facilitators do not have experience with the current group's type of organization or problem, they should share that relevant information, noting how the lack of experience may or may not hinder their effectiveness. If the client seems interested in the facilitator's qualifications but does not raise the issue, the facilitator may share that inference and ask whether the client would like to know the facilitator's qualifications. Later, when meeting with the entire client group, facilitators can describe their qualifications as part of their introduction to the group.

The second way to address the client's concerns about qualifications is to explore the concerns directly. For example, the facilitator can say, "You've asked me a number of questions about my facilitation experience, and I'm happy to answer them. I think it's important that you have an accurate view of whether I can help you. I'm wondering, are there particularly difficult issues the group is dealing with, or has the group had experiences with other facilitators that lead you to wonder whether I will really be able to help?" By discussing clients' concerns, facilitators learn more about clients' problems, help clients determine whether they think the facilitator is qualified, and demonstrate effective facilitation.

Concerns About the Facilitator's Neutrality. Often, the facilitator is asked to help a group that is in conflict over a controversial issue, such as gun control. When contacting the facilitator, the client may ask the facilitator's position on the issue. To act consistently with the values of valid information and free and informed choice, the facilitator must respond to the question. Yet doing so may lead some members of the group to consider the facilitator biased and less effective. To not answer the question, however, may decrease the trust certain members have in the facilitator. But the question remains: how can facilitators generate valid information and free and informed choice without having clients consider them non-neutral?

One way is to distinguish facilitators' personal opinions from their professional actions. If clients and the facilitator believe that the facilitator can act neutrally despite a personal opinion on the issue, the client may find the facilitator acceptable.

Alternatively, when asked about a position on an issue, the facilitator can inquire how the position would affect the client. In this way, the facilitator can determine whether the client's concern is the issue of neutrality or some other issue, such as not wanting to financially support a facilitator who holds certain positions on the issue. By exploring the interest behind the client's questions, the facilitator can better help the client make an informed choice.

To return to the client's question about the facilitator's position, facilitators may want their responses shared with the entire group. In this way, all group members have the same information and can also make an informed choice about hiring the facilitator. Here the advantage of meeting with the entire client group as soon as possible becomes clear. If the contact person reacts strongly to the facilitator's personal opinion, the contact person may either recommend or not recommend the facilitator based on this, without giving group members the benefit of addressing their concerns directly to the facilitator. In practice, however, it is often not feasible for the facilitator to meet initially with the full client group.

On some occasions, a facilitator is asked to help a special interest group in which all members hold a position on one side of a controversial issue, for example, the pro-choice position on abortion. Here too, the group may inquire about the facilitator's position, and here too the approach described is valid. While the group may be uncomfortable hiring a facilitator whose personal beliefs are at odds with the group's, facilitators who strongly support the group's position face another threat to their effectiveness. In their eagerness to see the group succeed (thereby advancing their cause as well), they may be tempted to leave the facilitator role and rescue the group by taking on some of the group's responsibilities. Or, their strong interest in the subject matter may lead them to focus on the content of the discussion to the exclusion of the process.

I was once asked to facilitate a meeting of more than one hundred female representatives of groups supporting one side of the abortion issue. The client requesting my services had seen me work before and was satisfied that I could be effective in this setting. At the end of our initial conversation, I asked for a day to consider her request. In considering it, I realized that although she was comfortable having a man facilitate a group comprising only women, and although she was a primary sponsor of the facilitated session, I would be ineffective if the group in general did not feel the same way. I conveyed this to her in our next phone call and found that, in the meantime, a female facilitator had volunteered her services for the session. Given the purpose and sensitivity of the session, I suggested that she could probably be a more effective facilitator.

The example raises the issue of acceptance by the client. Although I may have been able to act impartially and neutrally, as a male I may not have been acceptable to the entire group, which would have undermined my effectiveness and ultimately the group's effectiveness. The same issue can be relevant when the facilitator is of a different race or religion than members of the client group.

How do facilitators find out whether they are acceptable to the group? Clearly, asking the contact client or planning group members is necessary but not sufficient. Ultimately, the question of the facilitator's acceptability is for the full client group to decide.

Facilitator-Leader Roles

Without a facilitator, the group leader typically manages the process when the group meets. The leader sets the agenda, decides when to change the topic of the conversation, and, in formal groups, recognizes those who want to speak. The addition of a facilitator raises the question of who will manage the group process. It should be clear that when facilitators manage the process, they do not do so unilaterally but by identifying choices that the group needs to make.

There are several ways to allocate this role between the leader and facilitator. First, the leader can continue to manage the process, and the facilitator can facilitate by augmenting the leader's role. This method makes the least use of the facilitator's skills and is most likely to maintain the same processes that normally occur in the group. The approach is useful when the group wants to use the facilitator to help the leader improve her or his skills.

Second, the facilitator can manage the process, while the leader continues to play a role distinct from other group members'. This is the flip side of the first method. Third, the leader can play the same role as other group members, and the facilitator can manage the process. The third method is useful in short-term basic facilitation when leaders want to diminish their influence in the group discussion and increase the influence of other group members. Finally, all group members can take responsibility for managing the process, including the leader and facilitator. This is the most effective method for developmental facilitation, because it decreases the group's dependence on the facilitator.

Member Roles

If facilitation will cause members' roles to vary from those normally expected of them in the group, the differences should be discussed. Changing the relationship of two of the three roles—leader, members, and facilitator—can easily affect the relationship with the third role. For example, if the facilitator takes over managing the process from the leader so the leader can act more as other group members, the result may be that other group members relate differently to the facilitator and leader. This has two implications. First, **the different group roles and relationships need to be defined (or redefined) as a system, so they do not cause role conflicts.** Second, **all members need to understand every role and relationship in the group.** The latter implication is another reason for sharing all relevant information.

I experienced the consequences of ignoring these implications in facilitating a city council-manager group. A colleague and I observed that the mayor called on council members to speak in a way that led to a series of unrelated monologues rather than a dialogue. We had clarified our facilitator role with the group members but not with the mayor. As a result, when we tried to intervene to encourage a dialogue, we found ourselves engaged in a conflict with the mayor over who should manage the process. We later compounded our error by reaching an agreement with the mayor regarding our respective roles, without including the rest of the group in the discussion. Consequently, when the mayor began playing his agreed-upon role, certain council members inferred that the mayor was abdicating his leadership position, because they had had no involvement in the agreement and did not know what roles the mayor and we had agreed to play.

What Ground Rules Will the Group Follow?

A group's process is more effective when members explicitly identify and commit to follow expectations about how they will act. The expectations are known as *ground rules*. Chapter Four describes a specific set of ground rules in detail. The contract need not identify the specific ground rules the group will use. In fact, the group often decides on a set of ground rules after the contract is developed. However, the contract should note that the group will agree on a set of ground rules. Although the facilitator may have discussed the use of ground rules before the contracting stage, the ground rules are usually agreed upon when the full client group is present. In basic facilitation, this usually occurs during the introductory part of the first meeting. In developmental facilitation, the process begins in the first meeting, but the set of ground rules emerges over time.

Ground Rules for Attendance

Unlike the ground rules that members agree to follow within the group discussion, ground rules for attendance are important to include in the contract, especially for single-session facilitations. Under what conditions should the facilitator decide not to facilitate? **It is important to have all members present when the group either needs to make decisions that require the full commitment of all members to implement effectively or when the absence of a member will significantly reduce the information available for making a quality decision.**

Requiring that all group members be present also conveys the message that the facilitation is an important process. A group's unwillingness to commit to full attendance can be an indication of insufficient motivation to make the process effective. For example, county officials asked me to facilitate a joint meeting of the board of social services and the board of county commissioners. For several reasons, I was ambivalent about requiring full attendance. I had conducted a similar retreat for the same groups the previous year, and we had set a minimum number of sessions for required attendance (not full attendance). When that number was not met, I continued to facilitate the retreat. I anticipated that attendance would again be a problem, but I did not raise the issue because I was concerned about alienating the initial client contact, who was influential with similar groups that were also my clients. In a conference call to plan the retreat, the social services director (the initial contact) mentioned that the chair of the board of commissioners was not going to be able to participate in the conference call. Again, I thought about but did not suggest that we reschedule the call when everyone could participate. As it turned out, the chair did not attend the retreat. This made other board members reluctant to make certain commitments, which defeated the purpose of the retreat. The example is an illustration of cues that facilitators usually get from the client that foreshadow problems that will occur. Facilitators ignore the cues at their—and their client's—expense.

When a group faces a difficult conflict, the member or members who are reluctant to attend are often those expressing a minority viewpoint. Sometimes, they are concerned that if they attend, the majority will pressure them to concede. The majority often responds by asking to meet without those members, believing that the majority can resolve a conflict with the minority absent. If facilitators agree to meet without the reluctant members, they set the group up to fail. Without full attendance, the group is likely to scapegoat the minority and escalate the conflict.

Unfortunately, requiring full attendance can lead to a tyranny of the minority in which the majority feels that its meeting is being held hostage by the minority. Once members frame the issue as a power struggle over who controls whether the facilitation occurs, members of the majority are likely to push for a meeting with less than full attendance as a way to assert their power, even if they realize the group's objectives cannot be accomplished with the minority subgroup absent.

With large groups—perhaps in excess of twenty—full attendance is less necessary. Large groups make it difficult, if not impossible, for every member to contribute meaningfully to the discussion and decisions. The absence of one or several members may make little practical difference in the process or outcomes. Instead, it is important that each subgroup and set of interests be represented. For example, in a management retreat that includes the top sixty members of an organization, the absence of just three people could be critical if they were the only representatives of one particular function.

For some facilitators, the hardest part of the attendance ground rule is following through. It takes courage to tell a client group that has gathered at a site (or even worse, traveled a distance) that the retreat must be canceled, because one or more members are absent. A facilitator can, however, do several things to make the conversation less difficult for everyone. First, the facilitator can remind the client that the reason for agreeing to full attendance is to avoid increasing the client's problems. This helps facilitators remember that if they give in to the client's pleas for violating the agreement, they risk harming the client. In other words, if the reason for full attendance was valid when planning the retreat, all things being equal, it is still valid five minutes before the retreat is scheduled to begin. Second, the facilitator can state the attendance ground rule clearly in planning conversations and in the contract and mention that it applies even if members need to cancel on the day of the retreat. Third, the facilitator can emphasize that if a member cannot attend and the group wants to reschedule the session, the facilitator will be as flexible as possible in accommodating the new meeting schedule.

How Will Decisions Be Made?

The decision about what rules will be used for making decisions is a central one. Will the group make decisions by consensus, two-thirds vote, majority rule, or some other way? Will all decisions in the session be made using the same rule, or will the decision rule depend on the type of decision? Even more basic, will any decisions be made in the sessions? The questions should be raised in the contracting stage but do not need to be decided until the full group meets.

There is a paradox inherent in this ground rule. To answer the question of how decisions will be made, the metaquestion of how the group will make a decision about how to make decisions must be answered first. This problem cannot be solved because the metaquestion continues infinitely. To get out of the paralyzing loop, group members must somehow just decide how to make decisions as if they already had a decision rule to guide them (Smith & Berg, 1987).

Ground Rules for Confidentiality

Facilitators need to reach agreement with clients about when they will treat as confidential information that individual members or subgroups share with the facilitator. Confidentiality has advantages and disadvantages. It enables facilitators to learn things that they may not otherwise find out about the group or to learn something earlier than otherwise possible, but confidentiality prevents facilitators from using that information to intervene in the group. Maintaining confidentiality increases client trust in the facilitator but maintains the mistrust among group members that led members to want to have the information considered confidential in the first place. Finally, confidentiality maintains group members' ability to work together at some level but fails to increase the group's effectiveness by keeping relevant information out of its realm.

Confidentiality creates a dilemma. By agreeing to protect the interests of the individual seeking confidentiality, the facilitator may fail to serve the interests of the full client group. In this way, agreeing to keep an individual conversation confidential can reduce the facilitator's effectiveness with the full client group and thus create a conflict with the facilitator's professional objectives and ethical values.

Clients can bind the facilitator to confidentiality explicitly or implicitly (Golembiewski, 1986). A colleague and I met with a mayor and city manager to plan their expectation-setting retreat. At the end of the meeting, the mayor stood up and casually said to us, "Just don't tell the council members I was involved in planning this retreat. If they knew, they wouldn't support it." For reasons I still do not entirely understand, neither my colleague nor I responded to the mayor's statement—we just let it pass as if he had not said it. The mayor explicitly stated that we should not disclose his participation in the planning process. By not responding, we had implicitly (and inappropriately) agreed.

In other situations, a client does not explicitly request confidentiality, but the facilitator may end up granting it, albeit ambivalently. This occurs when the facilitator infers that the client does not want the information disclosed and the facilitator does not test the inference with the client. Unlike the explicit example of the mayor, here the facilitator is largely responsible for creating the bind. For example, during a break in a meeting, the mayor may approach the facilitator and say, "What's really behind this conversation is that some of us think the manager is getting out in front of the council on some issues. He needs to lay low for a while."

Whether facilitators agree to maintain confidentiality, either as a result of a client's explicit request or implicitly because of the facilitators' untested inference, the consequences are similar. Facilitators limit their ability to disclose the conversation held with the individual "promised" confidentiality. The facilitator cannot say in front of the group, "Mayor, you talked with me about the issue of the manager's getting out in front. How is that related to the group's discussion?" Facilitators may also limit themselves from making any interventions that even appear to rely on information from a "confidential" conversation.

Dealing effectively with the issue of confidentiality means anticipating the issue and raising it "before we find ourselves being told things that put us in conflicts between protecting our client's interests and respecting our commitment to confidentiality" (Gellermann, Frankel, & Ladenson, 1990, p. 175). One way to accomplish this is to reach agreement with clients early in their relationships with the facilitator. In deciding when to discuss confidentiality, facilitators need to balance the likelihood of awkwardness from raising the issue too early with the probability of finding themselves in a confidentiality conflict.

Until an agreement is reached, once a client finishes a sentence that begins, "Just between you and me," it is no longer possible to disclose the client's information to the group without the client's believing that confidentiality has been breached. When a person with whom the facilitator has no agreement about confidentiality begins to tell the facilitator something while requesting it remain confidential, the facilitator should stop that person. The facilitator should then explain that by agreeing in advance to hear information the facilitator will not be able to use, the facilitator's usefulness to the group may be reduced. The facilitator can then offer a choice—does the member want to disclose the information without any agreement of confidentiality? The facilitator can also discuss with the member why the member is reluctant to tell the group something the member believes is important for the facilitator to know. If the facilitator can help the member find a way to raise the issue with the group, the facilitator has helped the group deal with an undiscussable issue.

Some facilitators specify that unless they explicitly agree to keep something confidential, clients should assume the facilitators will use their judgment in sharing information with the larger group. Others agree in advance on the kinds of information they will and will not keep confidential.

The agreement about limits of confidentiality should include more than conversation; clients can bind facilitators without talking with them. While consulting to a group of employees, I received an unsolicited letter at my office from one member of the group. The letter described some problems that were occurring in the group but that had not been discussed openly. I inferred that the writer believed that the group was not addressing important issues it needed to address. I also wondered whether I had been ineffective with the group for not helping to bring those issues to the surface and whether the client thought the same. Because our agreement on confidentiality did not address the situation, and because I did not talk to the letter writer after receiving the letter, I implicitly agreed to treat the letter confidentially. Unfortunately, I also did not raise the issue in the group, because I was reluctant to take responsibility for raising a group member's issue.

Facilitators also need to identify the conditions under which they will reveal to people outside the client group information accepted in confidence. Facilitators often discuss their work with professional colleagues in order to increase their effectiveness. Such consultation is appropriate "when discussion with them is confidential and compatible with the interests of [the] clients and informants" (Gellermann, Frankel, & Ladenson, 1990, p. 175). Facilitators may use information obtained through work with clients in their "writings, lectures, or other public forums only with prior consent or when disguised so that it is impossible from [the facilitators'] presentations alone to identify the individuals or systems with whom [the facilitator has] worked" (Gellermann, Frankel, & Ladenson, 1990, p. 175).

An important group to consider is the news media. One option is for the facilitator not to talk with the media at all. This encourages the client to take total responsibility for working with the media and reduces the facilitator's risk of violating confidentiality. But it also requires the client to answer questions about the facilitator, which the facilitator is more qualified to do. A more effective option is for the facilitator to agree to talk with the media but only about the role of facilitator. This helps the reporter (and ultimately the public) understand the process of facilitation without the facilitator's discussing the client's situation. For example, the facilitator might discuss generally how groups benefit from the use of a facilitator, without discussing the problems that the client group is trying to solve.

Groups also need to agree on what information they will keep confidential and what information they will share either in the larger organization or outside it.

How Will the Group Assess Its Progress?

Groups need some way to assess progress toward their objectives. In single-session or short-term facilitation, self-critiques enable the group to evaluate its progress during and at the end of the sessions. For long-term facilitation, self-critiques are useful, but methods such as surveys and analysis of relevant organizational records provide the group with other types of data. For example, a group of employees that is meeting to increase the quality of its service could survey a sample of customers over time or measure how long people wait to be served. It is not necessary for the contract to identify the specific ways by which progress will be measured. The client often does not know what specific changes it wants to create before facilitation begins, and even if it did, details are not necessary. However, it is important that the contract identify that progress will be measured and the broad ways in which this may be done.

How Will the Facilitator's Performance Be Assessed?

Facilitators also need some feedback from clients about their performance. This can be addressed in self-critiques conducted at the end of each meeting. By participating in the critique, the facilitator is a model of effective behavior. In addition, clients should be encouraged to give feedback to the facilitator at the time the relevant behavior occurs.

What Are the Facilitator's Fees and Other Charges?

The contract should clearly state the facilitator's professional fee, whether it is charged on a daily, hourly, or project basis, and whether the fee includes charges for other expenses, such as preparation time, travel, meals and lodging, and materials. Geoffrey Bellman's (1990) book, *The Consultant's Calling*, offers useful ideas for determining consulting fees.

How Long Will the Contract Be in Effect?

For short-term basic facilitation, the length of the contract is obvious. However, for a group that seeks to create more significant change, it is usually not possible to determine exactly how long the group will need to meet to accomplish its objectives. In this case, the contract should specify some time period after which the client and facilitator will discuss whether the contract should be renewed.

When and How Can the Contract Be Changed?

Changing the contract requires the agreement of the facilitator and the client. In practice, this means that whenever the facilitator or a member of the client group is dissatisfied with the agreement, that person raises the issue. For example, clients sometimes call the day before a retreat to see whether the facilitator will still facilitate if one member is unable to attend. On other occasions, a client (or the facilitator) may need to reschedule or cancel a meeting. In still other cases, a client may ask the facilitator to expand the work with the group or to facilitate additional groups.

The ultimate contract change occurs when the client unilaterally decides to stop using the facilitator before the end of the agreed-upon period. If the meeting schedule is set in advance, the client may reschedule or cancel a few meetings before telling the facilitator. If the next meeting date is not scheduled until after the most recent meeting has occurred, the facilitator may never get a call for the next meeting. The latter situation happened once to a colleague and me. Because we had no agreement with the client about changing the contract and because we were dissatisfied with the group's progress, we did not discuss the situation with the full client group. Only months later, in an informal conversation with one of the group members, did we learn of the client's reasons for discontinuing the work.

To avoid the problem, a long-term facilitation contract should specify that the facilitator will be given an opportunity to talk with the client before the latter decides to end the work prematurely. The purpose of the meeting is not to persuade the client to continue the work—that is inconsistent with the core value of free and informed choice. Rather, the meeting enables the facilitator to hear directly why the client wants to end the facilitation. The conversation may identify such concerns as the lack of progress, the facilitator's competence, external pressures on the group, or members' fears of dealing with undiscussable issues. Such a conversation enables facilitators to help the client make a more informed choice about ending the facilitation and provides facilitators with feedback about their performance.

Canceling a contract is often preceded by more subtle changes. The client may delay returning the facilitator's phone calls, exclude the facilitator in planning certain meetings, or react differently to the facilitator's interventions. The changes may reflect issues addressed in the contract. They may also reflect implicit understandings or norms that have developed between the client and facilitator. In short, the client begins to treat the facilitator differently. This can happen subtly but quickly. **A facilitator should seek to recontract with the client as soon as the facilitator senses that the client is treating him or her differently** (Block, 1981). The longer the facilitator waits, the less influence he or she has in exploring the reasons for the change in behavior.

In one sense, the client and facilitator are continually renegotiating the contract—if not in print, at least verbally. Over the course of the facilitation, clients become clearer about their objectives, their objectives change, their level of motivation waxes and wanes, and their dependence on the facilitator changes as their own skills increase. To serve the client well, the agreement must be modified to reflect the client's changing needs.

To act consistently with the values of valid information and free and informed choice, **both the client and facilitator need to be able to change the contract (with agreement from the other party) as conditions change.** One reason for changing the contract is that group members become more informed about the ground rules that they initially said they wanted to use. For example, after the facilitator has identified several times when group members have acted inconsistently with their ground rules when dealing with nongroup members, group members may decide they do not want to contract to use the ground rules with nongroup members but only within the facilitated meetings.

How and When Should the Tentative Contract Be Conveyed to All Parties?

To be useful, the contract has to find its way into the hands of all members of the client group. Especially in short-term basic facilitation, this should occur before the first facilitated meeting.

Resource B Sample Agreement for Basic Facilitation

Institute of Government

The University of North Carolina at Chapel Hill
CB# 3330 Knapp Building
UNC-CH
Chapel Hill, NC 27599-3330
919-966-5381

Memorandum

To: Terry Copeland, city manager, City of Livingston
        Anna Macher, director of human resources
        Ken Ahura, director of public works
From: Roger Schwarz, assistant director
Date: June 13, 1993
Re: Top Management Group Retreat

This memo summarizes the agreement we reached during our planning meeting regarding the top management retreat.

    Time and location: The retreat will be held at the Quail Roost Center north of Durham. The retreat will begin at 9 A.M. on June 29, and the group will work until 9 P.M. The group will meet from 9 A.M. until 5 P.M. on the 30th. Meals will be served at the center.

    Attendance and rescheduling: The top management team members will participate in the retreat: Terry Copeland, Anna Macher, Ken Ahura, Kathy Washington, Lee Robeson, Vance Forsyth, Charlotte Umstead, and Dale Rosenbaum.

To enable full discussion of all participants' views and to ensure adequate support for any decisions reached in the session, the participants agree to attend the full session without interruptions. We have agreed to reschedule the retreat if any member is unable to attend.

Tentative objective and agenda: The objective of the retreat is to help the group improve its functioning by clarifying its roles and working relationships. To accomplish the objective, the group will discuss some general issues: the general role of the city manager and department heads and the city manager's expectations for the department heads and vice versa.

We will begin the retreat by introducing participants, agreeing on or modifying the tentative agenda, identifying participants' expectations for the retreat, and agreeing on ground rules for the retreat. We will conclude the retreat with a discussion of next steps and an evaluation of the retreat, including the facilitator's work.

The retreat objective and agenda remain tentative until the entire group of participants either confirms or modifies it.

Third-party roles and fees: I will serve as a substantively neutral facilitator for the group. I will not provide expert information on the substantive issues the group is discussing nor make decisions for the group but will help the group use effective process to discuss its issues. This will include helping participants to stay on topic, to see how their views are similar and different, to understand the assumptions underlying their discussions, and to identify solutions that meet all participants' interests.

I will supply flip charts and markers needed to facilitate the group's work. The Institute of Government's charge for facilitation is $x,xxx for the two-day session, plus expenses for travel, lodging, and meals.

Advance preparation: At the beginning of the retreat, the group will decide on a set of ground rules to guide its discussion. To prepare for making the decision, please read the enclosed article, "Groundrules for Effective Groups," which I wrote.

Notification of changes: Please contact me immediately if this memo is inconsistent with the agreement we have reached in our conversations. Terry Copeland will contact me in the event that any participant cannot attend the retreat. If events or circumstances require modifying our agreement, we will jointly decide how to make the changes.

Distribution of memo: So that all participants are fully informed about the retreat plans, Terry Copeland will arrange for copies of this memo and the ground rules article to be sent to all participants.

I look forward to working with you on June 29 and 30.

Resource C Sample Agreement for Developmental Facilitation

**Facilitation Agreement Between City of Livingston Top Management Team
and Roger Schwarz, Institute of Government**

The purpose of this agreement is to clarify and commit to the conditions that will govern the facilitation relationship between the City of Livingston's top management team and Roger Schwarz of the Institute of Government.

Goals and Objectives of Facilitation

The goals and objectives of the top management team and Roger Schwarz are set forth in the two sections that follow.

Management Team Goals. The goals of the facilitation are to develop a management team that manages and leads by using a shared set of values and beliefs that are consistent with the mission and vision statement of the organization and solves problems, makes decisions, and communicates effectively within that set of values and beliefs. This includes top management team members' relationships with each other, with other members of the organization, and with persons in the organization's environment.

The objectives constituting these goals are to

1. Develop a set of espoused values and beliefs that will guide members' actions
2. Increase members' abilities to identify the values and beliefs that underlie their actions

3. Increase members' abilities to identify inconsistencies between their espoused values and beliefs and the values and beliefs embedded in their actions
4. Increase members' abilities to design problem-solving, decision-making, and communication processes and structures consistent with their espoused values and beliefs
5. Increase members' abilities to act consistently with a set of ground rules derived from the values and beliefs
6. Increase members' abilities to communicate values and beliefs to other organizational members, as well as clients and others in the organization's environment

Consultant Goals. The primary goal of the facilitator is to help the management team achieve its goals in a way that over time reduces dependence on the facilitator. Other goals include:

1. Increasing the facilitator's effectiveness by obtaining feedback about how his behavior affects the client
2. Contributing to the field of organization development by using the facilitation data to publish research, theory, and practice regarding the facilitation process

Criteria for Deciding the Issues on Which to Work

The management team will give higher priority to working on issues that have characteristics that are likely to help the group achieve its goals and objectives. Issues have higher priority for discussion to the extent that they meet the following criteria:

1. The issue is fertile ground for learning about the team's or members' values and beliefs
2. The issue has a relatively high level of emotional content or is usually undiscussable
3. The issue is one in which most of the relevant information resides with management team members
4. The issue is one in which the group's knowledge may be significantly increased by the facilitator's presence
5. The issue can be discussed without the pressure of a need for immediate resolution. This criterion is based on the premise that when the group must use the meeting to make a decision, the group will be under pressure to reduce the time allotted to examining values and beliefs related to the decision

Ground Rules

The group has committed to using the ground rules described in the article "Groundrules for Effective Groups." In addition, the group may develop other ground rules throughout the facilitation process.

Information shared within the facilitated sessions will be considered confidential unless members agree otherwise. Information shared by one or more group members with the facilitator will not be considered confidential with respect to the other group members.

The facilitator has the right to use data from the facilitation process for professional writing, research, and presentations if the identities of the organization and management team members are disguised. The facilitator may use the data in undisguised form with the permission of the management team.

Role of Facilitator

The facilitator will serve as a substantively neutral third party for the group. The facilitator will not make decisions for the group but will help the group use and learn how to use effective group process, in part by using the ground rules. The facilitator will provide expert information on the group's substantive issues only when a member of the group has requested it and the group has agreed the facilitator should provide it. The facilitator and top management team will jointly control the facilitation process.

Evaluating Progress

The management team and facilitator may use the following methods to measure the team's progress toward achieving its goals and objectives and the facilitator's effectiveness:

1. Self-critiques at the end of each meeting
2. Tape-recorded facilitation sessions
3. Written communications from top management team members
4. Decisions made by top management team members
5. Dialogues written by top management team members
6. Self-reports of top management team members
7. Verbal and written feedback from employees
8. Surveys or interviews of employees

Facilitator Fees and Expenses

The City of Livingston will pay the Institute of Government $x,xxx for each half day of facilitation provided by Roger Schwarz. In addition, the city will reimburse the institute for travel, lodging, meals, and other direct expenses incurred.

Duration of, Changes to, and Process for Terminating Facilitation

The parties agree to meet approximately one half day per week for one year from the date of this contract. At that time, the parties will evaluate their progress and renew, modify, or terminate their agreement as needed.

At any time, either party may suggest changes in this agreement. Any changes in the agreement must be agreed to by both parties.

Nevertheless, either party may terminate this facilitation relationship at any time. However, before terminating the relationship, the parties agree to meet with each other to discuss the circumstances of termination and to conduct a final self-critique of the facilitation process.

We commit to facilitation services as described in this agreement:

City of Livingston
Management Team Members: Institute of Government:

_____   _____
Terry Copeland   date   Roger Schwarz   date

_____
Anna Macher   date

_____
Ken Ahura   date

_____
Kathy Washington   date

_____
Lee Robeson   date

_____
Vance Forsyth   date

_____
Charlotte Umstead   date

_____
Dale Rosenbaum   date

Resource D Guidelines for Using Experiential Exercises and Self-knowledge Instruments

Experiential exercises and self-knowledge instruments are macro interventions. Experiential exercises help groups learn about their process in the course of working on some simulated task. A popular example is the "lost on the moon" exercise in which the group pretends it is stranded on the moon. The group must leave the spaceship to try to get saved and has fifteen items it can take along. Each member must rank the fifteen items (for example, a flashlight, a parachute, a box of matches) in order of importance for their trip. Next, the entire group must agree on a single order. The exercise helps group members explore how their group processes (that is, problem solving, decision making, conflict management, and communication) influence their group's effectiveness.

Self-knowledge instruments (for example, group communication surveys, Myers-Briggs Type Indicator) help groups understand some aspects of their group dynamics or individual differences within the group.

The decision to use exercises or instruments to facilitate group process rests on several factors: consistency with the values and principles of group facilitation, effective use of time, and in the case of instruments, their validity and reliability.

Consistency with Values and Principles

To be consistent with the core values and principles of group facilitation, the instrument or exercise must generate valid information, enable participants to make free and informed choices, and lead members to be internally committed to those choices. Given these values, it is *inappropriate* to use an exercise or instrument when

1. It withholds information or relies on deception. For example, one personnel selection exercise is designed to identify how well members test assumptions and share information. Each member is given a sheet of paper with what looks like the same description of several job candidates and asked to select the best candidate. In fact, the best candidate can be selected only if members realize that each member's sheet has slightly different information and if they share that information. For the exercise to work, the facilitator must withhold from the group the information that each sheet is different.

    The problem with using deception is that it reduces trust in and the credibility of the facilitator. It reduces trust because deception is inconsistent with the core values. It reduces credibility because it sends the message that deception is justified when one is seeking pure outcomes or is driven by pure motives (in this case, learning). However, because individuals almost always consider their motives or outcomes pure, in practice using deceptive exercises has the effect of endorsing deception in general. Finally, the facilitator cannot be a credible model of helping groups reduce deception if the facilitator relies on deception in working with clients.

    There is one condition in which it is appropriate for the facilitator to use an exercise or instrument involving deception: if the group makes a free and (somewhat) informed choice to participate after the facilitator tells the group that deception is involved.

2. It is used to set the group up, that is, when the outcome is predetermined and controlled by the facilitator. For example, one puzzle exercise examines conflict by asking a group to put together a puzzle that, unbeknown to members, is missing a piece. Here too, the group can make a free and (somewhat) informed choice about participating in an exercise if it is aware that the outcome is predetermined.

3. It demands a level of personal risk greater than that for which participants contracted. An example is having members reveal their answers to survey questions about group trust.

4. The facilitator unilaterally chooses an exercise that underestimates the group's potential for openly sharing information.

5. It is inconsistent with the group's objectives.

6. The facilitator does not have time to process the results adequately.

7. It meets all the requirements, but the facilitator does not know what to expect in terms of the range of issues that might be raised by the exercise or instrument and is not confident about handling all the issues that might be raised.

Deciding Whether to Use Experiential Exercises

Even if an experiential exercise meets the conditions listed, it may not be the best choice for a learning exercise. The purpose of experiential group exercises is to create an experience on which group members can reflect and from which they can learn about their process. Experiential group exercises are based on a set of assumptions that is consistent with facilitation (Hall, Bowen, Lewicki, & Bowen, 1982, p. 3):

1. Learning is more effective when it is an active rather than a passive process.
2. Problem-centered learning is more enduring than theory-based learning.
3. Two-way communication produces better learning than one-way communication.
4. Participants will learn more when they share control over and responsibility for the learning process than when the responsibility lies solely with the group leader.
5. Learning is most effective when thought and action are integrated.

Experiential group exercises require a group task and interdependent group members who are trying to accomplish the task. The group task is typically artificial. That is, the group would not normally perform that task (or perform it in that way) in the course of their work. Or, in training classes in which participants do not constitute an intact work group, the task is artificial because the group is artificial.

In group facilitation, however, members are already in an intact work group and interdependent. The group is faced with many real tasks that the facilitator can use to help members reflect on and learn from. In fact, this is what developmental facilitation is all about. Therefore, the facilitator needs some additional purpose for using an experiential exercise.

One purpose is to make it easier for group members to examine their process by separating it from their real content issues. By reducing the investment members have in the content of the decision, they can reflect on the process more objectively and less defensively. But the advantage can also become a disadvantage. A group may discount the exercise results by arguing that the exercise does not adequately represent the group's situation. And, if one of a group's problems is that members get defensive, using exercises that reduce defensive behavior limits the opportunities for working on it. In other words, in some situations, members will learn more when the experience comes from the group's real tasks and members experience the full consequences of the group's process (Schwarz, 1985). When deciding whether to suggest an experiential exercise, the facilitator needs to consider the potential advantages and disadvantages. Finally, **experiential exercises are generally not an effective use of time for basic facilitation, the purpose of which is not to learn how to develop more effective process.**

Validity and Reliability of Instruments

Instruments should meet a minimum level of validity and reliability. While a discussion of test validity and reliability is beyond the purpose of this book, a brief overview of these terms is provided here.

There are two major types of validity—internal and external (Cook &

Campbell, 1979). When an instrument is *internally* valid, it measures what it is intended to measure. For example, if an instrument is intended to measure a person's intelligence, it measures intelligence only and not the person's conflict style or whether the person is an introvert or extrovert.

When an instrument is *externally* valid, its internal validity holds for different types of people and settings. When instruments are developed and tested for internal validity, they are tested using a sample of people, for example, five-hundred first-level supervisors in the banking industry. If the instrument is externally valid for a certain population, the instrument will work for that population, such as higher-level supervisors, elected officials, or people in other occupations. Whether an instrument is externally valid for a particular population can be determined only after the instrument has been used with that population (Cook & Campbell, 1979).

When an instrument is *reliable,* it can be depended on to give roughly the same results when a particular individual takes it more than once over a period of time (assuming no change in the individual). Reliability reflects the consistency of results over time and nothing else.

Instruments that are not valid or not reliable mislead people about the meaning of their scores. To determine whether an instrument is valid and reliable, the facilitator should first examine the instrument. Some authors provide the information in appendixes that explain the design of the instrument. Other authors make it available to those who request it.

Readers interested in using experiential exercises or self-knowledge instruments will find additional sources listed in Resource G.

Resource E Questions for Cofacilitators

Orientation/Style

1. The major values, beliefs, and principles that guide my facilitation are . . .
2. The major values, beliefs, and principles that other facilitators hold and that I strongly disagree with are . . .
3. When contracting with this type of group, I usually . . .
4. When starting this type of group, I usually . . .
5. At the end of a meeting with this type of group, I usually . . .
6. When someone talks too much, I usually . . .
7. When the group is silent, I usually . . .
8. When an individual is silent for a long time, I usually . . .
9. When someone gets upset, I usually . . .
10. When someone comes late, I usually . . .
11. When someone leaves early, I usually . . .
12. When group members are excessively polite and do not confront each other, I usually . . .
13. When there is conflict in the group, I usually . . .
14. When the group attacks one member, I usually . . .
15. When a group member takes a cheap shot at me or implies I am ineffective, I usually . . .
16. If there is physical violence or threats of violence, I usually . . .
17. When members focus on positions, I usually . . .

Note: Some questions are from Pfeiffer & Jones (1975).

18. When members seem to be off the track, I usually . . .
19. When someone takes a cheap shot, I usually . . .
20. My favorite interventions for this type of group are . . .
21. Interventions that this type of group usually needs but that I often don't make are . . .
22. In working with this type of group, the things I find most satisfying are . . .
23. The things I find most frustrating in working with this type of group are . . .
24. The things that make me most uncomfortable in this type of group are . . .
25. On a continuum ranging from completely supportive to completely confrontational, my intervention style is . . .
26. My typical "intervention rhythm" is [fast/slow] . . .

Experiences and Background

1. Discuss your experiences as a facilitator or cofacilitator. What types of groups have you facilitated? What were the content and process issues in the groups?
2. Discuss your best facilitation and cofacilitation experiences. What was it about the experiences that made them so successful?
3. Discuss your worst facilitation and cofacilitation experiences. What was it about the experiences that made them so unsuccessful?
4. Describe some of your facilitation behaviors that a cofacilitator might consider idiosyncratic.
5. Describe the issues that have arisen between you and other cofacilitators.
6. Describe the areas in which you are trying to improve your facilitation. How would you like the cofacilitator to help you improve?
7. What personal issues do you have that might hinder the ability of you and the other facilitator to work with each other or with the client?
8. Given what you know about the cofacilitator, what concerns do you have about working with that person?

Cofacilitator Coordination

1. Who will sit where in the group meetings?
2. Who will start the session? Who will finish it?
3. Will both of you need to be present at all times? How will breakout sessions be handled?
4. How will you handle the role of flip chart recorder?
5. How will you divide the labor (for example, primary-secondary, task-relationship, intervener-recorder)?
6. What kind of facilitator interventions and behaviors are inside and outside the zone of deference that each of you will grant the other?

7. Where, when, and how will you deal with issues between you?
8. What kinds of disagreements between you are you willing and not willing to show in front of the group?
9. How closely should you expect each other to adhere to the designated roles you have jointly agreed on?
10. What is nonnegotiable for each of you as cofacilitator?

Resource F For Internal Facilitators: Guidelines for Contracting with Your Supervisor

For internal facilitators and their supervisors, contracting reduces the potential role conflicts for the facilitator and increases the chance that the facilitator can serve the client's needs. **Facilitator-supervisor contracting should occur before the facilitator begins working with any internal client.** It reduces the chance that facilitators will find themselves in a conflict in which they must choose between meeting the needs of the client and maintaining their own place in the organization. (External facilitators who are supervised by someone can also benefit from a similar conversation with their supervisors.) Listed here is a series of questions and issues for facilitators and their supervisors to consider when contracting with each other. The items appear in questionnaire form in Exhibit F.1, at the end of the resource.

How will clients request my facilitation services? If the client initially contacts the facilitator, the facilitator's role is less likely to be misrepresented to the potential client, and others cannot commit the facilitator inappropriately. Requesting services directly from the internal facilitator also establishes the norm of dealing directly with the individual who can best provide valid information— a principle of effective facilitation. The supervisor and facilitator can also agree on how requests to the supervisor will be handled. For example, the supervisor may generally describe the facilitator's role to those requesting services and ask that the potential client contact the facilitator to discuss the specific situation.

Under what conditions may I decline or accept client requests for my services? There are numerous legitimate reasons for declining a client's request for help. The facilitator may not have the skills or time to help the client, or cannot be considered as substantively neutral on the topic for facilitation. Or, the client may want facilitators to act in ways that are inconsistent with their roles. The client group may have insufficient motivation or time to accomplish its objectives, or other factors within or outside the group may significantly reduce the likelihood of success. If facilitators cannot decline requests under these or other legitimate conditions, they should tell the client group that they will work with them but explain the factors that they believe will hinder the group in accomplishing its objectives.

Who will decide whether I can work with a client? Related to the last question is the question of who will decide whether the conditions warrant declining work with a client. Ideally, the decision should be made by those who understand the role of facilitator and can accurately diagnose the group's situation. If the facilitator's supervisor is also a facilitator, they can jointly make an effective decision.

In some cases, the supervisor may want the facilitator to decline a request although, from the facilitator's perspective, it meets all the necessary conditions for accepting the request. For example, the supervisor may consider the group relatively unimportant to the organization and not worth the investment. Alternatively, the supervisor may want the facilitator to accept a request that fails to meet the necessary conditions. Here, the supervisor may be responding to pressure to give the group a quick fix.

The difficulty arises when the supervisor and facilitator cannot reach a decision that integrates their interests. If consensus cannot be reached, one approach is to use the premise that the decision should be made by whichever individual is more likely to experience greater negative consequences from it. Therefore, when the facilitator wants to accept and the supervisor wants to decline the request, the supervisor should decide. In this case, the negative consequences that follow from not helping the group are more likely to be felt by the supervisor than the facilitator. In contrast, when the facilitator wants to decline and the supervisor wants to accept the request, the facilitator should decide. Here the negative consequences that follow from working with a group under questionable conditions are more likely to be felt, at least directly, by the facilitator. Alternatively, facilitators can decide when they believe that facilitation will not only be unsuccessful but also will harm the group.

What are my limits for contracting and terminating a contract with the client? Facilitators need to know the limits within which they can contract with the client without supervisor approval. For example, does the supervisor need to approve facilitation that will require more than a certain number of hours of commitment? Or, does the supervisor need to approve facilitation for certain levels or areas of the organization? Can the facilitator contract for a high-risk developmental facilitation without approval? By examining the section on elements of contracts, the facilitator and supervisor can jointly identify the relevant limiting conditions.

In some cases, facilitators may need to terminate a contract with the client. May they do so without discussing termination with the supervisor?

What client information will I have to share with you or others in the organization? In considering confidentiality, four immediate interests need to be considered—the client group's, the facilitator's, the facilitator's supervisor's, and the client group's supervisor(s)'. Facilitators are usually interested in a confidentiality agreement that enables them to use colleagues as a sounding board to increase their effectiveness. If the facilitator's supervisor is also a facilitator, the facilitator may want to use the supervisor for that purpose. Similarly, the supervisor is likely to be interested in group information for evaluating and helping either group members or the facilitator improve performance.

Part of the agreement involves how to respond when others seek information about the group. For example, after facilitators explain their interests in not sharing information with a nongroup member, should facilitators refer the nongroup member to their supervisor if the nonmember persists?

Will I be required to evaluate my client's performance? The facilitator experiences role conflict when asked by a nongroup member to evaluate the performance of a group member. Group members trust a facilitator partly because the facilitator does not have any power in the system to affect group members (or agrees not to use that power). Evaluating members means using that power and changes the dynamic. This is true even if the facilitator evaluates the group member positively.

The need to evaluate the process can be especially strong when members of a facilitated group spend a significant amount of their work time in the group. For example, I worked with a federal agency and its national union to establish a cooperative incentive program. A small union-management committee worked almost full time to administer the program. Managers often wanted the facilitator to evaluate members' contributions. In fact, the managers believed the members were performing well and were looking for more detailed evaluation data to support giving the members bonuses.

One way to avoid creating role conflict for the facilitator is not to evaluate members on their internal group process. Instead, those who seek to evaluate group members can base their evaluations on the individuals' behavior outside the group. Alternatively, the entire group can be evaluated on its task performance. Performance can be evaluated without observing the group's internal process.

How will my performance as a facilitator be evaluated? It is more difficult to determine how the facilitator's performance will be evaluated. The assumption underlying group facilitation is that effective group process contributes to higher quality and more acceptable group decisions. But because the group maintains free choice over its actions, the group's performance is not determined solely by the facilitator's performance. A facilitator can perform effectively, and the group may not achieve any of its objectives. Alternatively, a facilitator can perform poorly, and the group can still accomplish its objectives.

An effective way to evaluate facilitators is to either observe their performance or review tapes of the facilitation. (This requires agreement from the group and agreement about confidentiality regarding the tapes or group observations.) Both methods use valid information in the form of directly observable data. Tape recordings also enable the facilitator and supervisor to review the performance data, which eliminates problems with recall and is of value in using the evaluation developmentally. If facilitation is only a small part of the individual's responsibilities (part-time facilitating), evaluation may not be as important for purposes of reward.

What arrangements will be made regarding my other work when I am working with a client? Part-time facilitators can reduce role conflict by agreeing on how their non-facilitation responsibilities will be handled when they are facilitating. For example, facilitators may delegate their nonfacilitation responsibilities if possible, or the facilitator and supervisor might agree that the facilitator will be responsible only for priority nonfacilitation work. Depending on how quickly their other responsibilities must be handled, part-time facilitators sometimes work long hours to keep up with other work after a full day's facilitation. Because facilitation is exhausting work, the quality of the other work may suffer.

What special agreements do we need if I facilitate a group of which you (the supervisor) are a member? At some point, facilitators may receive a request to facilitate a group that includes their supervisor. Here the potential conflicts facilitators face are similar to those discussed elsewhere. However, the conflicts can be more difficult if the facilitator perceives the supervisor as creating role conflicts, not buffering them. In this case, the facilitator needs to raise the issue with the supervisor. Even if the supervisor does not create role conflicts for the facilitator, other group members may believe that the facilitator will favor the supervisor. In contracting with the full client group, the facilitator should raise the issue and ask the group to decide if it wants to work with the facilitator.

What will each of us do to ensure that relevant individuals understand and honor our agreement? In some ways, the facilitator's supervisor acts as a buffer, protecting the facilitator from conflicts that would undermine work with the client group. The ways in which the supervisor is willing to do this as well as the supervisor's limits to serving as a buffer are an important part of the agreement. The facilitator is also responsible for ensuring that relevant members in the organization understand the facilitator's role. Together, the facilitator and supervisor can decide what initiatives to take to accomplish the objectives.

What will we do if either of us believes the other has acted inconsistently with our agreement? Finally, the facilitator and supervisor need a way to confront one another when one believes the other has acted inconsistently with their agreement. Agreeing to such a process at the time of contracting makes it easier to raise the issue when a conflict does arise.

Exhibit F.1. Contracting Questions for Internal Facilitators and Their Supervisors.

1. How will clients request my facilitation services?
   a. Directly from me.
   b. Through you (supervisor).
   c. Either a or b.
   d. Some other way.
2. Under what conditions may I decline or accept client requests for my services?
   a. I do not have sufficient time.
   b. I do not have the skills.
   c. The content of the client's problem makes it difficult for me to act or be seen as substantively neutral.
   d. The client is insufficiently motivated.
   e. The client has insufficient time available.
   f. Other factors within the group reduce its chance of success.
   g. Factors outside the group reduce its chance of success.
   h. The client wants me to play an inappropriate role.
   i. Other conditions suggest that facilitating the group is inadvisable.
3. Who will decide whether I can work with a client?
   a. I decide with the client.
   b. I decide with the client and you (supervisor).
   c. We use some other way to make the decision.
4. What are my limits for contracting and terminating a contract with the client?
5. What information will I be required to share with you or others in the organization?
   a. Only information regarding the amount of time I spend with the client.
   b. General information (define *general*) about how the client or I am doing.
   c. Specific information about what occurs in meetings.
   d. Other information (define).
6. Will I be required to evaluate my client's performance?
7. How will my performance as a facilitator be evaluated?
8. What arrangements will be made regarding my other work when I am working with a client?
9. What special agreements do we need to reach if I facilitate a group of which you (the supervisor) are a member?
10. What will each of us do to ensure that relevant individuals understand and honor our agreement?
11. What will we do if either of us believes the other has acted inconsistently with our agreement?

Resource G Further Reading

Adams, J. L. (1986). *Conceptual blockbusting: A guide to better ideas* (3rd ed.). Reading, MA: Addison-Wesley. This book explains the different kinds of creative blocks that people face—perceptual, emotional, cultural and environmental, intellectual, and expressive—and provides techniques for overcoming the blocks.

Argyris, C. (1993). *Knowledge for action: A guide to overcoming barriers to organizational change.* San Francisco: Jossey-Bass, and Argyris, C. (1970). *Intervention theory and method: A behavioral science view.* Reading, MA: Addison-Wesley. Chris Argyris is one of the leading scholars in the field of organizational change. He developed the three core values that are used throughout *The Skilled Facilitator. Intervention Theory and Method* introduces the core values and includes verbatim transcripts from consulting sessions to illustrate how organizational change agents can work effectively with clients. *Knowledge for Action* uses a case study that includes extensive transcripts from consulting sessions to show how organizational change agents can help clients identify defensive behavior that limits learning and how change agents use the core values to help people create fundamental change in their organizations.

Bellman, G. M. (1990). *The consultant's calling: Bringing who you are to what you do.* San Francisco: Jossey-Bass. Geoffrey Bellman writes an engaging and personal account about what it is really like to be an organizational consultant and the joys, frustrations, worries, and issues that consultants face. He helps consultants think about how to integrate their personal values and identities with their work so that they can live balanced, meaningful lives.

Block, P. (1993). *Stewardship: Choosing service over self-interest.* San Francisco:

294

Berrett-Koehler. In this book, Peter Block introduces and explores a new model of stewardship—the notion of accepting responsibility and accountability for the well-being of the larger organization while simultaneously giving up the need to control or take care of others. The role of the facilitative leader has much in common with Block's concept of stewardship.

Bryson, J. M. (1988). *Strategic planning for public and nonprofit organizations: A guide to strengthening and sustaining organizational achievement.* San Francisco: Jossey-Bass. John Bryson provides a conceptually grounded step-by-step method for strategic planning in the public and nonprofit sectors.

Gambrill, E. (1990). *Critical thinking in clinical practice: Improving the accuracy of judgments and decisions about clients.* San Francisco: Jossey-Bass. Eileen Gambrill explains how clinicians, by improving their reasoning skills, can better serve clients by avoiding inaccurate assumptions, fallacies, and logical traps when working with clients.

Gellermann, W., Frankel, M. S., & Ladenson, R. F. (1990). *Values and ethics in organization and human systems development.* San Francisco: Jossey-Bass. This book provides a set of ethical values and principles that organizational consultants can use to guide their behavior with clients. Through extensive case studies, the authors explore various ethical dilemmas that consultants face in their work.

Hackman, J. R. (1986). The psychology of self-management in organizations. In M. S. Pallack & R. O. Perloff (Eds.), *Psychology and work: Productivity, change, and employment.* Washington, DC: American Psychological Association. Richard Hackman's chapter describes the different types of self-managed work groups, the conditions that foster and support effective self-management, and the role of leaders in self-managing groups.

Manz, C. C., & Sims, H. P., Jr. (1989). *SuperLeadership: Leading others to lead themselves.* Englewood Cliffs, NJ: Prentice-Hall. *SuperLeadership* describes a form of leadership that leaders use to facilitate the self-leadership of others. The authors describe strategies for becoming a superleader. The role of facilitative leader and the role of superleader are similar.

Pfeiffer, J. W., & Ballew, A. C. (1988). *Using instruments in human resource development.* San Diego, CA: University Associates, and Pfeiffer, J. W., & Ballew, A. C. (1988). *Using structured experiences in human resource development.* San Diego, CA: University Associates. The two books are part of the seven-volume *University Associates Training Technologies* by the same authors. The two volumes give practical advice for selecting, using, and avoiding problems when using experiential exercises or self-knowledge instruments.

Schein, E. H. (1988). *Process consultation: Its role in organization development* (Vol. 1, 2nd ed). Reading, MA: Addison-Wesley, and Schein, E. H. (1987). *Process consultation: Lessons for managers and consultants* (Vol. 2). Reading, MA: Addison-Wesley. Edgar Schein's two-volume set is a classic in the field of group facilitation (the first volume was originally published in 1969). Together, the two easy-to-read books describe process consultation and how a process consultant or manager contracts, diagnoses, and intervenes in a group. The books also discuss issues in group dynamics.

Schwarz, R. M. (1989). Groundrules for Effective Groups. *Popular Government, 54*(4), 25–30. This article explains the sixteen ground rules discussed in *The Skilled Facilitator*. I frequently provide clients with copies of the article during the planning process. Copies are available from the Institute of Government, Knapp Building CB #3330, The University of North Carolina at Chapel Hill, Chapel Hill, NC, 27599-3330; (919) 966-5381.

Senge, P. M. (1990). *The fifth discipline: The art and practice of the learning organization.* New York: Doubleday. In this important book of broad scope, Peter Senge explores the five disciplines necessary to create a learning organization: systems thinking, personal mastery, mental models, shared vision, and team learning.

Steele, F. (1982). *The role of the internal consultant.* Boston, MA: CBI. As the title states, this book describes the role of the internal organizational change agent, the issues that these employees face, and how to deal with the issues.

Von Oech, R. (1983). *A whack on the side of the head: How to unlock your mind for innovation.* New York: Warner Books. This highly illustrated, fun-to-read book identifies ten blocks to creativity and gives practical pointers for overcoming them.

References

Adams, J. L. (1986). *Conceptual blockbusting: A guide to better ideas.* (3rd ed.). Reading, MA: Addison-Wesley.

Alderfer, C. P. (1976). Group processes in organizations. In M. D. Dunnette (Ed.), *Handbook of industrial and organizational psychology.* Skokie, IL: Rand McNally.

Alderfer, C. P. (1977). Group and intergroup relations. In J. R. Hackman & J. L. Suttle (Eds.), *Improving life at work.* Santa Monica, CA: Goodyear.

Alderfer, C. P. (1990). Staff authority and leadership in experiential groups. In J. Gillette & M. Mccollom (Eds.), *Groups in context: A new perspective on group dynamics.* Reading, MA: Addison-Wesley.

Allport, F. H. (1967). A theory of enestruence (event structure theory): Report of progress. *American Psychologist, 22,* 1–24.

Argyris, C. (1970). *Intervention theory and method: A behavioral science view.* Reading, MA: Addison-Wesley.

Argyris, C. (1982). *Reasoning, learning, and action.* San Francisco: Jossey-Bass.

Argyris, C. (1985). *Strategy, change, and defensive routines.* Boston: Pittman.

Argyris, C. (1987). Reasoning, action strategies, and defensive routines: The case of OD practitioners. In R. W. Woodman & W. A. Pasmore (Eds.), *Research in organizational change and development* (Vol. 1, pp. 89–128). Greenwich, CT: JAI Press.

Argyris, C. (1990). *Overcoming organizational defenses: Facilitating organizational learning.* Needham Heights, MA: Allyn & Bacon.

Argyris, C. (1993). *Knowledge for action: A guide to overcoming barriers to organizational change.* San Francisco: Jossey-Bass.

Argyris, C., Putnam, R., & Smith D. M. (1985). *Action science: Concepts, methods, and skills for research and intervention.* San Francisco: Jossey-Bass.

Argyris, C., & Schön, D. A. (1974). *Theory in practice: Increasing professional effectiveness.* San Francisco: Jossey-Bass.

Argyris, C., & Schön, D. A. (1978). *Organizational learning: A theory of action perspective.* Reading, MA: Addison-Wesley.

Bandler, R., & Grinder, J. (1982). *Reframing: Neuro-linguistic programming and the transformation of meaning.* Moab, UT: Real People Press.

Barnard, C. I. (1938). *The functions of the executive.* Cambridge, MA: Harvard University Press.

Bateson. G. (1972). *Steps to an ecology of mind.* San Francisco: Chandler.

Beer, M. (1980). *Organization change and development: A systems view.* Santa Monica, CA: Goodyear.

Bellman, G. M. (1990). *The consultant's calling: Bringing who you are to what you do.* San Francisco: Jossey-Bass.

Benne, K. D. (1964). History of the t-group in the laboratory setting. In L. P. Bradford, J. R. Gibb, & K. D. Benne (Eds.), *T-Group theory and laboratory method.* New York: Wiley.

Blake, R. R. (1964). *The managerial grid: Key orientations for achieving production through people.* Houston, TX: Gulf Publishing.

Blake, R. R., & Mouton, J. S. (1983). *Consultation (2nd ed.).* Reading, MA: Addison-Wesley.

Block, P. (1981). *Flawless consulting.* San Diego, CA: University Associates.

Block, P. (1993). *Stewardship: Choosing service over self-interest.* San Francisco: Berrett-Koehler.

Brown, L. D. (1983). *Managing conflict at organizational interfaces.* Reading, MA: Addison-Wesley.

Bryson, J. M. (1988). *Strategic planning for public and nonprofit organizations: A guide to strengthening and sustaining organizational achievement.* San Francisco: Jossey-Bass.

Chilberg, J. C. (1989). A review of group process designs for facilitating communication in problem-solving groups. *Management Communication Quarterly, 3,* 51–70.

Cook, T.D., & Campbell, D. T. (1979). *Quasi-experimentation: Design and analysis issues for field settings.* Skokie, IL: Rand McNally.

Cyert, R. M., & March, J. G. (1963). *A behavioral theory of the firm.* Englewood Cliffs, NJ: Prentice-Hall.

Dies, R. R., Mallet, J., & Johnson, F. (1979). Openness in the coleader relationship: Its effect on group process and outcome. *Small Group Behavior, 10,* 523–546.

Eiseman, J. W. (1978). Reconciling "incompatible" positions. *Journal of Applied Behavioral Science, 14,* 133–150.

Ellis, A., & Harper, R. A. (1975). *A new guide to rational living.* North Hollywood, CA: Wilshire Book.

Festinger, L. (1957). *A theory of cognitive dissonance.* Stanford, CA: Stanford University Press.

Fisher, R., & Ury, W. (1983). *Getting to yes: Negotiating without giving in.* New York: Penguin.

Fisher, R. J., & Keashly, L. (1988). Third-party interventions in intergroup conflict: Consultation is *not* mediation. *Negotiation Journal, 4,* 381–394.

Friedman. P. (1989). Upstream facilitation: A proactive approach to managing problem-solving groups. *Management Communication Quarterly, 3,* 33–50.

French, J. R. P., Jr., & Raven, B. (1959). The bases of social power. In D. P. Cartwright (Ed.), *Studies in social power.* Ann Arbor, MI: Institute for Social Research.

Gambrill, E. (1990). *Critical thinking in clinical practice: Improving the accuracy of judgments and decisions about clients.* San Francisco: Jossey-Bass.

Gellermann, W., Frankel, M. S., & Ladenson, R. F. (1990). *Values and ethics in organization and human systems development: Responding to dilemmas in professional life.* San Francisco: Jossey-Bass.

Goffman, E. (1959). *The presentation of self in everyday life.* New York: Doubleday.

Golembiewski, R. T. (1986). Invited commentary: "Promise not to tell"—A critical view of "confidentiality" in consultation. *Consultation, 5,* 68–76.

Gouran, D. S., & Hirokawa, R. Y. (1986). Counteractive functions of communication in effective group decision-making. In R. Y. Hirokawa & M. S. Poole (Eds.), *Communication and group decision-making.* Newbury Park, CA: Sage.

Hackman, J. R. (1986). The psychology of self-management in organizations. In M. S. Pallack & R. O. Perloff (Eds.), *Psychology and work: Productivity, change, and employment.* Washington, DC: American Psychological Association.

Hackman, J. R. (1987). The design of work teams. In J. Lorsch (Ed.) *Handbook of organizational behavior.* Englewood Cliffs, NJ: Prentice-Hall.

Hackman, J. R. (1989). Work teams in organizations: An orienting framework. In J. R. Hackman (Ed.), *Groups that work (and those that don't): Creating conditions for effective teamwork.* San Francisco: Jossey-Bass.

Hall, D. T., Bowen, D. D., Lewicki, R. J., & Hall, F. S. (1982). *Experiences in management and organizational behavior* (2nd ed.). NY: Wiley.

Hall, J. H. (1969). *Conflict management survey.* The Woodlands, TX: Teleometrics International.

Harrison, R (1970). Choosing the depth of organizational intervention. *Journal of Applied Behavioral Science, 6,* 181–202.

Hayakawa, S. I. (1972). *Language in thought and action* (3rd ed). New York: Harcourt Brace Jovanovich.

Hirokawa, R. Y. (1988). Group communication and decision-making performance: A continued test of the functional perspective. *Human Communication Research, 14,* 487–515.

Hirokawa, R. Y., & Gouran D. S. (1989). Facilitation of group communication: A critique of prior research and an agenda for future research. *Management Communication Quarterly, 3,* 71–92.

International City Management Association (1991). *Future challenges, future opportunities: The final report of the ICMA futurevisions consortium.* (Insert in *Public Management,* 1991, *73*). Washington, DC: International City Management Association.

Janis, I. L. (1972). *Victims of groupthink: A psychological study of foreign-policy decisions and fiascos.* Boston: Houghton Mifflin.

Kaplan, A. (1964). *The conduct of inquiry: Methodology for behavioral science.* San Francisco: Chandler.

Kaplan, R. E. (1979). The conspicuous absence of evidence that process consultation enhances task performance. *Journal of Applied Behavioral Science, 15,* 346–360.

Katz, D., & Kahn, R. L. (1978). *The social psychology of organizations* (2nd ed.). New York: Wiley.

Kerr, S. (1975). On the folly of rewarding A, while hoping for B. *Academy of Management Journal, 18,* 769–783.

Kiesler, C. A. (1971). *The psychology of commitment: Experiments linking behavior to belief.* San Diego, CA: Academic Press.

Knapp, M. L. (1972). *Nonverbal communication in human interaction.* Troy, MO: Holt, Rinehart & Winston.

Krantz, J. (1990). Group relations training in context. In J. Gillette & M. Mccollom (Eds.), *Groups in context: A new perspective on group dynamics.* Reading, MA: Addison-Wesley.

Levinson, H. (1972). *Organizational diagnosis.* Cambridge, MA: Harvard University Press.

Manz, C. C., & Sims, H. P., Jr. (1984). Searching for the "unleader": Organizational member views on leading self-managed groups. *Human Relations, 37* (5), 409–424.

Manz, C. C., & Sims, H. P., Jr. (1989). *SuperLeadership: Leading others to lead themselves.* New York: Prentice-Hall.

Manz, C. C., & Sims, H. P., Jr. (1993, August). *Business without bosses: Real-life stories about self-managing work teams.* Paper presented at the annual meeting of the Academy of Management, Atlanta, GA.

Marrow, A. J. (1969). *The practical theorist: The life and work of Kurt Lewin.* New York: Teachers College Press.

McConnell, J. V. (1986). *Understanding human behavior* (5th ed.). Troy, MO: Holt, Rinehart & Winston.

Merton, R. K. (1957). *Social theory and social structure.* New York: Free Press of Glencoe.

Moore, C. W. (1986). *The mediation process: Practical strategies for resolving conflict.* San Francisco: Jossey-Bass.

Moulton, J., Robinson, G. M., & Elias, C. (1978). Sex bias in language use: "Neutral" pronouns that aren't. *American Psychologist, 33,* 1032–1036.

Nisbett, R., & Ross, L. (1980). *Human inference: Strategies and shortcomings of social judgment.* Englewood Cliffs, NJ: Prentice-Hall.

Osborn, A. F. (1953). *Applied Imagination: The principles and problems of creative thinking.* New York: Charles Scribner's Sons.

Paulson, I., Burroughs, J. C., & Gelb, C. B. (1976). Cotherapy: What is the crux of the relationship? *The International Journal of Group Psychotherapy, 26,* 213–224.

Pfeiffer, J. W., & Jones, J. E. (1975). Co-facilitating. In *The 1975 annual for group facilitators* (pp. 219–229). San Diego, CA: University Associates.

Roy, D. F. (1960). "Banana time": Job satisfaction and informal interaction. *Human Organization, 18,* 158–168.

Schein, E. H. (1969). *Process consultation: Its role in organization development.* Reading, MA: Addison-Wesley.

Schein, E. H. (1985). *Organizational culture and leadership.* San Francisco: Jossey-Bass.

Schein, E. H. (1987). *Process consultation: Lessons for managers and consultants* (Vol. 2). Reading, MA: Addison-Wesley.

Schein, E. H. (1988). *Process consultation: Its role in organization development* (Vol. 1, 2nd ed.). Reading, MA: Addison-Wesley.

Schein, E. H. (1990, August). Models of consultation: What do organizations of the 1990s need? Address to the 1990 annual meeting of the Academy of Management, San Francisco.

Schön, D. (1983). *The reflective practitioner: How professionals think in action.* New York: Basic Books.

Schwarz, R. M. (1985). Grounded learning experiences: Treating the classroom as an organization. *Organizational Behavior Teaching Review, 9,* 16–30.

Schwarz, R. M. (1989). Groundrules for effective groups. *Popular Government, 54* (4), 25–30.

Schwarz, R. M. (1991). Consulting to council-manager groups. *Public Administration Quarterly, 14,* 419–437.

Senge, P. M. (1990). *The fifth discipline: The art and practice of the learning organization.* New York: Doubleday.

Smith, K. K. (1989) The movement of conflict in organizations: The joint dynamics of splitting and triangulation. *Administrative Science Quarterly, 34,* 1–20.

Smith, K. K. (1990). On using the self as instrument: Lessons from a facilitator's experience. In J. Gillette & M. Mccollom (Eds.), *Groups in context: A new perspective on group dynamics.* Reading, MA: Addison-Wesley.

Smith, K. K, & Berg, D. N. (1987). *Paradoxes of group life: Understanding conflict, paralysis, and movement in group dynamics.* San Francisco: Jossey-Bass.

Snyder, M., & Swann, W. B. (1978). Behavioral confirmation in social interaction: From social perception to social reality. *Journal of Experimental Social Psychology, 14,* 148–162.

Spich, R. S., & Keleman, K. (1985). Explicit norm structuring process: A strategy for increasing task-group effectiveness. *Group and Organization Studies, 10,* 37–59.

Steele, F. (1982). *The role of the internal consultant.* Boston, MA: CBI Publishing.

Steiner, C. M. (1974). *Scripts people live: Transactional analysis of life scripts.* New York: Bantam Books.

Sundstrom, E., De Meuse, K. P., & Futrell, D. (1990). Work teams: Applications and effectiveness. *American Psychologist, 45*, 120–133.

Sutton, R. I., & Shurman, S J. (1985). On studying emotionally hot topics: Lessons from an investigation of organizational death. In D. N. Berg & K. K. Smith (Eds.), *Exploring clinical methods for social research.* Newbury Park, CA: Sage.

Svara, J. (1990). *Official leadership in the city.* New York: Oxford University Press.

Thomas, K. W., & Kilmann, R. H. (1974). *Thomas-Kilmann conflict mode instrument.* New York: Xicom.

Von Oech, R. (1983). *A whack on the side of the head: How to unlock your mind for innovation.* New York: Warner Books.

Vroom, V. H., & Yetton, P. W. (1973). *Leadership and decision making.* Pittsburgh, PA: University of Pittsburgh Press.

Wall, J. A. (1981). Mediation: An analysis, review, and proposed research. *Journal of Conflict Resolution, 25,* 157–180.

Watzlawick, P., Bavelas, J. B., & Jackson, D. D. (1967). *Pragmatics of human communication: A study of interactional patterns, pathologies, and paradoxes.* New York: W. W. Norton.

Wells, L. W. Jr. (1990). The group as a whole: A systemic socioanalytic perspective on interpersonal and group relations. In J. Gillette & M. Mccollom (Eds.), *Groups in context: A new perspective on group dynamics.* Reading, MA: Addison-Wesley.

Yalom, I.D. (1985). *The theory and practice of group psychotherapy* (3rd ed.). New York: Basic Books.

Zeithaml, V. A., Parasuraman, A., & Berry, L. L. (1990). *Delivering quality service: Balancing customer perceptions and expectations.* New York: Free Press.

Index